The Poetry of John Keats

Metaphysical Elements

Vishwanath Khali

ATLANTIC

PUBLISHERS & DISTRIBUTORS (P) LTD

Published by

ATLANTIC

PUBLISHERS & DISTRIBUTORS (P) LTD

7/22, Ansari Road, Darya Ganj,
New Delhi-110002
Phones : +91-11-40775252, 23273880, 23275880, 23280451
Fax : +91-11-23285873
Web : www.atlanticbooks.com
E-mail : orders@atlanticbooks.com

Branch Office
5, Nallathambi Street, Wallajah Road,
Chennai-600002
Phones : +91-44-64611085, 32413319
E-mail : chennai@atlanticbooks.com

ISBN 978-81-269-1732-7

Printed in India at Nice Printing Press, A-33/3A, Site-IV, Industrial Area, Sahibabad, Ghaziabad, U.P.

Dedicated to

My reverend parents

Sri Shridhar Prasad Khali and Smt. Sateshwari Devi,

Who not only gave me life but also inspiration to

live life creatively

Preface

John Keats was an English romantic poet. According to O'Neill and Mahoney, "Along with Lord Byron and Percy Bysshe Shelly, he was one of the key figures in the second generation of the Romantic movement." Although his poems were not generally well received by critics during his life, his reputation grew after his death to the extent that by the end of the 19th century he had become one of the most beloved of all English poets. He has had a significant influence on a diverse range of later poets and writers.

The poetry of Keats is characterized by sensual imagery, most notably in the series of odes. Today his poems and letters are some of the most popular and analyzed in English literature. Romantic poets, because of their theories of literature and life, were drawn to lyric poetry. They even developed a new form of ode, often called the romantic meditative ode.

Jack Stillinger describes the typical movement of the romantic ode thus:

> The poet, unhappy with the real world, escapes or attempts to escape into the ideal. Disappointed in his mental flight, he returns to the real world. Usually he returns because human beings cannot live in the ideal or because he has not found what he was seeking. But the experience changes his understanding of his situation, of the world, etc.

Douglas Bush noted that "Keats's important poems are related to, or grow directly out of...inner conflicts." For example, pain and pleasure are intertwined in 'Ode to a

Nightingale' and 'Ode on a Grecian Urn'; love is intertwined with pain, and pleasure is intertwined with death in 'La Belle Dame Sans Merci,' 'The Eve of St. Agnes,' and 'Isabella'. Cleanth Brooks defines the paradox of the theme of 'Ode to a Nightingale' somewhat differently:

> The world of imagination offers a release from the painful world of actuality, yet at the same time it renders the world of actuality more painful by contrast.

The romantic aspect of his poetry has been the focus of attention in the bulk of studies and books on Keats. Since romanticism is an important aspect of Keats's poetry, it has been discussed in an exclusive chapter in this book. However, Keats's poetry has also been studied from a different perspective, i.e. the metaphysical aspect. The term 'metaphysical' was first used by John Dryden in the contesxt of poetry, in his 1693 work, *Discourse of Satire*, to describe the style of certain poets earlier in the 17th century. Later, Samual Johnson popularized the term in 1779. Metaphysical poetry implies the poetry in abstract and highly complex form. The chief metaphysical poets include John Donne, Richard Crashaw, Andrew Marvell, George Herbert, and Henry Vaughan. The group shares certain traits, but their themes, structures, and assorted tones in their poetry vary widely.

The metaphysical poets defined and compared their subjects through nature, philosophy, love, and musings about the hereafter—a great departure from the primarily religious poetry that had immediately followed the wane of the Elizabethan era. Poets shared an interest in metaphysical subjects and presented similar means of investing them.

Beginning with John Dryden, the metaphysical movement was a loosely woven string of poetic works that continued through the 18th century, and concluded when William Blake bridged the gap between metaphysical and romantic poetry. The poets sought to minimize their place within the poem and to look beyond the obvious.

The book studies Keats from the point of metaphysics, which is found unconsciously or unwitingly woven in the text of his poems like 'Ode on a Grecian Urn', 'Hyperian' and

'Endymion'. The famous lines "Beauty is truth, and truth beauty...", in 'Ode on a Grecian Urn', are a powerful and most convincing statement to convey the message that Keats was not talking about physical beauty but about heavenly beauty when it is associated with truth because truth here is the ultimate reality. Keats was perhaps unwittingly dealing with the metaphysical when he was relating beauty with truth.

The book not only explains what is metaphysics, in detail, but also briefly discusses Keats's life and major works. Keats's letters, with their keen intellectional questioning and concern with moral and artistic problems, contributed to his re-assessment. His letters throw light on his own poetic practices and provide insight into his writing in general. T.S. Eliot calls Keats's letters as "the most notable and the most important ever written by any English poet". Thus, an exclusive chapter has been devoted to the letters that provide an insight into the metaphysical aspect of the poet's life.

The book will be useful for the students and teachers of English literature, particularly poetry, and researchers in these fields. To those who wish to know about the romantic elements in Keats's poems and the metaphysical aspcets in his poems, his letters and his life, the book will provide for a richly rewarding reading.

Vishwanath Khali

Acknowledgements

I wish to put on record my respectful thanks to Prof. S.S. Deo, Head, Dept. of English, HNB Central University, Srinagar (Garhwal), for giving me, as my D.Phil supervisor, invaluable suggestions during the course of my study. My heart-felt thanks are also due to Prof. Kapil Kapoor, English Dept., JNU, and Prof. (retd.) G.K. Srivastav, Head of English Dept., Allahabad University, for their encouragement.

My thanks are due to my parents, my brothers, sisters, father-in-law, and all my close relatives for their constant help and support during the course of my study.

I take the opportunity to thank Dr. D.P. Kothiyal for support. I fondly remember Dr. B.P. Dimari, our college librarian, and Mr. Jagdish Rawat for the help they extended to me in the form of some valuable books.

I also wish to extend my thanks to my wife Mrs. Anju Khali for her moral support and encouragement, enabling me to concentrate on my research on a regular basis. I am also thankful to my dear kids Pooja, Sonali and Rahul for their love and encouragement for the work.

Last but not least, I am grateful to Atlantic Publishers & Distributers (P) Ltd., New Delhi for the interest evinced in publishing this book.

Vishwanath Khali

Contents

1

What is Metaphysics

'Metaphysics' is a branch of knowledge with an objective to determine the real nature of things. In other words, the main objective of 'metaphysics' is to deal with real nature of things with to regards to the meaning, structure, and principles of the things as they are. Although the study is conceived as referring to anything highly subtle and theoretical and thereby subject to criticism, it is presented by metaphysicians "as the most fundamental and most comprehensive of inquiries, inasmuch as it is concerned with reality as a whole".[1]

Thus, 'metaphysics' can be regarded as a study which deals with matters relating to human existence with regards to 'ultimate reality'. *The New Encyclopedia Britannica* defines the term as "the philosophical study whose object is to determine the real nature of things—to determine the meaning, structure and principles of whatever is insofar as it is".[2] It has been defined as 'branch of philosophy dealing with the nature of existence, truth and knowledge', by *Oxford Advanced Learner's Dictionary.*[3] In other words, it is a branch of knowledge that deals with matters relating to higher purposes of life. In a way, it talks about matters beyond 'physical life', which limits itself to the physical aspects only. So, the chief concern of 'metaphysics' is to try to explore the mystical nature of 'life' that makes it uncertain, inexplicable and mysterious.

Etymologically speaking, 'metaphysics' is a difficult term to comprehend. However, in general it means, "what comes after physics".[4] Aristotle distinguished two tasks for the understanding of the term: first, to investigate the nature and properties of what exists in the natural world, and secondly to inquire into the characteristics 'Being as such' and to inquire into the character of "the substance that is free from movement".[5] In other words, it was the 'most real of all things', the intelligible reality on which everything in the world of nature was thought to be dependent.

In Aristotelian treatise it is known as 'Physica'[6] as it lives with the matters belonging to the sensible or the physical world. Second task related to the matters belonging to the world beyond physical limits. Hence, it was also known as 'theology', referring to God as "unmoved mover in His system".[7] Therefore, the subject is named as "Metaphysica".[8] As a matter of fact, the term 'metaphysics' has been derived from Aristotle's famous book *Metaphysical.*

For the purpose of distinction between the two treatises, the *Physical* has to be described as more empirical, just because it deals with the things that are objects of the senses, the subject matter of the *Metaphysics* is the "eternal, free of movement, separately existent".[9] However, there is a marked connection between the first and the second treatises, as the inquiries about the nature carried out in the *Physical* lead on naturally to the more fundamental inquiries about 'Being as such' that are taken up in the *Metaphysical* and go along with the latter to make up a single philosophical discipline.

Aristotle's views were influenced by his master Plato, although the disciple had his disagreements with his master, with regards to the manner of approaching the metaphysical matters, although the basic ideas were commonly shared by the both. Plato, the disciple of the early Greek philosopher Parmenides, known as the "father of metaphysics"[10] had sought to distinguish opinion from knowledge. "Opinion, for Plato, was a form of apprehension that was shifting and unclear, which was similar to seeing things in a dream. Knowledge, by contrast, was wholly lucid. It carried its own guarantee against error, and the objects with which it was concerned were eternally what they were, and so unchangeable."[11] Philosophy was thus a call to recognize "the existence and the overwhelming importance of a set of higher realities that ordinary men entirely ignored. That there were such realities, was a fundamental tenet in the discipline that later became known as metaphysics".[12]

The study of metaphysics can be carried under four points: (1) An inquiry into what really exist, (2) The science of reality as opposed to appearance, (3) The study of the world as a whole, and (4) A theory of first principle.

There is a common belief among metaphysicians that it is an inquiry into what exists and what is truly real. Are dream objects real, in the way chairs and trees are? It is easy enough to confuse any common man with questions like these. It is equally difficult for the metaphysician to come up with more satisfactory answers of his own. Many metaphysicians have relied on the internally related notions of substance and quality, for the determination of reality. They have argued that what is "substantial truly exists, although every substance has qualities and stands in relation to other substances. A tree, for example, qualifies for substance, as it just a thing that has qualities and stands in relations. However, the height of the tree would none exist unless the tree existed."[13]

For metaphysicians, "metaphysics seeks to define what is ultimately real, as opposed to what is merely apparent".[14] In everyday life, people distinguish between the real size of the sun and its apparent size. Again, a cloud appears to consist of some white substance, although in reality it is a concentration of drops of water. In general, men are often inclined to allow that scientist knows the real constitution of things as opposed to the surface aspects with which ordinary men are familiar. So, "the ultimate realities that the metaphysicians seek to are precisely things as they are—simple and unchangeable, and therefore stable objects of knowledge. Also, it is genuine as opposed to sham, original in contrast to derivative, self-dependent rather than dependent on the existence of something else".[15]

When Aristotle sought to inquire into the most real of all things, or the original and perfect being, he was looking for something that, in contrast to the everyday thing of this world, was truly 'self-contained' and thereby 'self-caused'. As a result, most importantly, reality for the metaphysician is "intelligible as opposed to opaque".[16] Therefore, appearances are not only deceptive and derivative, they make no sense when taken at their own level. To arrive at what is 'ultimately real' is to produce an account of the facts that does them full justice.

Consequently, the metaphysician believes that everyday ways of thinking will not suffice for a full and coherent description of what falls within experience. Hence, the argument that 'appearances' are unreal, because they are 'unstable' and 'unintelligible'. In view of the metaphysician, both common sense of ordinary man and the science are unable to comprehend the 'ultimate reality', because of their dependence on the 'visible proofs', which are mere appearances in the eyes of metaphysicians. As a result, in the eyes of a metaphysician "the world of scientist, restricted as it to what can be dealt with in quantitative terms, it is a poor thing in comparison with the rich if untidy world of everyday life".[17]

The need for metaphysics arises because some people want to know not only what the scientist makes of the world but also what significance to give to his account. They experience the world at different levels and in different capacities. "They have a moral and a legal, an aesthetic and a religious life on top of their scientific life".[18]

But there are philosophers who appear to see no mystery here. They argue that "there can be no question of the possibility of, say, moral or religious vision of the world that rivals the scientific vision".[19] They believe that the morals and religion are the matters of practice, not of theory, and in this way they do not oppose science but complement it only. However, the practice of the moral life is believed to proceed on assumption that can hardly be accepted if science has taken the last word about what is true. Accordingly, it becomes necessary for the metaphysician to produce some rational assessment of the truth of the different forms of experience.

Therefore, the "conception of metaphysics as offering an account of the world or, of experience as a whole, accords more obviously with the practice of those who see ultimate reality as immanent, or inherent in what is immediately known, than of those who take it to be transient, or beyond the limits of ordinary experience".[20]

As regards the science of first principle, there seem to be conflicting opinions, as far as metaphysics and mathematics are concerned. Plato, in his famous book *The Republic* contrasted these two attitudes very effectively. According to him, "the mathematician lays down or hypothesizes certain things as true and then proceeds to deduce their consequences without examining them further".[21] But, clearly, as the theory is developed on account of a hypothesis, it is false. However, the metaphysicians' claim hold some strength when they say that their business is to "justify the ultimate assumptions of the science, and also there are no unjustified assumptions"[22] as far as 'the science of first principle' is concerned. Perhaps the most celebrated issue in classical metaphysics is concerned with the existence of God. God in this connection is the name of 'the perfect being' or 'the most real of all things'. The question is whether it is necessary to recognize the existence of such a being as well as of things that either are or might be objects of everyday experience. A number of famous arguments have been offered from the time of Greeks in favour of the view that such recognition is necessary. The most original was the argument of St. Anselm (11th century), who said that "that than which nothing greater can be conceived must exist in fact as well in thought, for if it existed only in thought and not in fact, something greater than it could be conceived, namely the same thing existed in fact".[23]

Therefore, God must exist, because the idea of God is the idea of that "than which nothing greater can be conceived". This argument was later known as "the ontological proof".[24] Relatively few theologians like Descartes, Spinoza, Leibniz and Hegel, etc. accepted it in principle. But most of them preferred to put their case for God's existence on the ground of 'empirical philosophy'. St. Thomas Aquinas, for example, argued that "to explain the fact of motion in the world, the existence of a prime mover must be presupposed".[25]

He further argues that "to account for contingent or dependent being the existence of something that is necessary or self-contained must be presumed; that to see why the world is orderly and why the different things in it fit together harmoniously, a situation that might not have obtained, a Creator who fashioned it on these lines must be postulated—adding in each case and this all men call 'God'".[26]

The argument needs to be discussed in somewhat greater detail, because it has a plausibility and lies at the basis of many different kinds of metaphysical schools, such as that of Hegel and of Aquinas. It begins with the innocent-looking statement that 'something contingent exists, such as oneself, the world in general'. In describing oneself or the world as contingent, one means only that thing in question does not exist through itself alone. Rather, it owes its existence to the activity of some other thing as a person owes its being to its parents. So to say, the contingent things are not 'self-complete'. They demand the existence of something else, if they are to be explained.

Thus, "the move is made from contingent to necessary being. It is felt that the contingent things, of whatever order, cannot be endlessly dependent on other contingent things but must presuppose a first cause that is self-complete and so exists necessarily."[27] In Hegel, however, the necessary being is not a separate existent but, "an order of things, where the loose facts of everyday life and even of science are said to point to a system that is all-embracing and in which everything is necessarily what it is".[28]

The relationship between 'soul, mind and body' has also been an area to which the metaphysicians attached a great importance. Plato, in this connection, believed in the 'immortality of human soul'. According to him, "The soul was an entity that was fundamentally distinct from the body, although it could be and often was affected by its association with the body, being dragged down by 'the leaden weight of becoming'. The soul was simple, not composite, and thus not liable to dissolution as were material things".[29]

Carrying the argument of the relation of 'soul, mind and body' forward, Plato says that:

> It (the soul) had the power of self-movement, again in contrast to material things. Ideally, the soul rules and

> guides the body, and it should ensure that this situation persisted by seeing that the bodily appetites were kept to the minimum, necessary for the continuance of life. The true philosopher made his life a practice for death, because he knew that after death the soul would be free of bodily ties and would return to its element.[30]

However, Aristotle, differing a little bit with his master, defined soul "in terms of functions, like the soul of a plant was concerned with nutrition and reproduction, that of an animal with these and with sensation and independent movement, that of a man with all these and with rational activity".[31] Thus, the soul, according to Aristotle, was the form of some body, and the clear implication of this was that it would disappear as the body in question dissolved. To be more accurate, the soul was the principle of life in something material. That is to say, it needed the material element to exist, although it was not itself either material or immaterial, but an abstraction.

Metaphysics, however, seems to have undergone a change in recent times as it is the 'mind' (not soul) and 'body' that is heard of, in recent times. The old problem of 'the relationship of soul and body' has given way to the problem of 'mind and body'. Most subsequent discussion of this subject has been influenced by the thoughts of Descartes, whose arguments come mainly through his *Meditations de Prima Philosophia* (1641). He had argued that "there was a total and absolute distinction between mental and material substance. The defining characteristic of matter was to occupy space, whereas that of mind was to be conscious or, in the broader sense of the term, to think.... Material substance was, so to say, all one, although packets of it were more or less persistent, mental existing in the forms of individual minds, with God as the supreme example".[32] In other words, the mental and the material orders were each complete in themselves under God.

That is to say, Descartes believed that 'mind' is real as against the 'body' whose existence is 'doubtful'. He admitted that "sensation and imagination could be understood only if referred to the mind-body complex and that acts of pure intellect and of will belonged to the mind as it was in itself".[33]

However, he did not claim to have a philosophical proof of the immortality of the soul, which would require "the assurance of revelation".[34] But, he did succeed in establishing the separate existence of 'mind'.

However, in order to reach a better and smooth understanding of the term metaphysics, it needs to be analyzed alongside philosophy. As far as "philosophy" is concerned, even it does not have any fixed opinion about it. According to one opinion, throughout its long and varied history in the West, "Philosophy has meant many different things. Some of these have been a search for wisdom of life—an attempt to understand the universe as a whole; an examination of man's moral responsibilities and his social obligations; an effort to fathom the divine intentions and man's place with reference to them; a rigorous examination of the origin, extent, and validity of man's ideas; an examination of the values of truth, goodness, and beauty…".[35]

Therefore, it is difficult to determine whether any common element can be found within this diversity of thought and whether any single meaning can be discovered for philosophy that could serve as a universal definition. It is so, perhaps, because philosophy, firstly, is a reflective, or meditative activity; and secondly, it has no explicitly designated subject-matter of its own but is a method of mental operation that can take any area or subject matter as its object.

Thomas Aquinas (13th century), George Berkeley (18th century) and Soren Kierkegaard (19th century), all saw philosophy as a means "to assert the truths of religion and to dispel the materialistic or rationalistic errors"[36] that, in their opinion, had led to its decline. Pythagoras in ancient Italy, Rene Descartes in the late Renaissance and Bertrand Russell in the 20th century have been primarily mathematicians whose views of the universe and of human knowledge have been vastly influenced by the concept of number.

Some philosophers such as Plato and Thomas Hobbes have been obsessed by "problems of political arrangement and social living, so that whatever else they have done in philosophy has been stimulated by a desire to understand and to change the social and political behavior of men".[37]

The history of Western philosophy reveals in detail the serious activity of many philosophers, reflecting deeply upon the nature of their experience. But, while discussing the subject, certain characteristic oppositions have also occurred, such as the "division between dualists and pluralists in metaphysics; between Materialists and Idealists in cosmological theory; between Rationalists and Empiricists in the theory of signification; and between partisans of logic and partisans of emotion in the search for a responsible guide to the wisdom of life".[38]

As a matter of fact, "Philosophy among the Greeks slowly emerged out of religious awe into wonder about the principles and elements of the natural world. But as the Greek populations left the land to shift to the cities, interest also shifted from nature to social living. Matters of laws and civic values became more important. Cosmological speculations gave way to moral and political theorizing, and the preliminary and somewhat fragmentary questionings of Socrates and the Sophists turned in a great positive construction of Plato and Aristotle. With the political and social fragmentation of the succeeding centuries, however, philosophizing once again shifted from the norms of civic involvement to problems of salvation and survival in a chaotic world".[39]

The dawn of Christianity brought to philosophy new tasks. Augustine, for example, dealt with problems of the creation, of faith and reason, of truth. However, the waning of the middle Ages became the Renaissance. As a result, philosophy became secularized. The new fact that emerged was that of the "mystery of the natural world".[40] In a way, philosophy turned to the foundations of physical science, initiated by Newton, in 17th century. The 19th century came with a philosophical diversity, particularly between "Positivism and Existentialism"[41] that characterize the present situation in philosophy.

Since ancient Greek philosophers focused upon the origin and the nature of the physical world for the first time, it will be worthwhile to consider their views. The first of them was

'Thales (6th century BC)'[42], "to give a purely natural explanation of the origin of the world, free from all mythological ingredients declaring that everything had come out of water—an explanation based on the discovery of fossil sea animals".[43]

Thales's disciple, Anaximander, tried to give a more elaborate account of the origin and development of the ordered world (the cosmos). According to him, "it developed out of the *apeiron*, something both infinite and indefinite (without distinguishable qualities). Within this *apeiron* something arose to produce the opposites of hot and cold. These at once began to struggle with each other and produced the cosmos. Cold that partly dried up became solid earth, and that partly remained turned into water, and that partly evaporated turned into air and mist."[44] Anaximander was also "the first to realize that upward and downward are not absolute directions, but the downward means towards the middle of the Earth and upward away from it, so that the earth had no need to be supported by anything as Thales had believed".[45]

Anaximenes, Anaximander's successor, believed that "air was the origin of all things".[46] However, his position was thought as a step backward because, like Thales, he placed a special kind of matter at the beginning of the development of the world. But neither Thales nor Anaximander specified the way in which the other things arose out of water or 'apeiron'. Anaximenes declared that "the other types of matter arose out of air by condensation and rarefaction. In this way, what to Thales had been merely a beginning became a fundamental principle that remained essentially the same through many transmutations."[47] He further says:

> The term *arche* (beginning) acquired the new meaning of 'principle', a term that henceforth played an enormous role in philosophy down to the present day. This concept of a principle that remains the same through many transmutations, is furthermore, the presupposition of the idea that nothing can come out of nothing and that all comings to be and passings away that men observe are

> nothing but transmutations of something that essentially remains the same eternally.[48]

However, in the field of theoretical philosophy, Plato's contribution was remarkable. His philosophy is based on his "theory of ideas",[49] which he derived from Socrates, who used to ask "what it is that makes men say that a certain thing or action is good or beautiful or pious or brave; and he had asked what people are looking at when they make such statements".[50]

But Plato at times made Socrates ask such tricky questions as to what is the Eidos or the idea—i.e., the image—that a man has before him when calls something 'good'. A definite answer was never given, however, because no abstract definition would be adequate, the purpose being rather to make his predecessor aware of the fact that he somehow does look at "something indefinable",[51] when making such statements.

What was at first simply seen as a way of 'somehow expressing something that is difficult to express' developed into a definite theory of ideas when Plato made the discovery that something could be observed in the field of 'mathematics'? Explaining the ways and means of mathematics, Plato held that "no two things in the visible world are perfectly equal, just as there is nothing that is perfectly good or perfectly beautiful. Yet equality is one of the most fundamental concepts not only in mathematics but also in everyday life—the foundation of all measurements. Hence, like the notion of good and the beautiful, it appears to come from different world, a world beyond that of the senses."[52]

All the things, according to Plato, that men perceive with their senses appear to be very imperfect copies of the 'Eternal Ideas'. The most important and fundamental of all, however, is the 'Idea of the Good'. It is 'beyond being and knowledge'. 'Being' in this connection does mean existence, but being something—a man, a lion, a house—being recognizable by its quality or shape. Without such shapes, which are copies of ideas, there would be complete chaos, in which nothing would be recognizable.

Furthermore, it is impossible to build up any system of knowledge without constantly preferring what is formed and thus, recognizable to what is not, what is true to what is false, a sound logical conclusion to a logical fallacy, even an elegant scientific demonstration to a clumsy one; i.e., without considering the former as good and the latter as bad. In this sense at least, there is no such thing as value-free science.

In the famous chapter "Myth of the Cave"[53] in the book *The Republic*, Plato compared the ordinary person to a man sitting in a cave looking at a wall on which he sees nothing but the shadows of the real that are behind his back. Similarly, he compared the philosopher to man who has gone out in the open and seen the real world of ideas. The philosopher, Plato thinks, is the one who knows the "real reality".[54] Therefore, he conducts his life accordingly.

So, we can say that 'metaphysics' and 'philosophy' go together, as far as the 'ultimate nature' of human life is concerned. Both the studies suggest that there is some supreme power, the 'ultimate reality' or some 'invisible force' governing each and every particle of the universe as well as the minutest activity of man, and thereby each and everything present in the universe needs to be discussed in that light, in order to realize the 'highest purpose' of life.

Hence the description of the 'metaphysics' given by the some other thinkers is that it is a science that "seeks to define what is ultimately real, as opposed to what is merely apparent".[55] The contrast between 'appearance' and 'reality', however, is by no means peculiar to metaphysics. In everyday life, people distinguish between the real size of the sun and its apparent size. Or, for that matter, a cloud appears to consist of some white substance, although in reality it is a concentration of drops of water.

The study of science *vis-à-vis* metaphysics also deserves attention, in order to reach the 'ultimate truth' of life. In this case, 'science' too falls short of the goal, because of its dependence for the 'truth' on the 'physical proofs'. In general, people are inclined to allow that scientist knows the real constitution of things as opposed to the surface aspects with which ordinary men are familiar. It will not suffice, therefore, to define 'metaphysics' as knowledge of reality as opposed to appearance. But the student of metaphysics believes that the 'ultimate reality' lies beyond the physical appearance of a thing. According to him, the physical aspect of a 'matter' is only the carbon copy of the reality behind it. This is the opinion mainly responsible for the birth of the branch of knowledge known as 'metaphysics'.

Therefore, the 'ultimate realities' that the metaphysicians seek to know are precisely things as they are—simple, unchangeable, and therefore stable objects of knowledge. 'Ultimate reality', therefore, is genuine as opposed to artificial, original in contrast to derivative, self-dependent rather than dependent on the existence of something else. Which is why, when Aristotle, or for that matter the medieval philosophers attempted to established the characteristics of what they called "the end *realissimum* ('the most real being'), or the original and the perfect being, they were looking for something that, in contrast to the everyday things of this world, was truly self-contained and could accordingly be looked upon as self-caused".[56]

The metaphysicians also strongly believe that reality is 'intelligible as opposed to opaque'. Appearances, according to them, are not only deceptive they also make no sense when taken for analysis. To arrive at what is ultimately real is to produce an account of the facts that does them full justice. Therefore, the assumption is that one cannot explain things satisfactorily if one remains within the world of common sense. Consequently, the metaphysician has to move out of the world of common sense into the world of inner experience in order to arrive at the 'ultimate reality'. This can best be done by associating the whole existence with the ultimate reality—i.e. God.

As a result, the metaphysician goes to claim that everyday ways of thinking are not sufficient for a full and coherent description of what falls within experience, thus arguing that appearances are unreal, because they are unstable and unintelligible. However, the opinion held by the metaphysicians faces a challenge against the fact that the time and space as well as things undergo a change. But they firmly abide by their ideas.

The most celebrated issue, thus, in metaphysics is its concerns with the 'existence of God'. God in this connection is the name of 'the perfect being' or 'the most real of all things'. The question is whether it is necessary to recognize the existence such a being as well as of such things that either are or might be objects of everyday experience. A number of arguments have been advanced from the time of Greeks in favour of the thesis that such recognition is necessary. One of these is the one put forward by St. Anselm in the 11th century, which says that, "that than which nothing greater can be conceived must exist in fact as well as in thought, for if it existed only in thought and not in fact, something greater than it could be conceived, namely the same thing existing in fact".[57]

Therefore, God necessarily exists, because the idea of God is the idea of that 'than which nothing greater can be conceived'. In the same way, St. Thomas Aquinas, another 13th century celebrated philosopher, argued that "to explain the fact of motion in the world, the existence of a prime mover must be presupposed; that to see why the world is orderly and why the different things in it fit together harmoniously, a situation that might not have been obtained".[58]

Another favourite aspect of metaphysical study is the 'soul and body relationship'. Plato, the great philosopher, believed in the immortality of the human soul as against the temporary nature of body. "The soul was", he thought, "an entity that was fundamentally distinct from the body. The soul was simple, not composite, and not liable to dissolution as were material things. Moreover, it had the power of self-movement again in contrast to material things".[59] Ideally, the soul should rule and guide the body and as Plato thinks, it could ensure that this situation persisted by seeing that the bodily appetites were kept to the minimum extent necessary for the continuance of life. The true philosopher, as Plato says in *Phaedo*,[60] made his life a practice for death, because he knew that after death the soul would be free of bodily ties and would return to its native element.

However, Aristotle defined soul in terms of functions. The soul of a plant, according to him, was concerned with "nutrition and reproduction, that of an animal with sensation and independent movement, that of a man with all these and with rational activity".[61] As a result, the soul was, in each case, the form of some body, and the clear implication of this was that it would disappear as the body in question dissolved. To be more accurate, the soul was the principle of life in something material and therefore it needed the material element to exist. Although the soul was, to put it straight, neither material nor immaterial but abstract.

But, the theory of metaphysics has its own problems as well. The main difficulty with the metaphysicians is the problem of establishing that there is something answerable to his conception of what is 'ultimately real' and identifying it. Different metaphysicians approach the problem differently. Some feel that the ultimately real is plural, the other think that there is only one ultimate reality. Other sect of thinkers has argued that what is truly real must be utterly transcendent of the things of this world and occupy a "super-sensible realm accessible only to the pure intellect",[62] while other has thought of 'ultimate reality' as immanent in experience.

Still, 'metaphysics' is one of the most significant studies about life, as the metaphysicians have a tendency to look into the 'mysteries of life' so that the actual intentions of the Creator could be apprehended in totality. They want to feel and realize the 'invisible'. The very belief of the Omnipresence or the permanence of the 'invisible' inspires them to make it a recurrent subject of their study. In other words, they want to inquire as to 'why' the man was born and not 'how', as it is a matter relating to science, which is based on concrete evidences, and therefore, limited in approach.

As a result, 'metaphysics' begins where 'science' ends, as metaphysician asks the vital and profound questions as to what kind of a life man should lead so as to find an answer to the question of 'why' does he come to this world, and once in the world, what should be his primary objective to achieve in life. In other words, should the man continue to lead the 'worldly life' with 'worldly pursuits' in mind and an attempt to achieve them, or, should he look beyond them and go into 'metaphysical pursuits', which relate to the very creation and working of the system of the whole in the way as it is made to work by the 'Divine Power', and try follow it in thought as well as in action.

2

Life and Works of John Keats at a Glance

John Keats was born on 31 October 1795 at Finsbury, London, where his father, Thomas Keats, was living with his wife Frances Jennings, as the head ostler in a Livery Stable. John was the first child of his parents. There followed two brothers, George and Tom, and a sister Frances Mary. After the death of the father Thomas, the children were sent to live with their grandparents, John and Alice Jennings, at Ponder's End, Enfield. His father had died in the month of April, 1804, after falling from the back of a horse. John was hardly nine years of age at that time. As a result, the children were looked after by their grandfather Mr. John Jennings. However, after Jennings's death on March 1805, children moved to Edmonton along with Alice Jennings, their grandmother. In 1810, Alice Jennings appointed John Nowland Sandall and Richard Abbey as the children's guardians. Sandall also died in 1816, leaving Abbey the only guardian.

"The parents (of Keats) were ambitious for their boys, and would have liked to send them to Harrow, but thinking this beyond their means, chose the school kept by a Mr. John Clarke at Enfield."[1] John, the eldest son, too was educated at the school of Mr. John Clarke, at Enfield. From the above estimate, it is quite clear that Keats had witnessed a very hard times in his childhood, in the form of losing his father in an early age, leaving it on his mother's shoulder to look after the family. But, the days became more difficult, when his mother,

Frances Keats, "married one Mr. William Rawlings, after his father's death".[2] Although, she must have been forced to take the decision of the remarriage because of the acute "practical and financial problems".[3] However, the event must have left a very negative impression on the tender mind of Keats. In fact, he was apparently very upset on having Mr. William Rawlings as his stepfather.

But, fortunately for Keats, the marriage did not succeed for some unknown reasons. The marriage must have caused unhappiness between the couple, for it was soon followed by separation. Evidently, the whole episode must have cast such bitter memories in the young mind of Keats that his 'letters' have no mention of his stepfather. (It is notable that the 'letters' cover almost every aspect of his personal life, as analyzed in the chapter related to it except the mention of his stepfather.) However, the separation brought happiness and hope to Keats, as he was upset by his mother's decision of remarriage, even though it was because of financial problems.

As a result, Jennings's separation with William Rawlings brought her back to her children. This was the opportunity that Keats was waiting for, when he would see his mother back. As if not to waste the opportunity, "Keats did every thing in his power to make sure that his mother (Mrs. Jennings) would never go away again from them, and he vowed to achieve this by excelling in one of the areas where success would surely guarantee her love. So, when he returned to school in January 1809, it was with the iron determination to carry off all the first prizes in literature by a considerable distance. Books and hopes of emotional security had become identified."[4]

All the family details, at this stage, go to show the kind of unfortunate childhood John Keats had to spend, because of the unfortunate turn of events in the family. This must have obviously played in his mind when he grew older. But once at school, Keats seemed to have forgotten all about the unfortunate past. Very soon at the school, he made friends with Charles Cowden Clarke, the Headmaster's son. And in the space of eighteen months he turned studious, read at mealtimes, did holiday tasks and started to take interest in Greek mythology. But the destiny brought him to the field of literature. He had learned to love reading, could enjoy Virgil, and took great delight in Greek mythology. At school itself, he translated a large part of *Aeneid* into English, and shortly after leaving school finished the entire epic.[5]

In 1812, he borrowed Spencer's *Faerie Queen* from Cowden Clarke and was fascinated by it. Keats now came into contact with people like Leigh Hunt and Hayden, and realized that poetry and not surgery was his true vocation. Encouraged by his literary friends he began to write seriously. In March 1817, he brought out the first collection of his 'Poems'. A year later came the publication of 'Endymion'.

Keats was greatly impressed by his schoolmaster, Mr. Clarke, who was well-read, particularly in 'renaissance poetry'. With him Keats started sharing his reading. This was necessary, and even inevitable preparation, and was an important aspect of the informed but passionate response to tradition that is a hallmark of Keats's maturing genius. Keats also makes clear that "these studious hours in the arbour offered pleasure, companionship and, above all, access to the world of the imagination that was now becoming an imperative for him".[6] The poet shared his reading of *A Midsummer Night's Dream* and *Macbeth* with the schoolmaster. On reading *Macbeth*, the poet offered the "boyish opinion that no one would dare read *Macbeth* at two o'clock in the morning".[7]

Clarke introduced Keats to Milton also, to his depiction of the rout of the fallen angels as well as to that aspect of "Paradise Lost". Keats's engagement with Milton was to become as profound as his knowledge of Shakespeare. It was from Clarke that he also learned that epic poem "Paradise Lost" was considered to be the 'king' of the genres, something 'round, vast, and spanning' like the rings of Saturn illustrated in his copy of Bonnycastle. The idea of the epic poem would always fire Keats's ambition.[8] It was Keats's reading of "Paradise Lost" that eventually inspired him to write *Hyperion*.

Another contemporary by whose poetry Keats was highly impressed was Leigh Hunt. Regarding his poetry, Keats himself declares that "reading his (Hunt's) poetry has freed his immortal spirit".[9] However, Leigh Hunt's influence is taken up for discussion later in the chapter.

Anyway, "the relation between Keats and his brothers, nurtured at Clarke's school and in the absence of parents, was deep, affectionate, and for Keats himself, a sustaining and necessary security. But, while his personal life rested on these foundations, his response to the public world was also beginning to grow."[10]

Keats was very handsome-looking person and had attractive features. "In character he was enthusiastic, full of strong feelings and warm affections. He was small in stature, but he was brave and sturdy.... His features were beautiful, and the ardour of his nature was visible in his expression. At school he made a valuable friend in Charles Cowden Clarke, son of the headmaster, and the friendship was maintained after Keats's hospital studies had begun."[11] Possession of *Faerie Queen,* however, can be said to be a turning point in Keats's poetic career. To Keats, the book was a revelation, as not only the adventures and visions, but the music of the stanza and above all the imagery and epithets gave him uncontrollable delight.

Clarke's school, however, offered Keats the outlet where he could his use his vigorous energies in an air of freedom. "He delighted in the buffoonery and pranks of his friends. He became a renowned fighter.... Such outbursts were occasionally ungovernable, they suggests something more in Keats than mere animal high spirits. Tough as he was, he had been hurt, and his vulnerability made him quick to sympathize with others in pain."[12]

As a result, "his mind started opening to the beauty of nature. The villages of Enfield and Edmonton of Keats's childhood days were still full of rural charm. He needed just this ordinary unspoilt countryside to stir him to rapture. Certain things affected him extremely, said his friend Severn, "Particularly when 'a wave was billowing through a tree'. The tide! tide! he would cry delightedly, spring on to some stile, or upon the low bough of a wayside tree and the passage of the wind upon the meadow grasses or young corn, not stirring till the flow of air was around him, while an expression of rapture made his eyes gleam and his face glow."[13] These new delights were to deepen into passion, preparing a foundation for Keats's entry into the world of Romantic Poetry in the time to come.

Even as he was studying medical science, Keats became attached to a literary circle, headed by a fluent poet and gifted essayist, James Henry Leigh Hunt. He began to write a few poems in the form of sonnets, descriptive lines, verse-letters, etc. The reception which his attempts received from his friends was highly encouraging, inducing Keats to venture upon publication. In 1817, the first publication appeared entitled *Poems*, attracting a fairly positive response from the readers. It turned out to be a decisive step, as Keats left the medical studies and plunged into what was an "anxious liberty of literary life,"[14] to Keats.

By now Keats was fully engrossed in the writing of poetry. Soon after *Isabella* was finished, he set out on a long walking-tour in the North, with his friend Charles Brown, to Cumberland, Western Isles and to the home of Burns, one of his other intimate friends. The visits gave Keats an unbounded delight. But the fatigue of the tour added with his family's tendency to tuberculosis brought about a fast deterioration in his health. As if it was not enough, soon after Keats's return to London harsh reviews of *Endymion*, appearing in *The Quarterly Review* awaited him to further increase his problems.

About the same time the poet became acquainted with a young and beautiful lady Miss Fanny Browne, living in Hampstead, with whom he soon fell violently in love. Both even got engaged but could not marry, partly because of Keats's poor health and partly because of his poor economic condition. But certainly, the unfortunate turn of events only helped to create hopelessness in his life. "The last year of his life was a painful struggle for health, and his ebbing strength was unequal to the intense strain of poetic composition.... His medical knowledge was sufficient to diagnose his own case: he knew that he must die."[15]

One day (February 1820), after a return from an outing in a chilly night, Keats was attacked by a spasm of violent coughing and spat out blood. His friend Brown, who was with him at the time, tells Mr. Bernard Groom of the calmness with which Keats faced the truth. There was indeed no hope of life. Miss Browne and her mother did whatever possible for him, but now it had become clear that his days are numbered.

Recounting the incident of coughing blood by Keats, his great friend Charles Brown says, "The young man who had studied medicine knew what this meant; 'Bring me the candle, Brown, and let me see this blood.' After regarding it steadfastly, he looked up in my face, with a calm of countenance I can never forget, and said, 'I know the colour of that blood; it is arterial blood;—I cannot be deceived in that colour: that drop of blood is my death-warrant; I must die.'"[16]

In view of the serious condition, Keats was advised by Joseph Severn to visit Italy for a change, and in the hope of betterment, he set sail for Italy in September, 1821, with one of his most devoted friends, Joseph Severn. The poet's fancy and natural brightness were still visible in his face, but the disease was irresistible and the poet died at Rome in February, 1821. He was buried in the Protestant Cemetery at Rome, in the presence of quite a few of his admirers and, of course, Joseph Severn, with an epitaph chosen by Keats himself, in a moment of bitter despair, which reads as follows: "Here lies the one whose name was writ in water".[17]

But, going back to his childhood days, as Keats grew older, he realized that poetry, and not medical studies, was his passion. As a result, he started writing a few poems-sonnets, descriptive lines, verse letters and the like. The reception which his attempts received was highly encouraging, and induced Keats into publication. In 1817, a volume appeared by the name of *Poems*. A decisive step had been taken. It was followed by his ambitious and daring poem *Endymion*, based on a fable of the moon-goddess Cynthia's love for Endymion, who happens to be a shepherd of Latmos. Now was the turn of *Isabella,* or *The Pot of Basil.* This work reveals the true poet, containing passages of exquisite beauty. In the winter of 1818 Keats went on to write *Hyperion,* a poem which "dares to challenge comparison with Paradise Lost".[18] January 1819 saw the completion of "The Eve of St. Agnes", a poem in which descriptive beauty reaches its height.

In the early spring of the same year Keats began to write odes, which were 'perfect embodiment of the poetic spirit'. In the month of April (1819) he produced the first of his complete odes, entitled "To Psyche". It was followed by one of his finest ever odes in English poetry, by the name "Ode to a Nightingale", composed in Hampstead garden in May. This very month witnessed the most mysterious and haunting of his works, "La Belle Dame Sans Merci". And in July the same year, he finished one of his narrative poems "Lamia".

Then came the publication of "Ode to Autumn" in the month of September. It was now the time for the landmark poem "Ode on a Grecian Urn", which appeared in January, 1820. In July (1820), in the midst of ever-failing health, Keats came with his long-cherished wish of the publication of the great volume with the proud announcement on the title page: "Lamia", "Isabella", "The Eve of St. Agnes", and "Other Poems", by John Keats, Author of *Endymion.*[19]

The most important poem that came in 1817 volume is *Sleep and Poetry.* Regarding the importance of the volume and Keats's future in poetry, one of the admires of Keats, Graham Hough comments that "it is an early attempt to formulate his poetic ideals, and is still written in Huntian manner. (It was actually composed in Hunt's house.) But it contains within itself the reason why this manner was not to satisfy Keats for long. The central part of the poem describes prophetically what he foresees to be his course in poetry, 'First the realm I'll pass/ Of Flora and old Pan: sleep in the grass/ Feed upon apples red and strawberries'...".[20]

However, Keats was not satisfied with the sensuous pleasures of nature only. He wanted to go beyond it. He wanted to explore the mysteries present behind making the nature so beautiful. Throwing light on this matter with regards to his poetry, Graham Hough says, "These lines and the twenty that follow describe a phrase of delighted communication with nature and with the external and obvious beauties of the world. He wonders whether he can ever bear to give up these sensuous ecstasies, but realizes in the same breath that they are only a stage in his progress."[21]

Talking about the pattern in his early poetry, published in 1817 as *Poems*, one of the biographers of the poet, Mr. Sidney Colvin says that "the element in which his (Keats's) poetry moves is liberty, the consciousness of release from those conventions and restraints, not inherent in its true nature, by which the art had for the last hundred years and more been hampered. And the spirit which animates him is essentially the spirit of delight: delight in the beauty and activities of nature, in the vividness of sensation, in the charms of fable and romance, in the thoughts of friendship and affection, in the anticipation of future, and in the exercise of the art itself which expresses and communicates these joys."[22]

On the creative front, in the early attempts Keats ventures some way in the direction of breaking the design of the regular couplet. As an innovative he "runs his sentences freely enough through a succession of lines.... He deals freely in double endings, and occasionally, breaks the run of a line with a full stop in or near the middle.... Somewhat more freely and adventurous alike in metre and in diction are the two poems, *Sleep and Poetry* and *I stood tip-toe*, which Keats wrote after he came back to London in the autumn. Both in substance and intention they are preludes merely, but preludes of genius, and although marked by many immaturities, as interesting and attractive perhaps as anything which has ever been written by a poet of the same age about his art and his aspirations. Possessed by the thrilling sense of that everything in earth and air is full, as it were, of poetry in solution, he has as yet no clearness as to the forms and modes in which these suspended moments will crystallize for him".[23]

In *Sleep and Poetry*, for example, "he tries to get into shape his conceptions of the end and aim of poetical behaviour, conjecture up the difficulties of his task, counts over the new achievements and growing promise of the time in which he lives, and gives thanks for the encouragement by which he has been personally sustained. In *I stood tip-toe* he runs over the stock of delight, traces in various phrases and aspects of nature a symbolic affinity, or spiritual identity, with various forms and kinds of poetry...and finally goes on to speculate on the moods which first inspired some of the Grecian tales he loves best, and above all the tale of Endymion and Cynthia, the beneficent wonders of whose bridal night he hopes himself one day to re-tell".[24]

At this point in time a sort of a warning voice from within him reminds the poet sadly "of the shortness and fragility of life, to which an answering inward voice of gay courage and hope replies. Keats could only think in images, and almost invariably in images of life and action",[25] as he exclaims:

> Stop and consider! Life is but a day;
> A fragile dew-drop on its perilous way
> From a tree's summit....[26]

The poetic growth and ambitions of Keats are dexterously described by the Sidney Colvin, one of the premier biographers of Keats, as he says, "then follows a cry...to carry out the poetic schemes which float before his (Keats's) mind; and here he returns to the ascending scale of poetic ambitions and sets it forth and amplifies it with a new richness of figurative imagery. First the realm of Pan and Flora, the pleasures of nature and the country and the enticements of toying nymphs...then the ascent to loftier regions where the imagination has to grapple with the deeper mysteries of life and experiences of the soul. Here again he can only shadow forth his ideas by evoking shapes and actions of visible beings to stand for and represent them symbolically.... He sees a charioteer guiding his horses among the clouds, looking out the while 'with glorious fear', then swooping downward to alight on a grassy hillside; then talking with strange gestures with trees and mountains, then gazing and listening, 'awfully intent', and writing something on his tablets with a procession of various human shapes, 'shapes of delight, of mystery and fear', sweeps on before his view, as in pursuit of some ever-fleeting music, in the shadow cast by a grove of oaks".[27]

Thus, the vision of the charioteer remained in Keats's mind as a symbol for the imagination and its energies. For the moment, as his poem goes on, the vision vanishes, and the sense of everyday realities seems like a muddy stream bearing his soul into nothingness. But he clings to the memory of that 'chariot' and its journey. And thereupon the poet turns to consider the history of English poetry and the dearth of imagination from which it had suffered for so many years. His composition in the form of a sonnet, "Is there so small a range/ In the present strength of manhood, that the high/ Imagination cannot fly freely, as she was wont of old",[28] is perhaps the best criticism on loss of imagination in the poetry of his times, after Wordsworth's that came seventeen years earlier.

Admiring Keats's exceptional qualities as a romantic poet, Sydney Colvin says that "controversy apart, if we have in us a touch of instinct for the poetry of imagination and beauty, as distinct from that of taste, reason, and 'correctness',—however clearly we may see the week points of the passage like this, yet we cannot but feel that Keats touches truly the root of the matter: we cannot but admire the ring and the power of his appeal to the element, his fine spontaneous and effective turns of rhetoric, and elastic life and variety of his verse. The congratulatory part repeats with different imagery the sense of the sonnet to Hayden beginning 'Great spirits now on earth are sojourning', and declares that fine sounds are once more floating wild about the earth, wherefore the Muses are glad and happy.... He will believe in and seek to enter upon a kingdom of poetry where all shall be gentle and soothing like lawn beneath a myrtle tree", declaring, "And they shall be accounted poet-kings/ Who simply sing the most heart-easing things".[29]

Then follows a momentary terror of his own presumptions, regarding the disease, disturbing the poet deeply. But he puts it away, defying despondency, as is evident in the following quote:

> For all his youth and lack of learning and wisdom, he has a vast idea before him and a clear conception of the end and aim of poetry...and then once more the sense of the greatness of the task comes over him, and he falls back for support on thoughts of recent friendship and encouragement. A score of lines follow, recalling happy talks at Hunt's over books and prints: the memory of these call up by association a string of the delights of nature: thence he recurs to the pleasures of sleep, or rather of a night when sleep failed him for thinking over the intercourse he had been enjoying and the place where he now rested—that is on the couch in Hunt's library....[30]

In fact, Keats's poetic creativity, apart from his own genius, was also largely shaped by literary giants like Shakespeare and Wordsworth. As for the contemporary influences, which are apparent in Keats's first volume, the name of Leigh Hunt comes first. The influence of Wordsworth, easily the greater poet, is also to be traced in it. By now Keats was diligent and a critical admirer of Wordsworth, as both of the earlier poems and of the *Excursions*, which had appeared when his passion of poetry was already at its height in the last year of his 'apprenticeship at Edmonton'. Keats is supposed to have been influenced by the fourth book of the *Excursions*, in which "Wordsworth treats the spirit of Greek religion and imagines how some of its conceptions first took shape...".[31]

Keats is supposed to have been so much influenced by Wordsworth that, in the views of Mr. Robert Bridges, "some of the ideas expressed by Keats in his own way in *Sleep and Poetry* run parallel with some of those expressed in a very different way by Wordsworth in Tintern Abbey, a poem which we know from other evidence to have been much in Keats's mind a year and half later. Wordsworth in the *Tintern Abbey* defines three stages of his own emotional and imaginative development in relation to nature: first the stage of mere boisterous physical and animal pleasure: then that of intense and absorbing, but still unreflecting, passion...and lastly the higher, more humanized and spiritualized passion doubly enriched by the ever-present haunting of 'still, sad music of humanity', and by the 'sense sublime/ Of something far more deeply interfused...".[32]

However, there was a difference of style and technique between the older and younger poet, even if there was a similarity of thought, as is evident in the following statement:

> Both by gift and purpose it was the part of Wordsworth to meditate and expound, while the part of Keats was to imagine and evoke. Wordsworth, bringing strong powers of abstract thinking to bear on his intense and intensely realized personal experience, expounds the spiritual relations of man to nature as he conceives them.... Keats, on the other hand, had a mind constitutionally unapt for abstract thinking. When he conceives or wishes to express general ideas, his only way of doing so is by calling up, from the multitudes of concrete images with which his memory and imagination are haunted, such as strike him as fitted by their colours and significance, their quality of association and suggestion, to stand for the symbolizing the abstractions working in his mind; and in this concrete and figurative fashion he will be found, by those who take the pains to follow him, to think coherently and purposefully enough.[33]

Still Keats's perception of nature was substantially different from Wordsworth's. Describing this difference of attitude between the younger and the elder poet, Mr. Colvin says that "Keats's sense of personal identity was ever ready to be dissolved and carried under by the strength of his imaginative sympathies. It is not the effect of nature on his personal self that he realizes and ponders over; what he does is with ever-participating joy and instantaneous instinct to go out into the doings of nature and lose him in them. In the result he neither strives for nor attains, as Mr. Bridges truly points out, the sheer intellectual lucidity which Wordsworth in his most impassioned moments never loses. But as, in regard to nature, Wordsworth's is the genius of luminous exposition, so Keats's, even among the immaturities of his first volume, is the genius of living evocation."[34]

In other words, it would be fair to say that Keats bears comparison with the great Wordsworth, only on account of his first attempts at poetry. So, if he lived longer as Wordsworth did, then he would have certainly achieved greater heights in the field of Romantic poetry than Wordsworth succeeded in achieving.

Another literary giant, by whom Keats was influenced, other than a poet, was William Shakespeare. He was so much fascinated by Shakespeare's plays and poetry that "he was reading and re-reading his Shakespeare with passion, and phrases from the plays come up continually in his letters, not only in the form of set quotations, but currently, as though they were part of his own mind and being".[35] His mind was so full of Shakespeare's plays, particularly *King Lear*, when he was out on a tour of Southampton, in the month of April in 1817,[36] that he bethinks him on his approaching birth-anniversary (April 23) in the following lines written to Reynolds:

> I'll tell you what—on the 23rd was Shakespeare born. Now if I should receive a letter from you, and another from my Brothers on that day 'twould be a parlous good thing. Whenever you write say a word or two on some Passages in Shakespeare that may have come rather new to you, which must be continually happening, notwithstanding that we read the same play forty times.[37]

As a matter of fact, John Keats was the last of the great romantic poets to have been born and the first to die. His brief but luminous career is one of the most significant one, in the field of English poetry. Stephen Coote reveals him 'as a man intensely aware of his troubled times'. From Coote's biography of the poet, he emerges "as a poet for whom beauty was inseparable from personal tragedy, and as one, who setting his face against an authoritarian church and state, tried to find a spiritual life free from the repressive conditions of the early nineteenth-century-England".[38]

The result was that the Keats that we know as a poet turned out to be a kind of a combination of "personal genius added with the storehouse made up of earlier geniuses like Homer, Virgil, Shakespeare and Wordsworth", in whose writings he had taken deep interest and had read them with such a passion as to re-live them while reading.

Therefore, Keats's life can be summarized as that of a poet whose had dedicated his life to the 'higher or sublimer' purposes, bothering least about his health. As a matter of fact, a systematic study of his life reveals him as one of the most investigating and innovative poets of all times, in so far as he had attempted to unravel the 'mysteries of life' in his poetry as well as in his letters. This belief is substantiated by the fact that Keats held on to his ideas, which apparently appear 'metaphysical' in nature, till the end of his life, despite his medical knowledge of the fatalness of his disease and thereby the shortness of his life. In fact, the closer the poet reached his last time, the more determined he seemed about his ideas.

Thus, Keats's life was that of a poet who was born to convey to the world the message that human being must utilize the life, which is temporary in nature, to the cause of exploring the 'mysteries of life' by constantly thinking and investigating about them. The early and untimely death of the poet also confirms his unusual 'imaginative capability' on account of which he succeeded in giving an expression to such 'deepest and most profound ideas' in his poetry, as are a rarity either with his predecessors, his contemporaries, or his followers. Which is why, the kind of an innovative and investigating nature that Keats had developed so early in his life, which is itself surprising as to how he had developed them so early, it is certain that he would have undisputedly become the 'greatest and the most original' of all poets that the history of English poetry had given to the world, but for his premature death. Lord Tennyson, the trend-setter for Victorian era, also had said something to this effect, regarding Keats's position in English poetry.

3

Romanticism and Keats

Keats holds a prestigious place amongst the romantic poets along with P.B. Shelley, Wordsworth and S.T. Coleridge, Lord Byron, and others, on account of his sincere and faithful treatment of nature in his poetry. And rightly so, all his poetry is replete with the description of nature, with all the chief characteristics of romantic poetry, like his love of nature, nostalgia for past (love of Greek mythology), love of beauty, etc., leading him to be rightly called a true romantic poet. Like all other romantics, Keats too dwells in the lap of nature to find solace, comfort and inspiration and beauty in life, as the world is a place, full of sorrow, grief and disappointment. ('Where to think is to be full of sorrow'.) But, nature is a place where sorrow cannot enter.

Therefore, the poet has a natural tendency to go to nature. Still, unlike Shelley, he does not merely get lost in the charms of nature, but develops a death-wish, when he happens to listen to the enchanting song of nightingale ("Ode to a Nightingale"), not to escape the miseries of life but to become one with nature. In other words, by dying physically, the poet wanted to become a part of eternity or which is permanent. This idea places Keats ahead of his contemporaries, as far as his approach to life is concerned.

As a matter of fact, "it was in his rambles afield and in his habitual afternoon and evening strolls to Enfield, his native land, that a delighted sense of the innumerable activities of natural life in the forest or brook began to possess Keats's mind, and to blend with the beautiful images from his readings in Greek mythology, and to be enhanced into a strange supernatural thrill by the 'recurring magic of moonlight'. It was only in adolescence that such delights can be drunk in, not with conscious study and observation but passively, and no youth ever drank them in more deeply than Keats. Not till later came for him the time when so awakened, define and develop themselves in consciousness and discover with effort and practice the secret of rightly expressing them in words."[1]

This was, perhaps, Keats's first step into his love of nature and the very first lesson of Romantic poetry.

However, the study of any poet cannot be done in isolation. As a result, Keats's poetry needs to be analyzed with those writing in his age, in the genre in which he himself was writing, namely, poetry. The easiest and an important name that comes to mind is that of P.B. Shelley, who was Keats's contemporary. Both of them sailed the boat of romantic poetry together, as far as period was concerned. Both had a passionate love of nature. Both were also in touch with each other through correspondence. And most of all, both had a great sense of respect for each other as contemporaries.

But, there are grounds on which Keats was in disagreement with Shelley, as far as his approach to poetry was concerned. Keats did not like Shelley's attitude of combining philanthropy with poetry. As a matter of fact, Keats did not hesitate even to advise his contemporary to concentrate only on poetry as a work of art and not to mix his poetry with philanthropy or other social matters, if he wanted to come out with pure poetry. The advice can be easily noticed in a letter written by Keats to Shelley, which is as follows:

> I received a copy of the *Cenci*.... There is only one part of it I am judge of—the poetry and dramatic effect, which by many spirits nowadays is considered the Mammon. A modern work, it is said, must have a purpose. Which may be the God? An artist must serve Mammon; You, I am sure, will forgive me for sincerely remarking that you might curve your magnanimity, and be more of an artist, and load every rift of your subject with ore. The thoughts of such discipline must fall like

> cold chains upon you, who perhaps never sat with your wings furled for six months together.[2]

Commenting on the letter and Keats's attitude to poetry, Graham Hough points out that "The letter reveals admiration but imperfect sympathy. Some of the reasons for this were irrelevant social ones; but the main reason is indicated above. Keats hardly shared at all in Shelley's political and social passions. He does not see the poet as trumpet that sings to battle, or the unacknowledged legislature of the world. 'An artist must serve Mammon'—that is his own art rather than humanity: and Keats is, therefore, the first of those in the nineteenth century who wished to carve out a separate kingdom for the arts, and this letter perhaps marks the beginning in England of the doctrine that was later to develop into 'Art for art's sake'. However, it is only the beginning.... Keats is never really happy in this belief and never works out its implications to his own satisfaction. Its significance for the study of Keats himself is that it shows him as above all the conscious artists, anxious to load his poetry as fully as possible with its own special kind of excellence. We see the result of it in the devoted critical care he gives to his own poetical development, the constant effort to correct faults in technique and emotional tone, to abandon harmful models and choose better ones, above all to think out the essentials of his own kind of poetry to the exclusion of everything else".[3]

"In fact, intellectually Keats was strongly in sympathy with Shelley and Byron. Indeed in religious philosophy he was more extreme, more wholeheartedly pagan than either. Byron, for all his cynicism, never freed himself from Christianity, and Shelley's transcendental fervour is far more obvious than his so-called atheism. But Keats had no religion than the religion of beauty, no God save Pan...."[4]

Perhaps his most notable divergence as a poet, from Shelley, is that he elects, as a rule, to deal with sensation rather than ideas, with concrete life than with abstract imaginings. Not that he eschews ideas, the 'Odes' eloquently refute such a suggestion. But when he elects to deal with ideas, he chooses such human things as love, sorrow, life and beauty. As a matter of fact, "his ideas, like his memory, become incarnate with the shaping splendour of the consummate Artist. And thus does he help us to realize, as no other poet has done since Shakespeare, the oneness of Truth and Beauty".[5]

Matthew Arnold was one of the most esteemed critics of Keats's poetry and mind. In one of his criticism of Keats's poetry, he says, "Keats as a poet is abundantly and enchantingly sensuous; the question with some people will be, whether he is anything else."[6] The statement is indicative enough to suggest that Keats could not be put in the traditional category of romantics. He was obviously more than that. He was, in other words, a kind of a 'metaphysical romantic'.

Arnold further says that "The truth is that the yearning passion for the Beautiful, which was with Keats, as he himself truly says, the master passion, is not a passion of the sensuous or sentimental man, is not a passion of the sensuous or sentimental poet. It is an intellectual and spiritual passion. It is 'connected and made one', as Keats declares that in his case it was, 'with the ambition of the intellect'. It is as he again says, 'the mighty *abstract idea* of Beauty in all things.' And in his last stage, Keats wrote: 'If I should die, I have left no immortal work behind me—nothing to make my friends proud of my memory; *but I have loved the principle of beauty in all things,* and if I had had time I would have made myself remembered.' He *has* made himself remembered, and remembered as no one merely sensuous poet could be; and he has done it by having 'loved the beauty in all things'."[7]

For Keats, to see things in their beauty are to see things in their truth and he knew it and in his immortal verse "Ode on a Grecian Urn" ('Beauty is truth, truth beauty.') he has said the same thing. "No, it is not all, but it is true, deeply true, and we have deep need to know it"[8], comments Arnold, and rightly so.

Elaborating on Keats's theory of beauty, Arnold says, "It is no small thing to have so loved the principle of beauty as to perceive the necessary relation of beauty with truth, and of both with joy. Keats was a great spirit and counts far more than many of his admires suppose, because this just and high perception made itself clear to him. Therefore a dignity and a glory shed gleams over his life, and happiness, too, was not a stranger to it."[9]

Dwelling on the 'higher element' of Keats's sensuousness, Arnold emphasizes that:

> The sensuous strain Keats had, and a man of his poetic powers could not, whatever his strain, but shows his talent in it. But he has something more and something better. We who believe Keats to have been by his promise, at any rate, if not fully by performance, one of the very greatest of English poets, and who believe also that a merely sensuous man cannot either by promise or by performance be a very great poet, because poetry interprets life, and so large and noble a part of life is outside of such a man. We cannot but look for signs in him (Keats) of something more than sensuousness, for signs of character and virtue. And indeed the elements of high character Keats undoubtedly, made efforts to develop them; the effort is frustrated and cut short by misfortune, and time, but for the due understanding of Keats's worth the recognition of this effort, of the elements on which it worked, is necessary.[10]

Deborah Pope explains Keats's attitude of life, which gets automatically reflected in his poetry. In one of his essays "The Dark Side of the Urn: A Re-evaluation of the Speaker in 'Ode on a Grecian Urn'", the critic says, "In his life and in his poetry, he (Keats) was struggling with the forces of self-assertion and submission, forces which Nietzsche was to believe gave rise to tragedy. The crisis was more than enough to tease a man out of thought, for poetic ecstasy demanded the initial spur of self-assertion in order to elevate the imagination and approach vision.... Yet, at some point, the ego must submit to the higher power or vision evoked. Therein lays the dilemma: the self-assertion needed to reach towards a vision, the imagination that seeks to step toward a truth, is itself the defeat of the effort by inevitably projecting its own reflection onto whatever it finds."[11]

An insight into his poetry reveals Keats's work as "always changing and developing".[12] However, it is not the same with his contemporaries. Wordsworth's poetry, or for that matter, that of Shelley, seem to confirm the ideas in the later poems, which had already been put in the earlier poems. But, Keats always seemed to be investigating into the nature of life and things. Therefore, from this point of view, he stands apart from his contemporaries. Indicating to this fact, Graham Hough, one of a significant critics on the poet, says that "...At his death he (Keats), seems to have been on the edge of a further growth. If Shelley had lived longer there would have been more of Shelley, but probably more of the same kind. We feel of Keats that there was much to come that would have been new and different.... There were so many conflicts unresolved at the time of his death. The relation of art, his own kind of art, to human life as a whole was a question that perplexed him from the beginning."[13]

The statement that 'if Shelley had lived longer, there would have been more of him but of the same kind' and that 'of Keats that there was much to come that would have been new and different', speaks volumes in terms of the innovativeness of Keats's poetry, as compared with that of Shelley's poetic theme. Which is why, the vital questions like the relation of art, his own kind of art, to human life as a whole was a question that perplexed Keats from the very beginning. What he says to Shelley in his letter can be analyzed in a different manner. For Keats, 'magnanimity' needs to be associated with the distresses of humanity for the essential growth of a poet.

Throwing light on Keats's social bearings in the light of his metaphysical concerns, Graham Hough says that Keats "lived in an age when a smack of the philanthropists, 'the friend to humanity', was expected of liberal and enthusiastic youth; and he began his career in a circle of liberal enthusiasts. Yet he cannot really worry himself about many of the things that worried them; he feels obscurely of a great liberal of the past that he was not quite a 'friend to humanity', in the contemporary sense, and we find him wondering 'whether Melton's apparently less anxiety for Humanity that proceeds from seeing farther or no than Wordsworth'.... He (Keats) ultimately concludes that 'a mighty providence subdues the mightiest minds to the service of the time being'. But, we might add, the whole tendency of Keats's work is to show that Providence does not always do so in the most obvious ways that the artist does not necessarily precede to the heart of humanity by the plainest and most trodden route."[14]

"We must remember", continues Hough, "too, what we all know, but perhaps without feeling it fully, that Keats's artistic intuition is far in advance of his ordinary experience—that at the time of his death the commonest problem of personal adjustment, even of a position in the world, were still, because of illness, because of poverty, not even on the way to a solution."[15] The statement clearly indicates that Keats's approach to poetry was quite different from his contemporaries. His poetic vision was not limited only to the sensuous aspect of nature, but beyond that, into heights of metaphysical considerations.

Keats was obviously not happy with the branding of his being called a 'sensuous poet'. Graham Hough makes the point clear when he says, "He (Keats) wonders whether he can ever bear to give up these sensuous ecstasies, but realizes in the same breath that they are only a stage in his progress."[16] The following lines from Keats's *Sleep and Poetry*, quoted by Hough, make the poet's intentions clear:

> And can I ever bid this farewell?
> Yes I must pass them for nobler life
> Where I may find the agonies, the strife
> Of human hearts.[17]

Describing Keats's progress as a poet with somewhat of a mystic or metaphysical temperament, Graham Hough says that in his mind, "a sort of a vision follows, in which 'shapes of delight, of mystery and fear' are seen, coming from the clouds and moving about the earth—symbolical of all the variety and passion of life, all that cannot be apprehended as sensuous beauty. This is the earliest statement of the problem that haunts Keats throughout his short life—the attempt to reconcile the loveliness of the world with its transience, its pleasures with its pain, the longing to enjoy the beautiful with the suspicion that it cannot be long enjoyed unless much that is not beautiful is faced. He was never to find a solution to these conflicts, and was never resigned as a modern poet might be, to write poetry of blank conflict: he was entering a new phase of exploration when he died...."[18]

The idea is strengthened further by Graham Hough, when he says that the whole tendency of Keats's work is to show that Providence does not always do so in the most obvious way, that the artist does not necessarily proceed to the heart of humanity by the plainest and the most-trodden route, and adds:

> We must remember...that Keats's intuition is far in advance of his ordinary experience—that at the time of his death the commonest problems of personal adjustment, even of a position in the world, were till, because of illness and poverty, not on the way to solution.[19]

But the utterances were yet largely prophetic; Keats was still in the realm of Flora, or the bright chamber 'Maiden-Thought'. It was only a matter of time before reaching that point where he could come out with that spiritual declaration in 'Ode to a Grecian Urn', saying with an air of finality that "Beauty is Truth, truth beauty—that is all ye know on earth." This was a thought-process which helped him to stand apart from other romantic poets, writing before or after him.

Bringing out the points of distinction of Keats's poetry from those of Shelley and Wordsworth, Graham Hough says, "So far, the most living thing in Keats's poetry has been the re-creation of sensuous beauty, first as a sense of delight for its own sake then as a symbol of life of the mind and the emotions. Speculative and philosophical interests always formed the major part of Shelley's experience, and the young Wordsworth for a time was hag-ridden by them: there is almost no trace of this in Keats.... (However) The academic education which he never had tends to foster abstract thought; but Keats would never have lived by it whatever his training. He not only cared little for, but positively resented intellectual truths which make demands upon the mind with being verifiable in immediate experience.... Keats almost hates a writer who tries to force the world and the reader to his own conclusions, and at times he felt that Wordsworth did so."[20]

For Keats, the "necessary precondition of poetry is submission of things as they are, without trying to intellectualize them into something else, submission to people as they are, without trying to indoctrinate or improve them".[21] Keats found this quality at its fullest in Shakespeare, as he says:

> It struck me what quality went to form a man of achievement, especially in literature—I mean Negative Capability that is when a man is capable of being in uncertainties, mysteries, doubts, without any irritable reaching after fact and reason.[22]

The way Keats wanted to enjoy nature it was not possible for him to do so, in the narrative of characters and events, as he had dreamt of doing in drama, or through the 'agony and strife of human heart'. The nature is "at its height in moments of immediate impassioned contemplation, when the life of the spirit is closely bound up with the objects of immediate sensuous experience. It was in such mood that the *Ode on Indolence* was written (1819)" in the poem not love, nor ambition, nor poetry makes it worthwhile to give up the luxurious enjoyment of the moment: none of them is:

> As sweet as drowsy nouns/And evening steep'd in honied indolence; O, for an age so sheltered from annoy, That I may never know how change the moons, Or hear the voice of busy common-sense![23]

These are "lines which might have served Matthew Arnold as the text for his sermon on Keats, the relaxed and the sensuous man",[24] comments Graham Hough. As if in a hurry, the poet comes with an instant reply when he says, "But what shocks the virtuous philosopher delights the camelian Poet."[25] Then Hough as if summarizing the philosophy of Keats's poetry, says that "it is all exquisite and all transitory; and out of the knowledge of this is born a longing for a world in which such moments could become eternal. All the Ode (of Keats) is closely bound up with themes of transience and permanency."[26]

Therefore, it will be in fairness of things to say that 'sensuousness' was only a phase of Keats's poetry towards a greater realization. In a way, it can be described as a beginning in the poet's journey into the realm of Flora to reach the heights of metaphysical reality. Graham Hough supports the argument as he says, "This is the earliest statement of the problem that haunts Keats throughout his short life—the attempt to reconcile the loveliness of the world with its transience, its pleasures with pain, longing to enjoy the beautiful with the suspicion that it cannot be long enjoyed unless much that is not beautiful is faced. He was entering on a new phase of exploration when he died."[27]

Traditionally, the romantic poets turn to nature for comfort and happiness, as they find worldly pain unbearable. The absence of joy, or the passing of it, is not acceptable to them. So, they hurry to the shelter of nature. But they must return to the same world where they actually live. Thus, for them there is always a conflict, either in poetry or outside it. And since they ask questions to which there is no answer, there is no likelihood to solutions. But, Keats stands apart from his fellow romantics in this regard. He appears more as a classical poet in so far as he dares to accept with resignation the passing of 'earthly joys', because of his tendency to metaphysical thoughts.

Keats, in fact, regards the human life an outcome of God's scheme of things. From this standpoint, joys as well as sorrows are bestowed by the Creator on human beings. As a result, both the situations stand equal in terms of application in life. Graham Hough supports the view when he says, "It (happiness) is all exquisite and all utterly transitory; and out of the knowledge of this is born a longing for a world in which such moments could become eternal. All the Odes (Keats's) are closely bound up with this theme of 'transience and permanency'...". Keats is known for his 'love of beauty', for his perception that everything in nature is 'beautiful'. That is why, he says, "A thing of beauty is a joy forever."[28] His concept of beauty, most of the times, is associated with the sensuousness only. However, his sense of 'beauty' is of a higher kind. It was, in fact, the 'Divine Beauty' he was seeking by way of his poetry. The idea is substantiated by Raghukul Tilak when he says, "It is not sensuous beauty alone that he (Keats) loves but it is the beauty of higher kind. As his powers matured he could identify Beauty with Truth, and later on with Power as well."[29]

Thus, 'beauty' for Keats was the moving spirit of his life and art. His deep sense of imagination made him see 'Beauty' as 'Truth', and he was at his best only in the presence of nature which was only a manifestation of beauty to him.

As a matter of fact, 'love of beauty' was a predominant factor in Keats's poetry. Even small objects that leave others unmoved and unaffected, thrilled the poet. He saw beauty in nature, women, art, literature, mythology and folklore and what not. Middleton Murry rightly remarks, "Beauty in all things—that was Keats's great poetic intuition, and of this beauty, the great human purpose to which he dedicated himself and for which he was prepared to die."[30]

The 'beauty' is seen by the poet "as mankind's truest spiritual activity, his one pledge of unfettered abundance and joy. Beauty is made into a universal, something transcendent in which the limitations of the day-to-day world can apparently be overcome. A sense of freedom and even a quiet religious awe flow through the famous passage as Keats suggests how the harmonious mind, turning with fresh wonder both to see and make the world in which it lives, delights in its own activity...man's truth lies in the shared insights of his subjectivity rather than the common miseries of his history. Truth is the joyful perception of what the senses can relish and the imagination enters into."[31]

However, towards the end of his career, Keats's poetry reveal his metaphysical thoughts more vehemently than before, as in the case of 'Ode on Grecian Urn' and 'Ode to a Nightingale' and *Hyperion*, etc. On the one hand, his health was failing him, but on the other, he was becoming more and more aware of the permanence of God, and the matters regarding His position. This point is duly conformed by Deborah Pope when she says that "Keats's later poems are increasingly tense, dramatic colloquies between some powerful representatives of a higher realm—more and more a realm where opposites are reconciled."[32]

In his youth, Keats was a man of varying moods and strong feelings, finding himself engrossed in the beauty of nature, whenever amidst it. But this 'imaginative curiosity' would extinguish as suddenly as it catches the poet's mind. He would 'become taciturn', comments Joseph Severn, his friend, "neither because he was tired, nor even because his mind was suddenly wrought to some bewitching vision, but from a profound disquiet which he could not and would not explain. The only thing that would bring Keats out of one of his fits of seeming gloomful reverie was the motion of the inland sea he loved so well, particularly the violent passage of wind across a great field of barley. These were moments when 'the natural world' corresponded to his inner need."[33]

Benjamin Bailey was one of the poet's dependable friends with whom he liked to share his readings of poets like John Milton and Wordsworth. It was Bailey himself who introduced the Keats with the genius of Wordsworth. Bailey's basic intention was to reveal "Wordsworth as the great imaginative and philosophic Christian poet, which he really is...while the notes the assiduous Bailey made on their conversation suggest that the greatest effect Wordsworth was to have on Keats at this time was through his profound sense of spiritual questioning, his awareness of confusion and misgiving, and of what, in *Tintern Abbey*, Wordsworth called 'burthen of the mystery'."[34]

Bailey was thus helping to draw Keats towards a more mature and puzzled knowledge of the world. Most of the times, the conversation between the two friends would turn to 'religion'. Interestingly, Bailey was 'a sincere believer', as against Keats's reluctance to be called a Christian in the strict sense of religion. But still, he tried to influence Keats in the direction of his own faith. It was so because, "Bailey's faith was a solution to the problem of evil, and it was this concept he tried to implant in Keats's mind as their conversation led to a deepening of Keats's always questioning sense of moral purpose. Obviously, Bailey was pleased by the result."[35] He expresses his pleasure, when he says, "He (Keats) promised me, and I believe he kept his promise, that he would never scoff religion."[36]

Keats's association with Bailey has a lot to do with the shaping of Keats's beliefs and thoughts. Evidently, he kept the friendship with Bailey without adopting his line of belief in religion, as he had wished him to do. But, it is clear that for most of his religious thoughts Keats owes a lot to Bailey. Although, it is also a fact that Wordsworth's 'burthen of the mystery' did attract Keats's attention a great deal, as regards the nature of the world. However, Keats's respect for Bailey suggests that he was greatly influenced by his thinking, in the matters of religion. "Both his friend's religious tact and his sincerity were of a high order, and, if Keats felt unable to follow him in faith, there is no question that Bailey influenced him by his example."[37]

As a person, Keats was "thoughtful, often grave", says A.C. Bradley, "sometimes despondent; but, he is full of the enthusiasm of beauty, of the joy and fear, the hope and the awe, that accompanied the sense of poetic power. He is the poet who looked, we are told as though he had been gazing on some glorious sight; whose eyes shone and whose face worked with pleasure as he walked in the fields about Hampstead; who is described watching with rapture the bellowing of the wind through the trees and over meadow-grasses and corns, and looking sometimes like young eagle and sometimes like a wild fawn waiting for some cry from the forest depths."[38]

Which is why for Keats "'A thing of beauty is a joy for ever'; who found 'the Religion of Joy' in the monuments of the Greek spirit, in sculpture and vases, and mere translations and mere handbooks of mythology; who never ceased to wonder at all that incarnate delight, and would to Severn (one of his closest friends) how essentially modern, how imperishable, the Greek spirit is—a joy forever."[39]

This is also where Keats was different from his contemporaries like Wordsworth or Shelley. He made full use of the Greek mythology in his poetry to describe the imperishable nature of the 'ultimate reality'. In fact, for Keats the Greek mythology came closest to stand for a comparison for anything that he thought was imperishable. In fact, Greek mythology was chosen by Keats to stand as a symbol for the matters of 'permanence or immortality'.

A marked change in terms of maturity can be noticed as the poet grows older. Now Keats starts looking beyond the limits of mere sensuous or the materialistic joy. Addressing the change, A.C. Bradley says, "Yet, as we have seen already, he was aware, and we find him becoming more and more aware, that joy is not the only word. He had read not for nothing Wordsworth's great Ode, and *Tintern Abbey* and the *Excursions*. We know it from *Endymion*, and the letter about the 'burden of the mystery' was written before the tour of Scotland. But after this we feel a more decided change, doubtless hastened by outward events. But, in personal life agonies, grief, and disappointments were awaiting the poet in form of the 'Blackwood and Quarterly' reviews of *Endymion*—reviews not less inexcusable because of their unjustified, bitter and undue criticism of the poem. Then came his brother's death. A few weeks later he met Miss Brawne. Henceforth his youth has vanished. There are traces of morbid feeling in the change, painful traces. His brother's death deepened his sympathies. He kept faith in his genius, but he felt that he must prove it. He became impatient of dreaming. Poetry, he felt, is not mere luxury and rapture, it is a deed. His gaze is as intent as ever—more intent; but the glory he would see walks in a fiery furnace, and to see it he must think and learn. He is young, writing at random, straining his eyes at particles of light in the midst of great darkness."[40]

In a period dominated by romantic spirit and nature, it was only natural that Keats too imbibed that spirit. But his treatment and outlook of nature was markedly different from his contemporaries. The difference can best be brought to light in comparison with Shelley. The two poets had a marked difference in 'manner' as well as in 'content', so far as writing of poetry is concerned. Basically, Keats did not like Shelley's attitude of mixing philanthropy with poetry. He also did not enjoy Shelley's deliberate philosophizing in poetry.

This difference of attitude and approach between the two contemporaries is nicely described by A.C. Bradley when he says that "For Keats, it may be said, was of all the great poets then alive the one least affected by the spirit of the time, or by that 'revolutionary' atmosphere of which I spoke in the previous lecture. He did not concern himself with the progress of humanity, or with the Manchester Massacres or the risings in Naples.... He worshipped Beauty, not Liberty; and the beauty he worshipped was not 'intellectual' but visible, audible, tangible. He was an artist, intent upon fashioning his material until the outward sensible form is perfectly expressive and delightful. In all this, he was at opposite pole to Shelley, so that he might keep his own unfettered scope; and he never speaks of Shelley cordially. He told him, too, that he might be more of an artist and load every rift of his subject with ore; and that while many people regard the purpose of a work as the God, and poetry as the Mammon, an artist must serve Mammon. And his practice, like his opinions, proves that, both in his strength and his limitations, he belongs to quite a different type."[41]

However, the difference or the contrast is preceded by marked similarities between the two poets. It may be true that Keats was untroubled by that sense of contrast between ideal and real which haunted Shelley and was so characteristic of time. But the similarities between the two can best be noticed by the two well-known Odes by both of them, namely, *To a Skylark* and the *Ode to a Nightingale*. Both the poems deal with the similar subject-matter—the bird as a symbol of perfection. As if to say that "Our human life is all unrest and sorrow, an oscillation between longing and satiety, a looking before and after. We are aware of a perfection that we cannot attain, and that leaves us dissatisfied by every thing attainable. And we die and do not understand death. But the bird is beyond this division and dissonance; it attains the ideal."[42]

One of the matters on which Keats and Shelley differed with each other was the concept of Beauty. For Keats "all things beautiful manifest it, and so far therefore are one and the same".[43] This idea of the unity of all the beauty comes out in many crucial passages in the poems and letters of Keats. The Goddess Cynthia in *Endymion*, for example, is the 'Principle of Beauty'. In the story she is identified with the Moon. So, Cynthia is an example of Beauty Incarnate. The Indian Maid or the others that Endymion comes across in his dream are only supplementary to the primary Beauty, i.e. Cynthia. But this is the kind of beauty that comes easily and is symbolic of sensuous pleasure. Up to this stage, the views of both Keats and Shelley are similar, with regards to beauty. The real difference lies when Keats associates beauty with suffering and pain, which is not the case with Shelley.

Analyzing the difference of attitude in Keats and Shelley, particularly with regards to 'beauty', A.C. Bradley says, "Indeed, the one Beauty is infinitely various. But its manifestation, for Keats, tend to fall into two main classes. On the one hand there is the kind of beauty that comes easily and is all sweetness and pleasure. In receiving it we seem to suppress nothing in our nature.... It is 'luxury'. But the other is won through thought, and also through pain. And this second and more difficult kind is also the higher, the fuller, the near to the Principle. That it is won through pain is doubly true. First, because the poet cannot reach it unless he consents to suffer painful sympathies, which disturb his enjoyment of the simpler and sweeter beauty, and may even seem to lead him away from beauty altogether. What, then, are the points, where, in spite of its evident resemblance to Shelley's, we feel a marked difference? In the first place Keats lays far the heavier stress on the idea that beauty is manifested in suffering and conflict. The idea itself is to be found in Shelley, but it is congenial to him; it appears almost incidentally and is stated half-heartedly.... And this was inevitable; for the whole tendency of Shelley's mind was to regard suffering and conflict with mere distress and horror as something senseless and purely evil, and to look on the whole world as naturally a paradise entirely free from them, but ruined by an inexplicable failure on part of the man."[44]

Thus, "the idealism of Keats is much more concrete. He has no belief either in Shelley's 'natural paradise' or in 'Godwinian perfectibility'. Pain and suffering have a meaning to him, as against Shelley for whom these are something of 'horror and evil'. Without pain and suffering, for Keats, the souls could not be made. When he sets the agonies and strifes of human hearts above a painless and luxurious loveliness, it is because they are more beautiful. Let art only be 'intense', let the poet only look hard enough and feel with force enough, so that the pain (in Keats's case) in his object is seen as truly as the vesture of great passion and action, all 'disagreeable' will 'evaporate', nothing will remain but beauty."[45]

In other words, the experience of pain and suffering, according to Keats, make things look more beautiful rather than that 'beauty' which is the symbol of pleasure and joy only.

The difference between Keats and Shelley also lies with regards to the treatment of 'pain and suffering'. If Shelley regards it as something of horror and 'purely evil', then Keats, as in *Isabella,* by no means supprésses the painful incidents and details. But the poem finishes up as a beautiful experience; the final impression is that of beauty. In the words of A.C. Bradley, "If the word beauty is used in his sense, not in the common contrasted sense, we may truly say that he (Keats) was, and must have remained, more than any other poet of his time, a worshipper of Beauty."[46]

The statement of A.C. Bradley about Keats's concern for truth, is worth-mentioning in which he says that "he (Keats) was far from being indifferent to truth, or for considering it unimportant for poetry. In an early letter, when he criticizes a poem of Wordsworth, he ventures to say that 'if Wordsworth had thought a little deeper at that moment he would not have written it', and that 'it is a kind of sketchy intellectual landscape, not a search after truth'."[47]

In fact, it speaks volumes about the poet's search for truth in his poetry. Commenting on *Endymion*, Keats himself says, "The whole thing must, I think, have appeared to you, who are a consecutive man, as a thing almost of mere words, but I assure you that, when I wrote it, it was the regular stepping of Imagination towards a truth."[48]

As a matter of fact, Keats had even contemplated to study 'metaphysics'.[49] Throwing light on this aspect, A.C. Bradley says that "Many passages show his (Keats's) conviction that for his progress towards this truth 'thought', 'knowledge', 'philosophy', are indispensable."[50]

Therefore, it is clear that Keats was far ahead and apart from his contemporaries like Wordsworth and Shelley, as he spares none of the two in his criticism, with regards to their attitude of life. As for Keats, he appears to be a man with utmost positive attitude towards life and God, with the gift of irreparable disease and thereby despair:

> Notwithstanding all this, by virtue of feeling for beauty of his perception of the vital connexion of beauty with truth, Keats accomplished so much in poetry, that in one of the two great modes by which poetry interprets, in the faculty of naturalistic interpretation, in what we call natural magic, he ranks with Shakespeare.[51]

Because of Keats's early death, he may not have carried his poetry to that stage where he could deal with the moral interpretation of life with authority. But in his criticism of life, he had given a hint that he was very much capable of doing what Shakespeare had done in his plays, if he had lived longer. Supporting the idea, Matthew Arnold says, "For the second great of poetic interpretation for that faculty of moral interpretation which is in Shakespeare, and is informed by him with the same power of beauty as his naturalistic interpretation, Keats was not ripe. For the architectonics of poetry, the faculty which presides at the evolution of the works like the *Agamemnon* or *Lear,* he was not ripe.... But in shorter things, where the matured power of moral interpretation, and the high architectonics which go with complete poetic development, are not required, he is perfect."[52]

For example, in *Ode on Melancholy* and the *Ode to Autumn*, the problems of the artist are in abeyance, and Keats returns to ordinary human experience, to the problems of happiness in life. "The Ode to Melancholy", says Graham

Hough "recognizes that sadness is the inevitable complement of the moments of intense sensuous happiness that so far have been the peaks of his experience."[53]

It is, therefore, vain to escape from the inevitable as to expect a light not to cast shadows. Melancholy, the poet thinks, springs from the transience of joy, and the transience of joy is a part of its nature. "The whole movement and vocabulary of the Odes suggest a rich, slow brooding over beauty and joy, with a full realization both of beauty and the pain that its disappearance will bring, but with an enjoyment of such intensity and depth that it makes the moment eternal, in quality if not in duration."[54]

Commenting on the nature and quality of the Keats's Odes, Graham Hough says, "It would be idle to try to turn the Odes into great philosophical poems. They come to no conclusion and make no synthesis. Keats does not wholly avoid confusion between *permanent value and value permanently accessible to the individual.* His temperament, with its eager love of life, would have been satisfied with a speculative solution like Yeats's belief in re-incarnation: but he would surely have dismissed it as too far fantastic: or like that of Mr. Donne, whose New Immortality, if I have not misunderstood it, suggests that after death a kind of consciousness persists, that is in permanent possession of its past experience.... Yet the Odes are not merely decorative and descriptive poems. The deep conflict from which they spring is both emotional and intellectual; yet they proceed solely by the methods peculiar to poetry, not by the aid of speculative intelligence. They are in fact supreme examples of Negative Capability, 'when a man is capable of being in uncertainties, mysteries, doubts, without any irritable reaching after fact and reason'."[55]

Keats found his real medium in odes, rather than in narrative poems. There was a strong possibility of the poet's journey into a different plane, which could have been mystical or metaphysical in aspect, as far as the subject-matter of his later poetry is concerned. The later poetry was certainly moving onto a plane which is beyond the physical limits of human life, as far as it attempted to deal with the theme of metaphysical interest, for example, the experience of love of a mortal with the Moon-Goddess, in *Endymion*. The love of a mortal with another mortal is a usual experience, but the love of a mortal with an 'immortal' (moon-goddess), is certainly more than that. It is a metaphysical experience.

Throwing light on this aspect, with reference to *Hyperion*, Graham Hough says that "they (the odes) are the summits of his achievement, for *Hyperion* was only the beginning of a phase that he did not live to complete. More than any other poet of his age he had the power of externalizing his experience, of finding adequate outward symbols for his experiences, instead of merely talking about them. This does not necessarily mean that he had the dramatic gift: indeed, his knowledge of human character and actions had hardly gone far enough for this to be possible. Sensuous beauty and meditation on sensuous beauty was the central experience of his life. It is in the Odes that he explores this most fully, and perhaps for the time exhausts it. It is not likely that he would have rested in this phase. Fighting against it all the time was the active and dramatic tendency we have noticed above, the desire to make 'the agony and strife of human hearts' the material of his verse. We must trace his further movement in this direction in the two versions of *Hyperion*."[56]

Allen Tate regards Keats a 'pictorial poet' for whom poetry is a medium of immortalizing the life. He says:

> Keats as a pictorial poet was necessarily presenting in a given poem a series of scenes, and even in the narratives the action does not flow from inside the characters, but is governed pictorially from the outside. He is thus a painting poet.... But like every great artist he knew that his problem was to work within his limitations, and to transcend them. He was a poet of space whose problem was to find a way of conveying what happens in time; for it is time in which dramatic conflict takes place; and it is only by conversion into dramatic actuality that the parts of the verbal painting achieve relation and significance." Tate conforms to the opinion held by Kenneth Burke, who says that 'the form of thought in

> Keats is mystical, in terms of eternal present'—I should add, in terms of the arrested action of painting.[57]

"When Keats adds to 'things as perceived'", says Tate, "what he adds? That it seems to me is the special problem of Keats. In the simplest language it is the problem of adding movement to a static picture, of putting into motion the 'languor which lingers in the main design' (Bridges) of even the later work."[58]

Talking about Keats's thoughts and beliefs, particularly in his Odes, in his essay "Keats and the Music of Autumn", Leonard Unger says that "Keats is not didactic here, nor does he claim didacticism for the bards. There earth-born souls, their works, teach wisdom in speaking of the lives of men, and in bringing to men, generation after generation, an intensified awareness and thrill of being alive. It is the same wisdom which the urn will continue to teach 'in the midst of other woes'. Keats believed that man's life, though rounded by a little sleep, is the stuff of which 'a thing of beauty' is made. Art takes its truth from life, and then returns it to life as beauty. The paradox that 'teases us out of thought' is that in a work of art there is a kind of life which is both dead and immortal. If there is heaven, Keats wanted it to be very much like earth...."[59]

Keats's work always shows the mark of progress, owing to his thoughtfulness. It may seem to be a contradiction that 'the writer of odes' was a surgeon by training. But, this is how the things are. Although, Keats might have exclaimed, 'O! for a life of sensations rather than thoughts.' Still, for him both the terms mean the same. He seems to have been a queer mixture of 'sensations' and 'thoughts'. As a result, he kept on experimenting in terms of his writing, at times trying his skills in story-writing or in drama, but without success. Throwing light on this tendency of Keats, Graham Hough says:

> Any poet whose work is as continually progressive as that of Keats must make these tentative and unfulfilled explorations. His most completely successful short narrative poem is the one where he remains most completely within the range of decorative romantic

> experience. This is *The Eve of St. Agnes*. It was written in the first flush of his acquaintance with Fanny Brawne, before illness and, perhaps, her lack of real sympathy, had made the hope of an idyllic and happy love impossible for him. It was full of dreamy sensuous happiness which finds its expression in a rich decorative pattern rather than in any precise delineation of passion and sentiment. The poetic equivalent for an emotion with Keats is commonly a picture: it is by the precision of his sensuous imagery—bright and clear, yet rich, like the figures in a painted missal-hat he commands the response he wants. This imagery is chiefly visual: (the clear pictorial quality explains his appeal to the pre-Raphaelite painters) but images of sound, of touch, even of taste, also play their part; and the reader who is content to respond simply to the rich sensuous surface of such a poem as *The Eve of St. Agnes* is in the end likely to understand Keats better than one who is too addicted to philosophical short cuts....[60]

"With our post-symbolist taste", says Hough, "we are too likely to be unappreciative of this sort of descriptive writing, even while we recognize its aptness. But, we should be wrong to think of it merely 'decorative'. The idea of a lucky love triumphant over obstacles could never express itself in Keats by the rhapsodic anatomizing of sentiment that we find in *Epipsychidion*; this succession of clear, bright images of sight, sound and touch is the only means by which his imaginative life can find its incarnation. Keats had been reproved for wishing once for life sensations rather than that of thoughts: the key to his poetry is that most of the time his sensations were thoughts, the kind of thought that could not be embodied in sensuous pictorial form was hardly possible for him."[61]

For example, the lover in 'The Eve of St. Agnes' is wakened by his beloved Madeline by playing "an ancient ditty long since mute/ In Province called 'La Belle Dame sans Mercy'.... The name appears to have fascinated Keats, and not long afterwards he wrote the poem of that name. It is thus dramatically conceived, and springs out of the atmosphere of

'The Eve of St. Agnes'. But it is a far less conscious poem, and springs perhaps from a different layer of mind. La Belle Dame is the fatal woman-figure, like Circe or Tannhauser's Venus, who haunts romantic literature. She is the opposite of the pure and ideal Madeline, and yet the same person; one of the many forms the woman image assumes in the unconscious imagination. The imagery and the phrasing have the perfect harmonious strangeness of a dream."[62]

Describing Keats's association with romantic poetry, with a different attitude, Graham Hough says, "if the essence of romantic poetry is to rely on sources of inspiration other than the rational intellect can supply, this poem ('The Eve of St. Agnes') may be justly considered as its quintessence, and its hidden source is shown in the magical compulsive rhythm, less opulent and deliberate than is usual with Keats, more unexplainably haunting."[63]

"The triumph of poetry lies in its ability to obliterate the need to reach for certainty and relish in ambiguities. Keats is the Man to whom an intellect is entrusted," argue Dr. Anupama Nagar and Dr. Amarnath Prasad, "and when he in a spirit of total surrender uses it to achieve the singular ideal of poetic-realization, then he can be referred to in Emersonian terms as *Man Thinking*."[64]

However, it will be interesting to analyze Keats's poetic-realization in the light of Orientalism. In this connection, the above-mentioned critics regard Keats as a man of disinterested action (karmayogi), from the point of Vedantic philosophy, as they say, "...Similarly the Man of disinterested action (karmayogi) has a determinate intellect, which is firmly established in God. In *Bhagwadgita*, the equal-minded Man is also referred to the philosopher (tattvagyananin) or one who has transcended three qualities of *sattva, rajas, tamas* (*gunateeta*). Keats by negating the capabilities emancipating from the ego-self (lower-self) transcends the physical/material limitations and attains like the tattvagyananin to the transcendental higher-self. Thus Keats's conception of a great Poet and Gita's Man of disinterested action are in spirit one and the same. Similarly the state of equal-mindedness in the

'Ode To Autumn' seeks to negate the extremities of life in order to manifest the true spiritual self of man. The poem advocates a philosophy of serene acceptance that goes hand in hand with the *sthitaprajana avastha*—the attitude of maintaining one's equipoise irrespective of all changes.... The idea of the shift from immortality to mortal powerlessness goes very well with the idea of deconstruction of an established order in 'Hyperion'. An Indian reader though would see the same as an instance of *vikalpa*, for only the best (alternative) stands the test of time. Again the 'Grecian Urn' carries a Center in itself which has to be deconstructed...."[65]

Praising Keats for his contribution to romantic poetry with his spiritual vision, Lord Tennyson, the most celebrated of Victorian poets, declares that, "Keats with his spiritual vision would have been, if he had lived, the greatest of all."[66]

It is, in fact, a rare gesture displayed by a successor (Tennyson) to his predecessor (Keats). Generally, a successor's tendency is to condemn his predecessor's achievement, so that he could succeed in setting a new trend. But, Tennyson's praise of his predecessor proves his greatness as a poet. Another critic, Prof. Stopford Brooke, describes Keats's Odes as 'pure gold'. Any poetry cannot be described as 'gold' only on account of its composition. It needs to carry a 'golden subject' in order to become a 'golden poetry'.

It is for this reason that when Stopford Brooke considers Keats's Odes as "above criticism, pure gold of poetry—virgin gold,"[67] he is justified in his praise. Yet another critic on the poet, Prof. Selincourt, says the same in using other words, about the quality of his Odes. He says, "in the odes he (Keats) has no master; and their indefinable beauty is so direct and so distinctive an influence on his soul that he can have no disciple."[68]

This kind of poetry is not possible without a philosophical attitude to life. Commenting on this aspect, Dr. Fatima Sugarwala, says, "Keats wrote from deep within, without social or commercial compulsions.... Like Longinus Keats believed that all art is sublime. An artist in reaching this stage of sublimity is all engrossed into 'ethereal musings'—a noble and heavenly thought which leads him to create a thing of beauty, that which is divine. Traditional scholarship views him as an artist who consciously transcended moral and political ideology to explore the realm of pure imagination.... Beauty to him was 'middle term that connects and reconciles two kinds of truth through the meditation of beauty, the truth of fact becomes the truth of affirmation, truth of life....' This interpretation of Beauty is the most positive approach to life. It sharpens all sense and widens all unimaginable horizons. As a result, it burns up everything within him, so that Beauty shines like a flame of his soul. When a poet reaches this stage then the heart sings, the mind make music, and the soul dances with delight. This magical impact of Beauty is 'Essential Poetry'."[69]

Thus, "Beauty to Keats was ideal, essential and everlasting. To him, Beauty which evoked truth and goodness gave rise to eternal poetry. Keats aimed at a greater perfection of beauty."[70] The term 'greater perfection of beauty' unmistakably indicates to the 'divine beauty'.

However, the last oft-quote lines of Keats's poem 'Ode on a Grecian Urn' ('Truth is beauty, beauty truth'), seen from the angle of Orientalism, can be compared with 'Satyam, Shivam, Sundaram'. Here, Satyam stands for the 'ultimate truth', Shivam means 'good', while Sundaram is 'beautiful'. These are the three qualities which go into the making of God. Dr. Fatima Sugarwala describes this ('Satyam, Shivam, Sundaram') as "sutra, considered as truly divine...and today it has been divinely knit into Indian culture, religion art and literature".[71]

Therefore, by comparison the 'Truth in Keats is 'Satyam', 'Beauty' 'Sundaram'. However, the second term Shivam (goodness) does not have a separate diction in Keats. But, for him, 'beautiful' cannot be but 'good' only. As a result, it is quite possible that Keats may have had some knowledge of Oriental philosophy, and thereby may have been tempted to finish the Ode with lines quoted above.

Dr. Fatima Sugarwala, who effectively attempts to analyze Keats's poetry in view of Orientalism, believes that:

> Keats was a spiritually minded person, interested in mysticism that transcended religion. At such level or

> from such a vantage, Keats tapped into a certain practice like the Zen Buddhists. The 'koans' are Zapanese riddles that have no answer unless they achieve the psychological or spiritual effect intended to gain pure experience of concrete reality. Keats is doing essentially the same thing, though in an inimitable Western way, and mixing it up with literary poetry and verse because of his Romantic beliefs in the purifying and the ethical powers of beauty and truth....[72]

In fact, the book *Recritiquing John Keats* "underlines the need of a comparative approach to holistically interpret John Keats.... Most of his ideas like the concept of 'negative capability'—(*nakaratmak samarthya*) lead to the freeing of the human mind from the fetters of bigotry and ideology through a quite different and superior use of intellectual faculties.... Today, in this era of rediscovery, rethinking and revaluation, there is emerging a mindset that would be able to appreciate better some of the deeper aspects of philosophical thoughts in Keats's poetry...."[73]

These ideas, however, are best expressed by the poet in his odes. The odes seem to be written in such a way as to give a feeling of coherent thoughts in them. Therefore, the odes need to be discussed in that light.

As a matter of fact, it can be said with a certainty that Keats had a definite thought-process in all of his Odes. It will be wrong to say that the 'Truth-Beauty' lines in 'Ode on a Grecian Urn' are not the outcome of the natural development of the earlier lines of the poem, a view held by the critics like T.S. Eliot and others. The poet does begin his career with his love for the 'Flora of nature'. But his journey as a poet does not end there. He wants to explore 'the dark passages of the mystery' before passing away from the world. His interest in such matters does neither diminish nor undergoes a change on account of his failing health and other miseries concerning his family.

Generally, a person, however mentally strong he may be, if gripped by such a fatal disease as was Keats, tends to become pessimistic in approach. But, it is just not the case with the poet. There are instances, referred to in chapter 2, studying his life and work, when Keats, after vomiting blood, could boldly say that the colour of the blood shows that his days were very near. Such boldness or plainness of expression can be made only by a man of a uncommon temperament. This goes to show that he had a particular thought-process, which he wanted to convey through his odes.

And, therefore, Leonard Unger brings out a pattern of similarity of thought among three odes, namely 'Ode to Autumn', 'Ode on Grecian Urn', and 'Ode to a Nightingale', in terms of the spirit of Romantic poetry that these odes represent, as well as Keats's innovativeness, as reflected in them. He says that "the imaginative aspect of structure which the three odes have in common illustrates opinions which are in accord with thought of Keats's times and which he occasionally expressed in his poetry. The romantic poets' preoccupation with nature is proverbial, and there are a number of studies relating their work and thought to the associationist psychology which was current in their times.

According to this psychology, all complex ideas and all products of the imagination were, by the association of remembered sensations, evolved from sensory experiences. Keats found this doctrine interesting and important not because it led back to the mechanical functioning of the brain and the nervous system, but because sensations led to the imagination and finally to myth and poetry, and because the beauty of nature was thus allied with the beauty of art. In the early poem that which begins, 'I stood tip-toe upon a little hill', Keats suggests that the legends of classical mythology were created by poets responding to the beauties of nature."[74]

That is to say, although Keats began his poetic career by just simply praising the beauty of nature, yet he goes on to transform that 'sensuous beauty' of nature into the 'Divine Beauty', by the power of imagination. In fact, he believes that the work of a sage or a poet is similar, as far as the realization of the beauty of nature is concerned, as is evident from one of his poems, which is worth-quoting. Some of the lines are as follows:

For what made the sage or poet write
But the fair paradise of Nature's light?
In the calm grandeur of a sober line,
We see the waving of the mountain pine;
And when the tale is beautifully staid,
We feel the safety of a hawthorn glade;
While at our feet, the voice of crystal bubbles
Charms us at once away from all our trouble:
So that we feel uplifted from the world,
Walking upon the white clouds wreath's and curl'd.[75]

So, Keats elevates a poet to the height of a sage, who is capable of taking part in spontaneity or the beauty of nature. In the 'Ode to Psyche', Keats undergoes,

> Similar experience for himself and contrasts it with those of the 'bards of old'. He has come upon Cupid and Psyche while he 'wandered in the forest thoughtlessly'. Although the times are 'too late for antique vows' and the 'fond believing lyre', he is still by his 'own eyes inspired'. If he cannot celebrate this symbolic deity with rites and shrine, then he proposes to do so with the service of imagination.... Conspicuous throughout Keats's work, blended and adjusted according to his own temperament and for his own purposes, are the *donees* of his time: a theory of the imagination, the Romantic preoccupation with nature, and the refreshed literary tradition of classical mythology. These are reflected by the structure of his most successful poems, and are the element in their interrelatedness.[76]

The unanimity of the theme and spirit also runs into the ode 'To Autumn'. It is shorter than the other odes, and simpler on surface in several respects. The nightingale sings of summer 'in full-throated ease', and the boughs in the flowery tale on the urn cannot shed their leaves 'nor ever bid the spring adieu'. The world in which the longer odes have their setting is either young or in its prime, spring or summer. Consequently, in these some directness of statement and a greater complexity are necessary in order to develop the paradoxical theme, in order to penetrate deeply enough the temple of Delight and arrive at the Sovran Shrine of Melancholy. The urn's 'happy melodist' plays a song of happiness, and the 'self-same' song of the nightingale is of summer.

One of these songs, however, has 'no tune', and the other is in either 'a vision or a waking dream', for the voice of the 'immortal bird' is finally symbolized beyond the 'sensual ear'. But the music of autumn, twittering of the swallows, remains realistic and literal, because the tensions of Keats's theme are implicit in the actual conditions of autumn, when beauty and melancholy are merging on the very surface of reality. Keats's genius was away from statement and towards description, and in autumn he had the natural symbol for his meanings. If 'To Autumn' is shorter than the other odes and less complex in its materials, it has the peculiar distinction of great compression achieved in simple terms.

Kenneth Allott also supports the idea of unanimity of thought in all the odes of Keats. Quoting Mr. Holloway, Kenneth Allott says that "the Odes collectively are 'a psychological document...of unique interest' because they 'prove to be a complex and detailed poetic revelation of what Keats knew himself as the creative mood', and he finds the main evidence for this view in certain repetition of phrase which in his opinion establish a distinctive unity for the six poems (he includes 'On Indolence'). With help of the *Letters* the creative mood the Odes is then revealed as a drowsy, luxurious indolence, a visionary ecstasy in which consciousness struggles with insight on the very edge of oblivion...."[77]

Talking about a 'unity of thought' in the three Odes, 'On Indolence', 'To Psyche' and 'To Nightingale', another important critic Holloway says that:

> Of these three Odes, 'On Indolence' in the main portrays a mood which the embryo of the 'melancholy fit', 'To Psyche' celebrates the deity of one of its forms (love-melancholy), and 'On Melancholy' displays its growth and intensity and climax. The other two Odes centre upon particular things which have evoked or represented

> the experience for Keats himself. To a very considerable degree they run parallel—though this has been overlooked by several critics or expressly denied.... Thus in the opening lines of 'To a Nightingale' the drowsy numbness is, once more, both an aching pain and a too-sharp happiness; hearing the song induces Keats to forget and also remember what is unhappy in life—it brings oblivion that, at a deeper level, is keener knowledge. Once again the senses are stilled, but to an 'embalmed darkness' that is even so a heightened sensuous awareness divining the surrounding sensuous wealth; and when Keats thinks of 'easeful Death' it is like 'nothingness' in 'On Indolence'—as the completion of this unique oblivion.[78]

In the analysis of 'Ode to Psyche' by Kenneth Allott, he also suggests a metaphysical approach undercurrent in the Ode, when he points out that "Psyche is the 'loveliest vision far', lovelier than the Moon or Venus, because she is a love-goddess with an understanding of troubled human experience, because she has known in her own person—as no true Olympian could ever know—suffering and seemingly hopeless longing. She is 'loveliest' because she is 'latest' (there is much in 'Hyperion' and 'The Fall of Hyperion' obviously relevant to this identification)—not an early and therefore simple personification of human nature subjected to an inevitable and cruel process of growing up and growing old."[79]

In fact, "one of the great symptoms of returning vitality in the imagination of Europe was its re-awakening to the significance and beauty of the Greek mythology. For a hundred years and more the value of that great mythology for the human spirit had been forgotten. There never had been a time when the names of the ancient, especially the Roman, gods and goddesses were used so often in the poetry as done by Keats. So far as the real effect upon men's minds is concerned, the Greek mythology was treated as 'dead'."[80]

Faiths may perish one after another, but each in passing away bequeaths for the enrichment of the time to come whatever elements it has contained of imaginative or moral truth or beauty. For example:

> The polytheism of ancient Greece, embodying the instinctive effort of the brightliest gifted human race to explain its earliest experiences of nature and civilization, of the thousand moral and material forces, cruel or kindly, which environ and control the life of man on earth, is rich beyond measure in such elements; and if the modern world at any time fails to value them, it is the modern mind which is insofar for a season dead and not they.[81]

Estimating the significant contribution made by Keats to the cause of romantic poetry in the whole of Europe in general, and in England in particular, Mr. Colvin says that:

> To rescue the mind of England from this mode of deadness was part of the work of the poetical revival of 1800 and onwards, and Keats was the poet who has contributed most to the task. Wordsworth could understand and expound the spirit of Grecian myths.... Shelley could feel and write of Apollo and Pan and Proserpine, of Alpheus and Arethusa, with ardent delight and lyric emotion. But it was the gift of Keats to make live by imagination, whether in few words or many, every ancient fable that came up in his mind. The couple of lines telling of the song with which Peona (in *Endymion*) tries to soothe her brother's pining are a perfect example of appropriate verbal music and of the imagination following out a classic myth, that of the birth and nurture of Pan, from a mere hint of its recesses and finding the human beauty and tenderness that lurks there....[82]

Which is why, when Keats interrupts for a passing moment, his tale of the might and mysteries of love, celestial or human, turns to images of war, and we find him able to condense the whole tragedy of the sack of Troy into three potent lines, which are as follows: "The woes of Troy, towers smothering o'er their blaze, iff-holden shields, far-piercing spears, keen blades, struggling, and blood, and shrieks."[83]

Many passages in *Endymion* give poetical expression to the same altering moods of "ambition and humility, of exhilaration, depression, or apathy, which he confides to his friends in his letters. One of the most striking and original of these pieces of figurative psychology studied from his own moods is the description of the Cave of Quietude in Book I. "There lies a den, Beyond the seeming confines of the space/ Made for the soul to wander in and trace/ Its own existence, of remotest glooms."[84]

However, Sidney Colvin's idea that Keats may have been influenced by Shelley's *Alastor* while writing *Endymion* was not right. Rather, the reverse was true. It was Shelley who seems to have been impressed by Keats, if not influenced, as he says:

> it is certain that Keats read and was impressed by *Alastor*: doubtless he also read *Hymn*.... That poem is a parable, as it enforces, as much of *Endymion* does, the doctrine that a poet cannot without ruin to himself live in isolation from human sympathies. But there the resemblance between the two conceptions really ends. In *Alastor* the poet, having lived in solitary communion 'with all that is most beautiful and august in nature and human thought and the world's past', is suddenly awakened, by a love-vision which comes to him in a dream, to the passionate desire of find and mating with a kindred soul.... The desire, ever unsatisfied, turns all his former joys to ashes, and drives him forth by unheard of ways through monstrous wilderness until he pines and dies....[85]

But, the theme of the poem (*Alastor*) is the quest of the poetic soul for perfect spiritual sympathy and its failure of what it seeks. Although Shelley does not make it fully clear whether the ideal of his poet's dream is a pure abstract idea or whether he is transcendentally expressing his own personal longing for an ideally sympathetic soul companion in the shape of a woman. But in any case his conception is fundamentally different from that of Keats in *Endymion*. However, the case is different with Keats, so far as *Endymion* is concerned. The poem is a reflection of an idea where the poet imagines about the possibility of a dream in which a human lover could yearn for the love of a goddess, namely the moon-goddess. Thereby, the poet dreams of a situation where the human being could realize his wish of loving a godly creature. This is why:

> The essence of Keats's task (in *Endymion*) is to set forth the craving of a poet for full communion with the essential Beauty in the world, and the discipline by which he is led, through the exercise of active human sympathies and the toilsome acquisition of knowledge, to the prosperous and beatific achievement of his quest.[86]

But, these are the kind of visions which may rise spontaneously in common in the minds of almost any pair of youthful dreamers. Shelley's poetic style is of course as much sounder and less experimental than that of Keats at this time as his range and certainty of penetrating and vivifying imagination are...less: he fad a trained and scholarly feeling both for the resources of the language and for its purity, and Keats might have learnt much from him as to what he should avoid. "But as we have seen," argues Colvin, "Keats was firm on his guard against letting any outside influence affect his own development, and would not visit Shelley at Marlow during the composition of *Endymion*, in order 'that he might have his own unfettered scope' and that the spirit of poetry might work out its own salvation in him."[87]

However, Colvin believes that if Keats was to criticize Shelley's *Hymn to Intellectual Beauty*, which was perhaps written under the influence of Plato, he:

> would have felt its strain of aspiration and invocation too painful, too near despair, to make much appeal to him, and that it would have seemed to him something abstract, remote, and uncomforting. His own imagination insisted on the existence of something in the ultimate nature of the universe to account for what he calls the 'wild and harmonized tune' which he found his spirit striking from all the scattered and the broken beauties of the world....[88]

Keats may have been indebted to Shelley with regards to *Endymion*. But there is an interesting small debt to be recorded on the side of Shelley to Keats. Shelley, notwithstanding his interest in Keats, did not read *Endymion* till a year or more after its publication. But once he had read the poem fully Shelley comments that "much praise is due to me for having read it, the author's intention appearing to be that no person should possibly get to the end of it. Yet it is full of the highest and finest gleams of poetry: indeed, everything seems to be viewed by the mind of the poet which is described here. I think if he had printed about fifty pages of fragments from it, I should have been led to admire Keats as a poet more than I ought, of which there is no danger."[89]

In May, 1820, Shelley wrote that "Keats, I hope, is going to show himself as a great poet; like the sun, to burst through the clouds, which, though dyed in the finest colours of the air, obscuring his rising."[90]

Anyway, so far as the debt is concerned, it is with regards to Shelley's *Prometheus Unbound*, some passages of which are supposed to have been inspired by *Endymion's*. Colvin says that "the derivation of this imagery from the passage of Keats seems evident alike from its general conception and sequence and from details like the anchors, beaks, targets, the prodigious primeval sculptures.... Another possible debt of Shelley to *Endymion* has also been suggested in the list of delights which the poet, in the closing passages of *Epipsychidion*, proposes to share with his spirit's mate in their imagined island home in the Aegean. If Shelley indeed owes anything to *Endymion* here, he has etherealized and transcendentalized his original even more than Keats did Ovid...."[91]

Throwing light on Keats's constant interactions with his fellow romantics regarding romanticism and matters concerning 'metaphysics', Maurice Bowra, one of the authorities on Romanticism, says that "this sudden flowering of genius is of course inexplicable, but at least it shows strange are the reactions of the creative spirit to circumstances.... In such conditions (of personal and family torments faced by Keats) might not be expected to start on a new form of poetry and to give to it an unprecedented richness. Yet this is what happened, and it is only another example of the unaccountable ways in which the creative spirit works. Perhaps something is due to the famous walk and talk which Keats had with Coleridge on April 11th, when Coleridge spoke, among other topics, of 'Nightingales, Poetry—on Poetical Sensation—Metaphysics', etc.[92]

The quality of 'Negative Capability' in Keats's poetry also keeps him ahead of his contemporaries. This type of feeling grows naturally into a strong wish to participate in the lives of others. This tendency makes his poetry absolutely objective in style. In such moments the poetry becomes a matter of impassioned contemplation, when the life of spirit is closely bound up with objects of immediate sensuous experience. 'Ode to a Nightingale' is perhaps the best example of Keats's negative capability, in his description of the perfectly happy world of the nightingale. However, it may be debatable as to what is the moral idea in Keats's poetry, or whether he deliberately makes use poetry to convey certain morals. Again, does his poetry gives the modern reader the total effect of major poetry, or is it relatively minor poetry that stirs our sensuous faculties only? are questions that require answers. But, as far as a distinction between his ideas and those of his contemporaries is concerned, Keats undoubtedly stands apart from them. N.S. Sahu supports the view when he says that "neither Wordsworth nor Shelley bear such ardour. Abstractions distinguishable from beauty, nature, liberty, love and truth with which imagination had little to do count much with both. The vision of Keats was never distorted by theories. He was a pure poet."[93]

No words could make this distinction between Keats and his contemporaries more clear and certain than those of Mr. Sahu which say that "not all poets were as fortunate as Wordsworth and Keats in finding that their discontents could be cured by contact with nature which lay at their doors, or that, by following their instinctive love of the visible things, they could find themselves in the presence of what they called 'eternity'. Others were content to dream dreams on the chance that they might some day prove true regardless of whether this happened or not...."[94]

So, Keats stands comparable only to Wordsworth, in the eyes of the critic, as far as his sensuousness was capable of making him realize what is known as 'eternity'. Considering his short span of life, rightly says Sahu, "there is no parallel to the varieties of styles with which Keats as a poet experimented. Yet it was never experimentation for its own sake. His poems, in terms of style, the experimentation Keats made, reveal a great honesty, greater openness to concrete life and the claims of experience towards greater fullness and richness of expression, and at the time a growing strength control and sensibility to the formal claims of his poetics."[95]

That is why, when "we read Keats's poetry, the question recur about life, about nature and worth of poetry, about the character, function and obligations of the poet, and finally about the relationship of imagination: Truth and Beauty. As a result, from the collection of his writings as a whole, a pattern of thought emerges, moving from simple, if vague concept of Beauty, through considerations of the conflicting elements of experience to a vision in which reconciliation and acceptance is possible."[96]

Therefore, "Keats's pursuit of rich, full sensuous effects is incidental to a more arduous quest, his search for fullness and completeness of meaning. Sensations powerful, though it is in Keats's poetry, is but a single element in a highly complex unity. Consequently, his fusion and transference of sensations are incidental to his deeper, more complex synthesis of poetic experience in which intellect, sense and emotions are inseparably interwoven."[97]

Therefore, it is enough to prove that Keats did not blindly follow the path of romanticism shown to him by his predecessors or contemporaries. He rather made use of romantic spirit to convey his deep thoughts in his poetry. His poetry has a lot to do with the metaphysical frame of his mind, which has a definite pattern of thoughts and themes, noticeable in the repetition of certain phrases like 'casements', 'death-wish', and 'Beauty', etc. throughout the poetry. As a result, Keats's romanticism is not exactly similar to that of his contemporary poets. But it was a kind of romanticism having to deal with matters relating to metaphysics. This is where Keats excelled his contemporaries, in so far as he made grave attempts to elevate the purpose of the romantic poetry from mere description of 'beauty' of nature to the 'principle of beauty in all things', which ultimately indicate to the 'Divine Beauty'.

The very statement that Keats's poetry is 'ever changing and developing', is enough to suggest that right from the beginning till the end of his life, Keats was deeply concerned with the metaphysical aspect of his life. Even his decision of not marrying in life is indicative of his unwillingness to take interest in mundane human activities of life, where one is bound by the limited pleasures. He regarded nature as a place capable of affording 'unlimited pleasures'. As a result, when he "elects to deal with ideas, he chooses such human things as love, sorrow, life and beauty, and presents them in concrete shape".[98] Loius Mac Niece was right in calling Keats a 'sensuous mystic'.[99]

Therefore, 'romanticism' for Keats was only a means to realize the 'limitless pleasure' through various moods of nature, which in the end is capable of taking him out of the mundane life into something more 'sublime and higher', which is very much a metaphysical subject. And this was where he not only differed from his contemporaries, but also excelled them, in attempting to make poetry a vehicle of 'higher purposes' in life.

To end the discussion, Keats's romanticism, therefore, was not the blind following of the romantic trends as was done by his contemporaries in the period dominated by romantic spirit. He remained unaffected by the spirit and, rather, used those trends to fulfill his purpose of making poetry a medium of 'higher thoughts' so as to explore the 'dark passages' of mystery, by way of 'sensations' and 'heightened sense of imagination', which were the ways, according to him, capable of realizing the 'ultimate truths' of life.

4

Keats's "Letters": An Insight into the Metaphysical Aspect of His Life

The letters of Keats are of more than merely biographical interest, although they do throw a great deal of light on his activities, his acquaintances and his way of life. As a matter of fact, "The recipients of the letters are few in number and in most cases are inmates of the writer. To these he writes as much of his inner as of his external life, working out his ideas and his feelings on a wide range of topics: literary criticism, the nature of poetry, the problem of suffering and evil and the problem of his own personality".[1]

Apart from various aspects of poetry, the letters also contain the poet's idea of 'suffering and evil', as mentioned in above statement. This makes an interesting reading as far as his metaphysical attitude is concerned.

By temperament, the poet seems to be concerned about his personal life as well as the general one, in terms of existence. His 'letters' are among the most interesting ever written by a poet. "They reveal a mind resolved to face fearlessly the problems of human destiny, and to shape its own interpretation of life. One sees in them how well-founded was Keats's ambition to produce, in time, 'a few fine plays'."[2]

In fact "Although Keats's letters have intrigued readers for generations, their specific placement within his overall corpus remains problematical. Most twentieth-century critics have seconded Eliot's claim that the rich aesthetic speculation in Keats's letters render them 'certainly the most notable and most important ever written by any English poet'. Consensus has been elusive, however, on the distinct relation between the letters and Keats's poems. More recently, W.J. Bate and Stuart Sperry have argued for a more complex reciprocity between letters and poems their major studies of Keats's development trace the formulation of aesthetic concepts in letters that anticipate and help generate similar constructions in the poetry."[3]

These more subtle juxtapositions of letters and poems have been further developed by David Luke and Susan Wolfson, both of whom discuss related patterns of mental action in two mediums. For instance, "Luke sees the letters open-minded speculation inspiring similar inquiry in Keats's correspondence, just as his poems raise questions to tease the thought of the readers. Wolfson stresses a creative process of intellectual discovery and qualification in the letters, 'doubling' habit off mental play that also informs much of Keats's best poetry."[4]

In her study of the 'Interrogative spirit', dealing with Keats's venturous ideas in his letters which 'qualify, subvert, and reformulate them, Wolfson describes these writings as 'creative events'. "The exact configuration of such 'events' bears many important resemblances to a specific pattern of conflict, visionary insight and qualification that controls much of the finest poetry written during the Romantic era. Keats of all the Romantics perhaps most strongly moved by such mentality made of its pattern a habitual frame of mind to foster poetry that dramatizes its countering movements."[5]

Throwing light on the factors for the emergence of the letters, Greg Kucich says that:

> Such activities of mind habitually prompt and inform marked rise in letter production during creative activity brought on by Keats's notorious poetic anxieties. The timing, complemented by decreased correspondence when poetic composition renews, suggests Keats's reliance on letters for creative exercise to rejuvenate flagging inspiration. His epistolary acts of mind never

> attain the formal discipline of their poetic counterparts, for the letters always remain casual, exploratory, and excursive. Yet this very absence of discipline, as Wolfson notes, was particularly stimulative during periods of creative frustration; and it often fostered a lyrical interiority whose dynamics traced out the doubling motions of the mind that recur so frequently in Keats's poems. Such internal dramas grant many of the letters memorable visions, and more significantly, they also shape a mental state conducive to artistic renewal. Keats's letters thus relieve creative blockage by initiating mental exercises directly productive of verse that shares in the same activity of mind. In this regard, they deserve recognition as integral parts of his total creative effort.[6]

We can says that "The growing intensity of this meditation (of writing letters) prompts a new visionary approach to despair in which highly imaginative language expresses a temporary sense of creative power. This development repeats the procedures of stimulating vision and creativity in Keats's earlier letters, but stronger treatment of psychological conflict intensifies the movement towards release, and the vision that emerges solve the conflict through a much more complicated mental operation. Instead of heightening and releasing tension, this visionary outlook redefines the entire problem and solves it by inverting its terms. Despair, seen from the inspired perspective, becomes a spur to higher artistic creativity, which finds no limits in its strengthened capacity. Keats's emerging revelation thus builds up confidence in the powers of a creative intrepidity fashioned be the agency of despair".[7]

Talking about his fight against despair, Keats writes to his brother: "However every ill has its share of good—this very bane at any time enable me to look with an obstinate eye on the Devil himself—ay to be proud of being the lowest of the human race as Alfred could be in being the highest. I feel confident I should have been a rebel Angel had the opportunities been mine. I am very sure that you do love me as your own Brother—I have seen it in your continual anxiety for me.... I know no one but you who can be fully sensible of the turmoil and anxiety, the sacrifice of all what is called comfort the readiness to measure time by what is done and to die in 6 hours could planes be brought to conclusions—the looking upon the Sun, the Moon, the Stars, the Earth and its contents as materials to form greater things—that is to say ethereal things—but here I am like Madman greater things that our Creator himself made!"[8]

Commenting on the contents and the implications of the letter, Greg Kucich says that

> Speaking with such a claim of god-like strength, this episode revolves letter's conflict by reformulating its components within a new imaginative context.... Specific formal patterns in this sequence, also refined beyond the earlier letter's mechanics, further suggest the mental intensity of Keats's lyrical moments of vision. The image clusters throughout this passage display a similar greater complexity in their sustained elaboration. Keats's feeling of defiance towards his own anxieties, for instance, yields the image of 'an obstinate eye on the Devil Himself'. This conception then leads to the figure of 'a rebel Angel' to portray Keats's stance against oppressive odds. And the association of such a demonic rebellion finally merges with a dominant concern of creative ambition to produce an image of Keats's triumphing over 'our Creator' in his building of an imaginative universe.[9]

The 'letters' also throw a great deal of light on Keats's obsession of writing a poem of an epic stature, like *Hyperion,* on the one hand and his conflict on his flirtation with a woman on the streets, Isabella Jones, on the other, added with his declining health. "The initiation of Keats's *annus mirabilis* with *Hyperion*, for example, depends significantly on epistolary acts. When poised to attempt this epic innovation during the autumn of 1818, Keats felt overwhelmed by the challenge. Mounting sickness, discouraging reviews, and his brother's fatal illness exacerbated the feeling of helplessness. In this morbid condition, Keats turned instinctively to letters for renewal. This act furnished in its visionary stage one on the letters' most engaging passages. Moreover, it shaped a productive mental condition for the beginning of *Hyperion* and the great year of astonishing creativity that followed."[10]

The sequence (in *Hyperion*) first recounts an encounter whose detail suggests Keats's interior conflict over the borders of mundane and epic, or sublime, experience. As is so habitual in these contemplations, the concerns focus on Keats's own partly thwarted desire for creative energy.

The scene, in the poem, "opens upon his (Keats's) recent accidental meeting in the street with Isabella Jones, a woman with whom he had once enjoyed an unspecified flirtation. As the episode unfolds, its details reveal a conflict between Keats's desire for some monumental experience and the restraining decorum of Isabella's behaviour. Having moved from the inhibiting propriety of his meeting with Isabella to a union with the wind and stars, Keats succinctly describes the mental procedures, enabling such an ascent. The 'mighty abstract idea of Beauty,' or the visionary imagination, transmutes the 'particles' of domestic happiness—'and amiable wife and sweet Children'—into more sublime experience.... Such an insight moves Keats, in the conclusion of this episode, to station himself confidently amid literary examplars of sublime passion—Achilles battling to avenge his beloved Patroklos, and Troilus yearning with anguish for Cressida."[11]

About this experience Keats himself says: No sooner I am alone than shapes of epic greatness are stationed around me, and serve my Spirits the office which is equivalent to a king's body guard—then 'Tragedy, with scepte'd pall, comes sweeping by.' According to my state of mind I am with Achilles shouting in the Trenches or with Theocritus in the vale of Sicily. Or I throw my whole being into Troilus and repeating those lines, 'I wander, like a lost Soul upon the Banks staying for waftage,' I melt into the air with voluptuousness so delicate that I am content to be alone.[12]

The contents of the letter quoted above eloquently reveal the poet's conflict between his small mundane life incidents and his ambitious poetic plans, like *Hyperion*, in which he completely identifies himself with the historic figures like

Achilles and the like. Apparently, the later part of the poet's psychology, which deals with the moments of his heightened imagination for the realization of the 'truth', was closer to his personality, as is clear in the following quote:

> Thus the rhetorical and imagistic patterns deepen this relation (of letter-writing) with the poetry by enabling the letter to act out, in poetic fashion, the very transformations it describes. Repetitions of words and phrases lend the passage a mounting intensity that seems to dramatize the mental elevation taking place during the composition.... The first sequence of images show a heightening of vision in its focus upon refined material comforts.... Situated within this cluster, however, is the more ethereal image of 'the morning Clouds' that anticipates the more transcendent level of associations in the next group of images: 'the wind is my wife and the Stars through my window pane are my children'. And this elevation of domestic comfort into more sublime attachments—with wife and children replaced by wind and stars—finally issues in the passionate images of Achilles, Theocritus, and Troilus, whose love seem, indeed, of cosmic proportions....[13]

The 'letters' contain many memorable passages, but few give us a more poignant sense of regret for the poet's early death than the one in which he compares life with a large mansion having many chambers, out of which he describes only about two, namely the Infant chamber and the Chamber of Maiden-Thought, with regards to the criticism of Wordsworth's lines composed a few miles above *Tintern Abbey*. Here, the picture of the decaying but mysterious nature of the human life is nicely painted. The reference of 'dark passages' indicate to the mystery surrounding the human life.

The lines, written to J.S. Reynolds, read,

> However, among the effects this breathing is father of is that tremendous one of sharpening one's vision into the heart and nature of Man—convincing one's nerves that the world is full of Misery and heartbreak, Pain, Sickness and oppression—whereby this Chamber of

> Maiden-Thoughts becomes gradually darkened, and at the same time, on all sides of it, many doors are set open—but all dark—all leading to dark passages. We see not the balance of good and evil; we are in a mist, we are now in that state, we feel the 'Burden of the Mystery'. To this point was Wordsworth come, as far as I can conceive, when he wrote *Tintern Abbey*, and seemed to me that his genius is explorative of those dark Passages. Now if we live, and go on thinking, we too shall explore them.[14]

To put it straight, Keats was destined to explore the dark passages of human existence but for his premature death. The death denied him the chance of exploring something more including some 'fine plays', of which he had dreamed and makes mention in the letter quoted above.

We find in his letters a peculiarly attractive personality of his own; devotion to his family; a deeply serious attitude to poetry and an unselfconscious delight in the pleasures of life. The letters to Tom form the main body of our knowledge of Keats's pleasure in northern expedition and his reaction to the stupendous scenes that he came across while travelling. Tom says that, "the grandeur of the scenery, far from making him feel small, enables to forget his stature completely as he feels himself at one with his surrounding".[15]

Keats regarded beauty as 'truest spiritual activity' (as discussed in previous chapter). As a result, he never mixed beauty with felinity or with sex. He was, rather disgusted at any attempt of such kind. Recounting his experience of a train journey to his friend John Hamilton Reynolds in a letter the poet says that "I saw some extensive Barracks which disgusted me extremely with the Government for placing such Nest of Debauchery in so beautiful place—I asked a man in the coach about this—and he said that the people had been spoiled...I did not feel very sorry at the idea of the Women being a little profligate."[16]

Keats was a staunch believer in the supremacy of God. But his basic objection was with the way religious fanatics took upon themselves the responsibility of conveying the message of

God to the common man, particularly the illiterates, and to force others to believe on His supremacy, according to their dictates. The poet was strongly critical of the terms like 'blasphemy' or 'eternal punishment', coined for those people who spoke against God. "The doctrine of the atonement (the idea of a religion based on sacrifice) was as abhorrent to Keats as it was to Hunt", says Stephen Coote, "who now proceeded to draw further parallels between his own ideal of paganism and his revulsion at Christian bigotry."[17]

Dwelling on the subject, Keats wrote to his brother George that, "They (the Christians) dealt in loves and luxuries, in what resulted from the first laws of nature, and tended to keep humanity alive—the later have dealt in angry debates, in intolerance, in gloomy denouncement, in persecutions, in excommunications, in wars and massacres, in what perplexes, outrages, and destroys humanity."[18]

In the tense political atmosphere of 1817 England, any attack on Christianity, as evidently made by Keats, could be viewed by conservatives as an attempt at subversion. And the fervour with which he was elaborating a description of an ideal society based on a revived paganism, not on the traditional tenets of established religion, was to be seen as a deliberate attempt to engage him with the very basis of the world in which he lived. Which is why, the poet was not liked by the authorities who were controlled by religious people.

Being a keen observer of the society, Keats had a lot of interest in the politics of his times. He was rather disappointed with the quarrels of the Wigs and Tories. In the midst of his financial and domestic problems, it was the pursuit of poetry and the fashioning of an alternative world of imagination that was Keats's abiding preoccupation, drawing from him fresh confessions both of his ambition and of his modesty. It was the period when Keats was engaged in writing the long narrative poem, *Endymion*. Writing to his painter friend Haydon about it in a moment of despair, he says, "I am sure that you love me as your own Brother—I have seen it in your continual anxiety for me."[19]

It was in response to Haydon's letter to Keats, in which he consoles and urges him to trust in God. Haydon says, "Every man of great views is at times thus tormented. My dear Keats go on, don't despair, collect incidents, study characters, read Shakespeare and trust in Providence."[20]

Keats himself describes the situation while writing *Endymion*. He says, "It will be a test, a trial of my powers of imagination and chiefly of my invention which is a rare thing indeed."[21] So to say, "It was a gift that could not be gained by effort. It was innate, the sign of a true poet and of the tradition to which Keats wished to belong."[22] It was something, Keats believed, the readers craved for. "Do not the lovers of Poetry like to have a little region to wander in where they may pick and choose, and in which the images are so numerous that many are forgotten and found new in a second Reading?"[23]

Plentitude, Keats thinks, is something pleasurable, something which stands against the hurry of the modern world. Dwelling on significance of the long poem, the poet says, "...a long poem is a test of Invention which I take to be the Polar Star of Poetry, as Fancy is the Sails, and Imagination the Rudder."[24]

The poet was a man of strong passions. He knew it and also knew it as his vulnerable aspect. So, because of this vulnerability, he would fight for small things. Owing to which, he would fight even with his brother George, in his childhood, when his brother tried to beat him. "Such outburst were occasionally almost ungovernable, and they suggested something more in Keats than mere animal high spirits",[25] recalls Stephen Coote. Recollecting the temperament of his brother George writes, "This response was wholly spontaneous. John's eyes moistened and his lips quivered at the relation of any tale of generosity or benevolence or noble daring...he had no fears of self-interference in the quarrels of others, he would at all hazards, without calculating his power to defend, or his reward for the deed, defend the oppressed."[26]

If George beat down John Keats, he also sustained him through his moods. If Tom was closer to him in his intellect, George was the brother who could bring Keats back to some moderate degree of contentedness. Writing to Charles Dilke George says, "He (John Keats) avoided teasing any one with miseries. Tom and myself, often asked for forgiveness; venting and discussing them gave him relief."[27]

Keats's letters to Benjamin Bailey from late October to early November tell a different story. While he congratulated his friend on an offer of a curacy, his own feelings were often pained and bitter. The poet was not happy with the world around him. He wrote to Bailey, "In this world there is no quiet nothing but teasing and snubbing and vexation."[28] The statement comes in the wake of Tom's deteriorating health. The anxiety was aggravated further by the Bishop of Lincoln's refusal of the offer of help to Keats by Bailey, when he needed it. To Keats this seemed an outrageous attack on a good man (Bailey), an exercise by the establishment in arbitrary power. Keats condemned this attitude of Churchmen by saying that, "The Stations and Grandeurs of the World have taken it into their heads that they cannot commit themselves towards an inferior in rank—but is not the impertinence from one above to one below more wretchedly mean than from the low to the high?"[29]

However, a letter written to Keats by a close friend like Bailey himself would throw a good light on Keats's character and temperament. One of such letters, written by Benjamin Bailey about him, at a time when both of them had spent some months together in Oxford, from mid August until the end of September, in 1817, does have a lot to say about the poet. The letter is as follows:

> I was delighted with the naturalness and simplicity of character, and was at once drawn to him by his winning and indeed affectionate manner towards those with whom he was himself pleased. Nor was his personal appearance the least charm of a first acquaintance with the young poet. How bore, along with the strong impress of genius, much beauty of feature and countenance. His hair was beautiful—a fine brown, rather than auburn, I think, if you placed your hand upon his head, the silken curls felt like the rich plumage

of a bird. The eye was full and fine, and softened into tenderness, or beamed with a fiery brightness, according to the current of his thoughts and conversation.... He sat down to his task,—which was about 50 lines a day,—with his papers before him, and wrote with as much regularity, and apparently as much ease, as he wrote his letters.... But he never forced himself.... When we had finished our studies for the day we took our walk.... He was struck I remember, with the simple statue there of Shakespeare. His enjoyment was of that genuine, quiet kind which was a part of his gentle nature; deeply feeling what he truly enjoyed, but saying little. On our return to Oxford we renewed our quiet mode of, until he finished the third Book of *Endymion*, and the time came that we must part; and I never parted with one whom I had known so short a time, with so much real regret and personal affection, as I did with John Keats, when he left Oxford for London at the end of September or the beginning of October 1817.... There was no reserve of any kind between us.... His brother George says of him that to his brothers his temper was uncertain; and he himself (Keats) confirms this judgment of him in a beautiful passage of a letter to myself. But with his friends, a sweeter tempered man I never saw. Gentleness was his roper characteristic, without one particle of dullness, or insipidity, or want of spirit.... But if any act of wrong or oppression, of fraud or falsehood, was the topic, he rose into sudden and animated indignation.... He had a soul of noble integrity: and his common sense was a conspicuous part of his character. Our conversations rarely or never flagged; during our walks...I have retained a few of his opinions on Literature and criticism which I will detail. The following passage from Wordsworth's Ode on Immortality was deeply felt by Keats, who, however, at this time seemed to me to value this great Poet rather in particular passages than in the full-length portrait, as it were, of the great imaginative and philosophic Christian Poet, which he really is, and which Keats obviously, not long afterwards, felt him to

> be.... Among the qualities of high poetic promise in Keats was, even at this time, his correct taste....[30]

The letter obviously does throw a great deal of light on Keats the man as well as the poet. If the letter was to be taken as an authentic document on the poet, as it richly deserves for, then the instant picture that comes to the mind is that of a man of strong character with attractive features but having a thorough gentility of heart. The letter also bears a testimony of how much Keats was liked by his companions. One of the various friends of Keats was Haydon, with whom too he liked to share his innate personal matters. And in turn, he always received a very positive and encouraging response. In a moment of despair experienced by the poet, Haydon wrote a letter of encouragement to him, which is as follows:

> Never despair while the path is open to you. By habitual exercise you will have habitual intercourse and constant companionship; and at every want turn to the Great Star of your hopes with a delightful confidence that will never be disappointed. I love you like my own brother: Beware, for God's sake, of the delusions and sophistications that are ripping up the talents and morality of our friend (Leigh Hunt). He will go out of the world the victim of his own weakness and the dupe of own self-delusions....[31]

The reply of the letter by Keats is even more interesting; in terms of frankness it carries. He says:

> You tell me never to despair—I wish it was as easy for me to deserve the saying—truth is I have a horrid morbidity of Temperament which has shown itself at intervals. It is I have no doubt the Greatest Enemy and stumbling block I have to fear—I may even it is likely to be the cause of my disappointment....[32]

Then referring to Haydon's warning in regard to Hunt Keats declares that he would die rather than getting deceived about his own achievements as is the case of Hunt. He says:

> There is no greater sin after the seven deadly than to flatter oneself into the idea of being a great poet: the

> comfort is, such a crime must bring its own penalty, and if one is a self-deluder indeed account must one day be balanced.[33]

Keats's letter to his sister Fanny, who was just fourteen years old, shows the poet's "elder-brotherly anxiety to get into touch with her to know her likings and dislikings."[34] It also tells about the importance that Keats attached to reading habit that he also expects from his sister. The letter is as follows:

> Let us now begin a regular question and answer—a little pro and con; letting it interfere as a pleasant method of my coming at your favourite wants and enjoyments, that I may meet them in a way of a brother. We have been so little together since you have been able to reflect on things that I know not whether you prefer the *History of King Pepin* to Buniyan's *Pilgrim's Progress*.... However in a few Letters I hope I shall be able to come at that and adapt My scribblings to your Pleasure. You must tell me about all you read.... This I feel as a necessity for we ought to become intimately acquainted, in order that I may not only, as you grow up love you as my only Sister confide in you as my dearest friend....[35]

And he goes on to tell her a story from the Greek mythology and asks her to also read herself about such stories in order to enrich her mythological knowledge. However, the story that he relates to his sister concerns a shepherd being loved by the Moon herself. The story later on makes the basis for writing of *Endymion*. He writes:

> Perhaps you might like to know what I am writing about. Many years ago there was a young handsome Shepherd who fed his flocks on a Mountain's side called Latmus, he was very contemplative sort of a person and lived solitary among the trees and plaines little thinking that such a beautiful Creature as the Moon was growing mad in Love with him.—However so it was; and when he was asleep on the grass she used to come down from heaven and admire him excessively for a long time; and at last could not refrain from carrying him away in her arms to the top of that high Mountain Latmus—while

> he was a dreaming...but I dare say you have read this and all the other beautiful tales which have come down from the ancient times of that beautiful Greece....[36]

In fact, there was a series on exchange of letters between Keats and his friends. "On November 22, 1817, Keats writes to Bailey a letter even richer in contents and more self-revealing, than this to Reynolds. It gives the indispensable key both to much in his own character and much of the deeper speculative and symbolic meanings underlying his work, from *Endymion* to the *Ode on Grecian Urn*. Beginning with a wise and tolerant reference to the Haydon trouble, and throwing out a passing hint of the distinction between men of Genius, who have not, and men of Power, who have, a proper individual self or determined character of their own, Keats passes at the close to an illuminating self-confession which is also a contrast between himself and his correspondent."[37]

The letter is as follows:

> You perhaps at one time thought there was such a thing as worldly happiness to be arrived at, at certain periods of time marked out,—you have of necessity from your disposition been thus led away—I scarcely remember counting upon any happiness—I look not for it if it be not in the present hour,—nothing startles me beyond the moment. The Setting-Sun will always set me to rights, or if a Sparrow comes before my Window, I take part in its existence and pick about the gravel. The first thing that strikes me on hearing a misfortune having befallen another is this—'Well, it cannot be helped: he will have the pleasure of trying the resources of his Spirit'—and I beg, my dear Bailey, that hereafter should you observe anything cold in me not to put it to the account of heartlessness, but abstraction....[38]

Commenting on the importance of the contents of the letter in work of art, Colvin says that:

> Readers of *Endymion* will recognize a symbolic embodiment of a mood akin to this in the Cave of Quietude in the fourth book. But the great value of the letter especially great as a help to the study of *Endymion*

> in general, it is in the long central passage setting forth his speculations as to the relation of imagination to truth, meaning ultimate or transcendental. He finds his clue in the eighth book of *Paradise Lost*, when Adam recounting to Raphael his first experiences as new-created man, tell how twice over he fell into a dream and awoke to find it true: his first dream thus confirmed in the result being how 'One of shape divine' took him by the hand and him into the garden of Paradise: his second, how the same glorious shape came to him and opened his side and from his rib fashioned a creature....[39]

In fact, It was no doubt that this second of Adam's dreams that was chiefly in Keats's mind. His way of explaining his speculations to his friend is quite unstudied and inconsecutive; he is, he says, "continually running away from the subject", or shall we say letting the stream of his ideas branch out into side channels from which he found it difficult to call them back? Yet their main current and purport will be found not difficult to follow: if only the reader will bear one thing well in mind: that when Keats in this and similar passages speaks of 'Sensations' as opposed to 'Thoughts' he does not limit the word to sensations of the body, of what intensity or exquisiteness whatsoever or howsoever instantaneously transforming them from sensation into emotion. What he means are "intuitions of mind and spirit as immediate as these, as thrillingly convincing and indisputable, as independent of all consecutive stages and formal processes of thinking almost the same things, indeed, as in a later passage of the same letter he calls 'ethereal musings'."[40]

The later part of the letter also deserves quoting, so as to know in more detail the poet's vital ideas. Keats says:

> O! I wish I was as certain of the end of all your troubles as that of your momentary start about the authenticity of the Imagination. I am certain of nothing but the holiness of the Heart's affection, and the truth of Imagination. What the Imagination seizes as Beauty must be Truth—whether it existed before or not—for I

> have the same idea of all our passions as of Love: they are all, in their sublime, Creative of essential Beauty. In a Word you might know my favourite speculation by my first book, and the little Song I sent in my last which is a representation from the fancy of the mode of operating in these Matters. The Imagination may be compared to Adam's dream, he awoke and he found it truth:—I am more zealous in this affair, because I have never yet been able to perceive how any thing can be known for truth by consecutive reasoning—and yet it must be. Can it be that even the Philosopher ever arrived at his Goal without putting aside numerous objections? However it may be, O for a life of Sensations rather than of Thoughts! It is 'a Vision in the form of Youth,' a shadow of reality to come—and this consideration has further convinced me, for it has come as auxiliary to another favourite speculation of mine,—that we shall enjoy hereafter by having what we called happiness on Earth repeated in a finer tone. And yet such a fate can only befall those whose delight is Sensation, rather than hunger as you do after Truth.[41]

Talking about his poetic ambition and his position as a poet, he writes to his brother George (April, 1817):

> As to what you say about my being a Poet, I can return no Answer but by saying that the High Idea I have of poetical fame makes me think I see it towering too high above me. At any rate I have no right to talk until *Endymion* is finished, it would be a test of, a trial of my Power of Imagination and chiefly of my invention which is a rare thing indeed—by which I must make 4000 lines of one bare circumstance, and then fill them with poetry....[42]

Keats was not one of those writers who imposed autobiography on their readers. In an age when poetry was often too subjective and egotistical, he showed the rare quality of the artist who lives chiefly in his creations. Anyone, he felt, was a fitter theme for poetry than the poet himself. His Letters are among the most interesting ever written by a poet. The

Letters, according to Bernard Groom, "reveal a mind resolved to face fearlessly the problems of human destiny, and to shape its own interpretations of life".[43] The letters have an important place as they show his awareness of the conflicts which he presented in his major works. Commenting on the importance of 'letters' Douglas Bush says that they are an "indispensable accompaniment to (Keats's) poetry".[44]

In one of his lectures, dwelling on Keats's 'letters', A.C. Bradley reflects that "the best of Keats's poems can be fully appreciated without extraneous help; but the letters throw light on all, and they are almost necessary to the understanding of *Endymion* and of some of the earlier or contemporaneous pieces. They clearly reveal those changes in his mind and temper which appear in his poetry." "The letters, thus, are full of the presences of an intellectual nature, not merely sensitive and delicate, but open, daring, rich, and strong...."[45]

A.C. Bradley's comments on Keats's letters with regards to his attitude to life and his poetic genius are significant. He says:

> Of Keats's character, as the letters manifest it, Arnold has written. While speaking plainly and decidedly of the weakness in those to Miss Brawne, Arnold brought together the evidence which proves that Keats 'had flint and iron in him', 'had virtue in the true and large sense of the word'. And he selected passages, too, which illustrate the 'admirable wisdom and temper' and the 'strength and the clearness of judgment shown by Keats, alike in matters of friendship and in his criticism of his own productions, of the public, and of the literary circles.... In spite of occasional despondency, and of the feelings of awe at the magnitude of his ambition, Keats, it is tolerable from these letters, had a clear and habitual consciousness of his genius. However, when Shelley wrote, hinting a criticism, but referring to himself as excelled by Keats in genius, he returned the criticism without the compliment. Yet, with all this, and with all his pride and his desire for fame, no letters extant breathe a more simple and natural modesty than these; and from end to end they exhibit hardly a trace, if any

> trace, either of the irritable vanity attributed to poets or of the sublime egotism of Milton and Wordsworth. He was of Shakespeare's tribe.[46]

Keats was always thinking of poetry. In September, 1817, staying away at Oxford, he wrote to his sister Fanny, "We lead very industrious lives—he (Bailey) in general studies, and in proceeding at a pretty good pace with a Poem ('Endymion') which I hope you will see early in the next year."[47]

Imagination was most powerful medium for apprehending 'truth and beauty', which according to Keats, were one and the same thing and finally lead to the understanding of what is known by the metaphysicians as 'ultimate reality'. In one of his letters to Benjamin Bailey Keats says, "The imagination may be compared to Adam's dream—he awoke and found it truth."[48] Imagination, he asserts, is truly a higher kind of perception.

The letters throw a great deal of light with regards to Keats's concept of happiness. The following letter bears a testimony to it, in which he says, "This morning I am in a sort of temper indolent and supremely careless. I long for a stanza or two of Thompson's *Castle of Indolence*. My passions are all asleep. If I had the teeth of pearl and the breath of lilies, I should call it languor, but as I am I must call it laziness. In this state of effeminacy the fibers of the brain are relaxed in common with the rest of the body, and to such a happy degree that pleasure has no show of enticement, and pains no unbearable power. Neither Poetry nor Ambition nor Love has any alertness of countenance as they pass by me. They seem rather like figures on a Greek vase—a man and two women whom no one but me could distinguish in their disguisement. This is the only happiness, and is a rare instance of the advantage of the body overpowering the mind."[49]

The sentence, 'This is the only happiness', expresses a settled conviction on Keats's part. "Happiness, he (Keats) feels", analyses Bradley, "belongs only to childhood and youth. A young man thinks he can keep it, but a little experience shows him he must do without it."[50]

The letters also throw light on the poet's insight into the characters of different human beings. In a letter, describing about one of his friends, Dilke, he says:

> Dilke is a man who cannot feel he has a personal identity unless he has made up his mind about everything. The only means of strengthening one's intellect is to make up one's mind about nothing—to let the mind be a thoroughfare for all thoughts, not a select party. The genius is not scarce in population: all the stubborn arguers you meet are of the same brood. They never begin on a subject they have not pre-resolved on. They want to hammer their nails into you, and if you turn the point, still they think you wrong. Dilke will never come at a truth so long as he lives, because he is always trying at it. He is a Godwin Methodist.[51]

These lines, according to A.C. Bradley, illustrate the poet's instinctive feeling that it is essential to the growth of the poetic mind to preserve its natural receptiveness and to welcome all the influences that stream in upon it. They illustrate also his dislike of the fixed theories held preached by some members of his circle.

Keats was against, as is obvious from the above quote, any fixed beliefs or opinions. The terms like 'knowledge' or 'philosophy' came to him with distaste. This does not mean that he was in any way against the pursuit of truth. What he objected was the "Methodist, the stubborn argument, and habit of bringing to the argument and maintaining throughout it a ready-made theory."[52] Which is why, he offers his own thoughts and speculations freely enough to Bailey, one of his close friends, and to his brother, Tom. These were the men, willing to probe with the poet any serious idea. The following passage, from a letter to George and Georgiana Keats, clearly bears a testimony of his theory of the world in metaphysical terms:

> The whole appears to resolve into this—that man is originally a poor forked creature, subject to the same mischances as the beasts of the forest, destined to hardships and disquietude of some kind or the other. If

> he improves by degrees his bodily accommodations and comforts, at each age, at each ascent, there are waiting for him a fresh set of annoyances—he is mortal, there is still a heaven with its stars above his head. The most interesting question that can come before us is, How far by the persevering endeavours of a seldom appearing Socrates mankind may be made happy. I can imagine such happiness carried to an extreme, what must it end in? Death—and who could in such a case bear with death? The whole troubles of life, which are now frittered away in a series of years, would then be accumulated for the last days of a being that, instead of hailing its approach, would leave this world as Eve left Paradise. But in truth I do not at all believe in this sort of perfectibility.[53]

Keats speculates further, "The nature of the world would not admit of this—the inhabitants of the world will correspond to itself. Let the fish philosophise the ice away from the rivers in the winter time, and they shall be at continual play in the tepid delight of summer.... How are souls to be made? How are these sparks which are God to have identity given to them —so as ever to possess a bliss peculiar to each one's individual existence? How but by the medium of a world like this? This point I sincerely wish to consider, because I think it a grander system of salvation than the Christian religion—or rather it is a system of Spirit-creation. This is affected by three grand materials acting the one upon the other for a series of years. These three materials are the *Intelligence*, the *human heart*, and the world or elemental space suited for the proper action of *Mind* and *Heart* on each other for the purpose of forming the *Soul* or *Intelligence destined to possess the sense of Identity*. I can scarcely express what I but dimly perceive—and I think I perceive it. That you may judge the more clearly I will put it in the most homely form possible. I will call the *world* a School instituted for the purpose of teaching little children to read. I will call the *human heart* the horn-book read in that School. And I will call the *Child able to read*, the *Soul* made from that School and its horn-book. Do you not see how necessary a world of pains and troubles is to a school and Intelligence and make it a Soul? A place where the heart must feel and suffer in a thousand diverse ways. Not merely is the Heart a horn-book, it is Mind's Bible, it is the mind's experience, it is the text from which the Mind or the Intelligence sucks its identity. As various as the lives of men are, so various become their Souls; and thus does God make individual beings, Souls, identical Souls, of the sparks of his own essence. This appears to me a faint sketch of a system of Salvation which does not offend our reason and humanity."[54]

Commenting on the subject-matter in the letter, A.C. Bradley rightly says, "Surely, when Keats's education is considered, this with all its crudity is not a little remarkable. It would not be easy to find anything written at the same age by another poet of the time which shows more openness of mind, more knowledge of human nature, or more original thought of power."[55] The words 'more power of thought' in the letter easily place Keats apart from his contemporaries, like Wordsworth or Shelley, as man as well a poet.

The contents of the letter as quoted above clearly indicate Keats's association with 'metaphysical thinking', with regards to life and God. His concept of 'Soul-making' is very much a matter which belongs to the domain of 'metaphysics'. In a way, Keats was a 'metaphysician by temperament' without knowing it or without feeling it necessary to proclaim him as such.

The understanding of the human nature is achieved better, Keats thought, with the help of 'imagination'. As for the human mind, he believed that it contributes to what it assumes to be direct perception of the physical world but what helps to understand the 'mysteries of the world' is imagination. Elaborating on the subject he writes to his brother Tom, "The excellence of every art is its intensity, capable of making all disagreeable evaporate, from their being in close relationship with Beauty and Truth."[56] As Keats grew older, "he believed more and more that no simple monistic system could explain life. We must keep an openness; we must not demand answers." This, according to Keats is the state in which we are most capable of apprehending Beauty, which is Truth.

Keats was very keen about keeping his personality away from his poetry. In a letter to Mr. Woodhouse Keats talks about characterless nature of the poet. Distinguishing himself from the poets of the "Wordsworthian or egotistical sublime", Keats says, "...it (his poetry) has no self...it has no character."[57] Commenting on the significance of Keats's 'letters', T.S. Eliot, the famous 20th century critic, says, "The letters of Keats are the most notable and the most important ever written by any English poet."[58] The comment speaks volumes about the 'letters' with regards to Keats's poetic art. He had come to believe that the expression of personal emotions is not the function of poetry. Rather, he should fuse it with the object he is describing.

Discussing the importance of Keats's letters in one of his lectures, A.C. Bradley says, "Written in his last four years by a man who died at twenty-five, they (letters) contain abundant evidence of his immaturity and his faults, but they disclose a nature and character which command on the whole not respect than affection, and they show not a little of that general intellectual power which rarely fails to accompany poetic genius."[59] The letters reveal Keats as a very serious and thoughtful man. They also remind us that he was at a disadvantage in intellectual training as compared with Shakespeare or the likes of the University Wits. They also reflect a strong influence of Leigh Hunt and his literary circle in his poetry.

Keats was a poet who preferred to live in his present rather that worrying about future or repenting over past. He had felt a glow in his face watching a rainbow in the sky, but happiness was not his cup of tea. Disclosing this reality to his close friend Benjamin Bailey in a letter to him, dated 22 November 1817, the poet confesses, in no uncertain manner that, "I scarcely remember counting upon any Happiness—I look not for it be not in the present hour—nothing startles me beyond the Moment.... The setting sun will always set me to rights—or if a Sparrow come before my Window I take part in its experience and pick about the Gravel."[60]

Most of all, the letters reveal the poet's mastery over knitting together the 'worldly beauty with the spiritual one', as is evident from a letter written to his brother Tom in 1817, on his meeting with a young Indian lady. It says:

> She is not a Cleopatra, but she is at least a Charmian. She has a rich Eastern look. When she comes into a room she makes an impression the same as the beauty of a leopardess.... Yet she is a fine thing, speaking in a worldly way: for there are two distinct tempers of mind in which we judge of things—the worldly, theatrical and pantomimical; and the unearthly, spiritual and ethereal. In the former, Buonaparte, Lord Byron and this Charmian, hold the first place in our mind; in the latter, John Howard, Bishop Hooker rocking his child's cradle, and you, my dear sister, are the conquering feelings.[61]

Keats's views, particularly on *Endymion*, speak volumes, as far as his metaphysical ideas are concerned. The speech of Endymion addressed to his sister Peona, for example, was of the utmost importance to Keats. Emphasizing on the importance of the ideas in the poem, he writes to his friend Taylor, "My having written that Argument will perhaps be the greatest Service to me of anything I ever did."[62]

In a letter written to Benjamin Bailey some months later, Keats reiterated his views when he said:

> I am certain of nothing but of the holiness of the Heart's affection and the truth of Imagination. What the imagination seizes as Beauty must be truth—whether it existed before or not.—I have the same Idea of all our Passions as of Love they are all in their sublime; creative of essential Beauty.[63]

Commenting on the motive of the passage of the poem, to Bailey, Keats says that it was a "regular stepping of the Imagination towards a Truth."[64]

It will be a mistake to suppose that he had no political interests. But, he was disappointed with the undemocratic attitude of the political parties and regarded politics as "the mere quarrels of Wig and Tory."[65] In fact, as the friends of

Keats were advanced liberals, his sympathies too went that way. In September, 1819, he wrote to his friend Brown, "I sincerely hope I shall be able to a mite of help to the liberal side of the question before I die."[66] Few days later, he tells Brown of his wish to work as a journalist for his livelihood. But he makes it a condition that he would write "on the liberal side of the question."[67] It shows Keats's determination and firmness with regards to his political ideas.

Being a liberal himself, Keats was particularly critical of Napoleon's political thinking, with regards to his imperialistic policies. Drawing an interesting scenario of the world in terms of politics, he says: "Notwithstanding the part which the liberals take in the cause of Napoleon, I cannot but think he has done more harm to the life of Liberty than any one else could have done. Not that the divine right gentlemen have done, or intend to do, any good. No, they have taken a lesson of him, and will do all the further harm he would have done, without any of the good. The worst thing he has done is that he has taught them how to organize their monstrous armies. The Emperor Alexander, it is said, intends to divide his Empire as did Diocletian, creating two Czars beside himself, and continuing the supreme monarch of the whole. Should he do this, and they for a series of years keep peaceable among themselves, Russia may spread her conquest even to China. I think it a very likeable thing that China itself may fall; Turkey certainly will. Meanwhile European North Russia will hold its horns against the rest of the Europe, intriguing constantly with France."[68]

Wounded by the dirty politics, the poet regarded politicians as "foxes of the present day ministry, destroying the liberties and 'gold and ripe-earned hopes' of the people".[69] Therefore, it was "vital to turn elsewhere, to bind up the wounded spirit with 'ethereal things', to seek the consolations of myth and nature, and sense the serene delicacy of a world transfigured by imagination. Imagination and beauty, in the context of *Endymion*, seem to provide a permanent form of that solace which the world of politics denied the poet."[70]

Keats may not have been an orthodox Christian, but he had an unfailing faith in the existence of God without showing it, which he calls the Eternal Being. In his pursuance of his principle of beauty in all things he even did not care the public opinion. In this case, he looks a perfect metaphysician, as far as his basic ideas are concerned. It is clear by a letter in which he describes his perception of God in the following words:

> I have not the slightest feel of humility towards the public or to anything in existence but the Eternal Being, the Principle of Beauty, and the memory of great Men... I would be subdued my friends, and thank them for subduing me; but among multitudes of men I have no feel of stooping; I hate the idea of humility to them. I never wrote one single line of poetry with the least shadow of thought about their opinion. Forgive me for vexing you, but it eases me to tell you: I could not live without the love of my friends; I would jump down Etna for any public good—but I hate a mawkish popularity. I cannot be subdued before them. My glory would be to daunt and dazzle the thousand jabberers about pictures and books.[71]

The ideas expressed in the letter are clear indication of how deep and profound was Keats's perception with regards to existence of God. It also proves that he was man of metaphysical thinking. Public opinion had no place for him in terms of writing poetry. Instead, the poet was interested in expressing the 'profound matters of substance' in his poetry. These matters undoubtedly relate to Keats's undeclared faith in the powers of God. His genuine religiosity can be noticed in his remark about Bailey in one of his letters to his brothers, which reads as follows, "That sort of probity and disinterestedness which such men as Bailey possess, does hold grasp the tip-top of any spiritual honours that can be paid to anything in this world."[72]

Supporting Keats's tendency to virtuous life, Matthew Arnold also says, "Signs of virtue, in the true and large sense of the word, the instinct for virtue passing into the life of Keats and strengthening it, I find in the admirable wisdom and of what he says to his Bailey on the occasion of a quarrel between Reynolds and Haydon: Things have happened lately of great perplexity; you must have heard of them; Reynolds and Haydon retorting and recriminating, parting for ever. It is unfortunate; men should bear with each other; there lives not the man who may not be cut up, aye lashed to pieces, on his weakest side. The best of men have but a portion good in them.... The sure way, Bailey, is first to know a men's faults, and then be passive. If, after that, he insensibly draws you towards him, then you have no power to break the link. Before I felt interested in either Reynolds or Haydon, I was well read in their faults; yet, knowing them, I have been cementing with both. I have an affection for them both, for reasons almost opposite; and to both must I of necessity cling, supported always by the hope that when a little time, a few years, shall have tried me more fully in their esteem, I may be able to bring them together."[73]

To approve of the above letter as a testimony of Keats's virtuousness Arnold quotes a letter of Butler in which he defines a virtuous man as that "endeavouring to enforce upon our own minds a practical sense of virtue, or to beget in others that practical sense of it which a man really has himself, is a virtuous *act*. And such an 'endeavouring' is that of Keats in those words written to Bailey. It is more than mere words; so justly thought and as discreetly urged as it is; it rises to the act of a virtuous *act*. It is proof of character."[74]

The same thing may be said of a letter written to one of his most trusted friends, Charles Brown, who always stood by Keats whenever he needed him in times of crisis, particularly financial one. Somehow, Keats felt that he must allow this state of things to continue. He was determined to contribute to a periodical literature for his earning, rather than looking for his friend for help, to protect his 'independence and his self-respect'. The contents of the letter to Brown are as follows:

> I had got into a habit of mind of looking towards you as a help in all difficulties. This very habit would be the parent of idleness and difficulties. You will see it is a duty I owe to myself to break the neck of it. I do nothing

> for my subsistence—make no exertion. At the end another year you shall applaud me, not for verses, but for conduct.[75]

The strength of Keats's character could easily be noticed in his criticism of his own productions, of the public, and of the literary circles. His reaction after the severe reviews of *Endymion* is worth-quoting. He says:

> Praise or blame has but a momentary effect on the man whose love of beauty in the abstract makes a severe critic on his own works. My own criticism has given me pain without comparison beyond what *Blackwood* or the *Quarterly* could possibly inflict; and also, when I feel I am right, no external praise can give me such a glow as my own solitary reperception and ratification of what is fine....[76]

Keats looked at the literary world with a lot of hate and anger, particularly after the severe criticism of *Endymion* in *Quarterly Review*. When Byron fancied Keats among the circle of 'literary jabberers', flattering them and flattered by them,[77] the poet comes out with an outburst, outwitting Byron:

> Just so much as I am humbled by the genius above my grasp, am I exalted and look with hate and contempt upon the literary world. Who could to be among the common-place crowd of little famous, who are each individually lost in a throng made up of themselves?[78]

Keats' attitude towards the public is that of a strong man, not weakling avid of praise, made to 'be snuffed out by an article'. He says: "I shall ever consider the public as debtors to me for verse, not myself to them for Admiration, which I can do without."[79]

Indeed, nothing is more remarkable in Keats than his clear-sightedness and his lucidity. Therefore, of his overpowering feeling for beauty, in spite of his sensuousness, and in spite of his gift of expression, Keats could say resolutely:

> I know nothing, I have read nothing; and I mean to follow Solomon's directions. 'Get learning, get understanding.' This is but one way for me. The road

> lies through application, study, and thought. I will pursue it.[80]

The resolution of 'application, study, and thought' on part of Keats indicate to his concerns of metaphysical matters without the guise of a philosopher.

Keats's respect for Milton's poetry and his thinking is also noteworthy, as far as his own thinking is concerned. He had a high respect for Milton, which is obvious from his following comments about him:

> Milton had an exquisite passion for what is properly, in the sense of ease and pleasure, poetical luxury; and with that it appears to me,, he would fain have been content, if he could, so doing, preserve his self-respect and feeling of duty performed; but there was working in him, as it were, the same sort of thing which operates in the great world to the end of a prophecy's being accomplished. Therefore he devoted himself rather to the ardours than the pleasures of song, solacing himself at intervals with cup of old wine.[81]

In his own poetry, too, Keats felt that a place must be preserved for "ardours rather than the pleasures of song", "although he was aware that he was not yet ripe for it",[82] comments Matthew Arnold. And in proof he gives the following lines of Keats: "But my flag is not unfurled on the Admiral-staff, and to philosophise I dare not yet."[83]

"Even in his pursuit of 'the pleasure of song', there is that stamp of high work which is akin to character", says Arnold, "which is character passing into intellectual production."[84] "*The best sort of poetry*"—Keats says, "that is all I care for, all I live for."[85]

Keats has been criticized for his weakness for 'feminine beauty'. Therefore, it would be interesting to discuss Keats's love for beauty, and for that matter the feminine beauty, which is an open secret. But, he seems to have been interested in those women who had thoughtful and intellectual mind. That is why he speaks with a candidness of "the opinion I have formed of the generality of women, who appear to me as children to whom I would rather give a sugar plum than my time".[86] Even to Fanny Brawne he can write "a flint-worded-letter, when his mind is heaped to the full with poetry". The letter is as follows:

> I know the generality of women would hate me for this; that I should have so unsoftened, so hard a mind as to forget them; forget the brightest realities for the dull imagination of my own.... My heart seems now made of iron.[87]

Nevertheless, Fanny Brawne deserves a mention in terms of understanding of Keats's experience of love with her, particularly during the last days of his life. The letter reflects a kind of conflict that the poet was undergoing, who knew that his last time was near. The letter deserves a reading, which is as follows:

> You have absorbed me. I have a sensation at the present moment as though I was dissolving—I should be exquisitely miserable without the hope of soon seeing you. I should be afraid to separate myself far from you. My sweet Fanny will your heart never change? My love, will it? I have no limit now to my love.... Your note came in just here. I cannot be happier away from you.... Do not threat me even in jest. I have been astonished that Men could die Martyrs for religion have shuddered at it. I shudder no more—I could be martyred for my religion—Love is my *religion*—I could die for that. I could die for *you*. My creed is Love and you are its only tenet. You have ravished me away by a Power I cannot resist; and yet I could resist till I saw you; and even since I have seen you I have endeavoured often 'to reason against the reason of my Love.' I can do that no more. The pain would be too great. My love is selfish. I cannot breathe without you.[88]

The letter speaks volumes about the poet's temperament and high character. The word 'Power' seems to have been used in capital letter because of some specific reasons. The word appears to mean the 'Divine Power'. From that standpoint, Fanny Brawne, the poet's beloved, becomes a worldly symbol for the poet to experience the 'divine love'.

Speaking about the importance of Keats's love-letters to Fanny Brawne, Sidney Colvin rightly comments that:

> ...More than any man, more certainly than any other unripe youth fretting in the high fever of unhopeful love, Keats has had to pay the penalty of genius in the loss of posthumous privacy for the most sacred and secret of his emotions. He thought his name would be forgotten, but posterity in an excess of remembrance has suffered no corner of his soul to escape the searchlight. Once preserved and printed, these love-letters of his cannot be ignored. Unselfish through and through, and naturally well-conditioned in all thoughts and feelings over which he had control he strives hard in them to keep to a vein of considerate tenderness, and the earlier letters of the series contain charming passages. But often, more often indeed than not from the first, they show him a prey, despite his best efforts to master himself and be reasonable, to an uncontrollable intensity and fretfulness of passion.... An enraptured but an untrustful lover, alternately rejoicing and chafing at his bondage, and passing through a hundred conflicting extremes of feelings in an hour, he finds in the fever of work and composition his only antidote against the fever of his love-sickness.[89]

Another letter to Fanny Brawne shows the piety and depth of Keats's feelings for her, which have no trace of carnality or sexuality, as is evident from the lines below:

> I am glad I had not an opportunity of sending off a Letter which I wrote for you on Tuesday night—'twas too much like one out of Rousseau's *Heloise*. I am more reasonable this morning. The morning is the only proper time for me to write to a beautiful Girl whom I love so much: for at night, when the lonely day has closed, and the lonely, silent, unmusical Chamber is waiting to receive me as into a Sepulture, then believe me my passion gets entirely the sway, then I would not have you those Rhapsodies which once I thought it impossible I should ever give way to, and which I have laughed

> at in another, for fear you should think me either too unhappy or perhaps a little mad.... I have never known any unalloy'd Happiness for many days together: the death or sickness of someone has always spoilt my hours—and now when none such troubles oppress me, it is you must confess that another sort of pain should haunt me. Ask yourself my love whether you are not very cruel to have so untrammeled me, so destroyed my freedom.[90]

However, Keats's ambition of achieving more heights in the field of poetry, which seemed quite a possibility, was crushed by his failing health. Sharing this bitter situation with Reynolds, he says:

> I think, if I had a free and healthy and lasting organization of heart, and lungs as strong as an ox's, as to be able to bear unhurt the shock of extreme thought and sensation without weariness, I could pass my life very nearly alone, though it should last eighty years. But I feel my body too weak to support me to the height; I am obliged continually to check myself, and be nothing.[91]

The portion of the letter in which the poet talks of passing his life 'nearly alone' could have been spoken by none other than a philosopher. Keats was by nature a solitude-loving man. Time and again, he gives an expression to his love of philosophy, with regards to his opinion on the 'Ode to Indolence'. In a letter written to Sarah, Jeffrey, on dated 9 June, 1819, he says:

> I have been very idle lately, very averse to writing; both from the overpowering idea of our dead poets and from my abatement of my love of fame. I hope I am a little more of a philosopher than I was, consequently a little less of a versifying Pet-Lamb. You will judge of my 1819 temper when I tell you that the thing I have most enjoyed this year has been writing an ode to Indolence.[92]

One more noticeable thing in the letter is that it was written only two years back before he died. And still the poet's search for happiness was not over. Rather, he seems to have been more drawn towards it despite increasing effect of the fatal disease. It only proves that Keats had an unusual sense of living, which is found in the persons of elevated thinking.

Giving yet another fine example of Keats's philosophical or metaphysical bent of mind, is the letter written by him to George Keats, on dated 19 March, 1819, in which he tells about the writing of 'Ode on Indolence'. The letter says:

> ...This morning I am in a short of a temper indolent and supremely careless: I long after a stanza or two of Thompson's Castle of indolence—My passions are all asleep from my having slumbered till nearly eleven and weakened the animal fibre all over me to a delightful sensation about three degrees on this side of faintness—I had teeth of pearl and the breath of lilies I should call it languor(*sic*) but as I am in Laziness—In this state of effimacy the fibres of the brain are relaxed in common with the rest of the body, and to such a happy degree that pleasure has no show of enticement and pain no unbearable frown. Neither Poetry, nor Ambition, nor Love has any alertness of countenance as they pass by me: they seem rather like three figures on a greek vase—a Man and two women—whom no one but myself could distinguish in their disguisement. This is the only happiness; and is a rare instance of advantage in the body overpowering the Mind.[93]

The last line in the letter 'rare instance of the advantage in the overpowering the Mind' tells the whole thing. A real, or for that matter, a rare happiness is possible, when the mind is in total control over body, which is what was the case with the poet at the time of writing of the letter.

Throwing light on the importance of Keats's letters in view of the growth of his mind and personality, Sydney Colvin says:

> Keats's letters to his brothers and in these winter months, with a few more to Bailey and Reynolds, give us lively glimpse of his social doings, and others, interesting in the extreme, of the inward growth and workings of his mind. He tells of a certain amount of common-place conviviality: an absurd dance and rackety supper at one

> Redhall's...but of this pastime he soon got tired and rather ashamed. His social relations began to extend themselves more than he much cared about, or thought consistent with proper industry. We find him dining with Shelley's friend...man of letters Horace Smith, in company with some fashionable wits, concerning whom he reflects, 'They only served to convince me how superior is humour to wit, in respect to enjoyment. These men say things which make one start, without making one feel.... They have all a mannerism in their eating and drinking, in their mere handling of a decanter. They talked of Kean and his low company', said I to myself. Sunday evenings were for a while set apart for dining with Haydon, and here, on the last Sunday of the year, Keats met Wordsworth for the first time.[94]

Keats's first meeting with the legendary Wordsworth also deserves a notice. When Keats met Wordsworth, he was understandably excited. He saw him for the first time on 28th December, 1817, in a dinner party hosted by Haydon in the honour of the great poet. Keats recalls the sweet memories of the party in the following words:

> On December 28th the immortal dinner came off in a painting-room, with Jerusalem towering up behind us as a background. Wordsworth was in a fine cue, and we had a glorious set-up,—on Homer, Shakespeare, Milton, and Virgil. Lamb got exceedingly merry and exquisitely witty; and his fun in the midst of Wordsworth's solemn intonations of oratory was like the sarcasm and wit of the Fool in the intervals of Lear's passion.... It was indeed an immortal evening. Wordsworth's fine intonations as he quoted Milton and Virgil, Keats's eager and inspired look, Lamb's quaint sparkle of lambent humour, so speeded the stream of consciousness, that in my life I never passed a more delightful time. All our fun was within bounds....[95]

Obviously, Keats was instantly influenced by the great poet. A fortnight after his meeting with Wordsworth Keats reaffirms his views to his brothers and to Haydon that "If there are three things superior in the modern world they *the excursion*, Haydon's Pictures, and Hazlitt's depth of Taste."[96]

But the more Keats saw of Wordsworth himself, the more critical he became of him of his egotistical thinking. He disliked the idea of a man like Wordsworth dining with the foolish Kingston and refusing to dine and meeting him (Keats) there. In one of his letters he regrets, after Wordsworth had gone that he has "left a bad impression wherever he has visited in town by his egotism, Vanity, and bigotry; yet he is a great poet if not a philosopher."[97]

The fullest expression of this critical attitude about Wordsworth occurs in a letter written to Reynolds at the beginning of February. The words in which he expresses his impatience of the several dogmatisms of Wordsworth and Hunt are vital in relation to his own concepts of poetry and of its right aim and working. The letter is as follows:

> It may be said that we ought to read our contemporaries, that Wordsworth etc., should have their due from us. But, for the sake of a few fine imaginative or domestic passages, are we to be bullied into a certain Philosophy engendered in the whims of an Egotist? Every man has his speculations, but every man does brood and peacock over them till he makes a false coinage and deceive himself.... We hate poetry that has palpable design upon us.... Poetry should be great and unobtrusive, a thing which enters into one's soul, and does not startle or amaze it with itself, but with its subject. How beautiful are the retired flowers! How would they lose their beauty were they to throng into highway crying out Admire me, I am a violet.... The ancients (poets) were Emperors of vast Provinces; they had only heard of the remote ones and scarcely cared to visit them. I will cut all this—I will have no more of Wordsworth or Hunt in particular.... I don't mean to deny Wordsworth's grandeur and Hunt's merit, but I mean to say we need not be teased with grandeur and

> merit when we can have them uncontaminated and unobtrusive.[98]

Commenting on the poetic growth of Keats through such letters as quoted above, the biographer, Sidney Colvin says that "These letters of Keats are full of similar first fruits of young reflection, thoughts forming or half-forming themselves in absolute sincerity as he writes, intuitions of his first-endeavouring mind on the search of vital truths of art and nature and humanity. Imperfect, half-wrought phrases often come from him which prove, when you have lived with them, to be more sufficient as well as more suggestive than if they had been chiseled into precision by longer study and more confident mind. For instance: 'the excellence of every is its intensity, capable of making all disagreeables evaporate from their being in close relationship with Beauty and Truth': a sentence worth whole treaties and fit, sketchy as it is, to serve as text to most of what can justly be discoursed concerning problems of art in relation to nature,—of realism, romance, and the rest."[99]

In fact, criticism of Wordsworth's poetry by Keats is an example of his genius and of his fearlessness of expression. It was not easy for Keats, or for that matter, for any of Wordsworth's contemporaries to criticize his poetry in view of his towering image. Therefore, Keats, being so younger a poet, makes bold to feel pity on a great poet like Wordsworth for limiting his sense of beauty to a small group of people, which, according to him, is not a healthy sign for a proper appreciation of art. He says:

> It has yet been a Mystery to me how and where Wordsworth went. I cannot help thinking he has returned to his Shell—with his beautiful Wife and enchanting Sister. It is a great pity that People should be associating themselves with the finest things, spoil them....[100]

This is by no means a small statement on part of Keats for his elder like Wordsworth. This is where Keats is original and straightforward in his expression. And this where his sense of beauty is far wider and broader than Wordsworth or any of his contemporaries. No doubt, his vision of beauty, thus, achieves a greater significance, in terms of genuineness.

Even Keats's idea of 'happiness' was also different from his contemporaries. In his opinion, the real joy cannot be felt without the feeling of sorrow. In a way, joy and sorrow are the two sides of the same coin. Once, writing to Reynolds, Keats resumed his habit of casting his fancies and reflections into rhyme. Beginning playfully, he tells his friend of an odd jumble of incongruous images that had crossed his brain, a kind of experience expressed by him elsewhere in various strains of verse, like *Fancy* in which the poem begins with lines beginning 'Welcome Joy, and Welcome Sorrow'.[101] It also shows that the real happiness cannot be achieved without welcoming sorrow, as it is interwoven with joy.

The 'letters' hold a key to those readers who want to get to the centre of Keats's mind or for the understanding his 'deepest poetry'.[102] In one of such a letters to Mr. Taylor, Keats discloses his intentions to be executed in the time to come in the following words:

> I find I can have no enjoyment in the world but the continual drinking of knowledge. I find there is no worthy pursuit but the idea of doing some good to the world.... There is but one way for me. The road lies through application, study and thought. I will pursue it.[103]

As a follow-up to the foregoing letter the poet continues from where he had left, as he writes to Reynolds:

> An extensive knowledge is needful to thinking people—it takes away the heat and fever; and helps, by widening speculation, to ease the Burden of the Mystery, a thing which I begin to understand a little, and which weighed upon you in the most gloomy and true sentence in our letter. The difference of high sensations with and without knowledge appears to me this: in the latter case we are falling continually ten thousand fathoms deep and being blown up again, without wings, and with all the horror of a bare-shouldered creature—in the former

> case, our shoulders are fledged, and we go through the same air and space without fear.[104]

'Sensations' for Keats were not merely 'bodily sensations' as contrasted with 'thoughts'. For him, they meant "not pleasures and experiences of the senses as opposed to those of the mind, but direct intuitions of the imagination as opposed to deliberate processes of the understanding; and that by 'philosophy' he does not mean metaphysics but knowledge and the fruits of reading generally."[105]

After finishing his dream-project, *Endymion*, Keats must have felt relieved and happy. But his happiness soon disappeared as he received a bitter and strong criticism at the hands of the press, namely 'Blackwood' and 'Quarterly Review' in particular. It was like adding insult to injury to Keats, whose health, apart from surrounded by his family problems, was fast deteriorating. As a result, he was falling into the grip of frustration. But, even in such deplorable mood, only a person of Keats's determination and strong will-power could show his worries about his family members and about his poetry. The letter written to Bailey tells every thing itself:

> ...I was in hopes some little time back to be able to relieve your dullness by my spirits—to point out things in the world worth your enjoyment—and now I am never alone without rejoicing that there is such a thing as death—without placing my ultimate in the glory of dying for a great human purpose...I have two brothers; one is driven, by the 'Burden of Society', to America; the other, with an exquisite love of life, is in a lingering state. My love for my Brothers, from the early loss of our parents, and even from earlier misfortune, has grown into an affection 'passing the love of women'. I have been ill-tempered with them—but the thought of them has always stifled the impression that any woman might otherwise have made upon me. I have a sister too, and may not follow them either to America or to the grave. Life must be undergone, and I certainly derive some consolation from the thought of writing one or two more poems before it ceases.[106]

The letter shows Keats as a person of strong mind and commitment. It is really surprising that a man should be thinking of a 'great human purpose' to be achieved, even as he knew as to how close he was to death. Only a person of an extraordinary thinking can talk like this.

Keats's response to the criticism of *Endymion* is an example of his mental strength, as he writes:

> I cannot but feel indebted to those gentlemen who have taken my part. As for the rest, I begin to get a little acquainted with my own strength and weakness. Praise or blame has but a momentary effect on the man whose love of beauty in the abstract makes him a severe critic on his own works. My own domestic criticism has given me pain beyond what 'Blackwood' or the 'Quarterly' could possibly inflict—and also when I feel I am right, no external praise can give me such a glow as my own solitary re-perception and ratification of what is fine.... Had I been nervous about its being a perfect piece, and with that view asked advice, and trembled over every page, it would not have been written; for it is not in my nature to fumble—I will write independently'—I have written independently *without Judgment*. I may write independently, and *with Judgment*, hereafter. The Genius of Poetry must work out its own salvation in a man: It cannot be matured by law and precept, but by salvation and watchfulness in itself. That which is creative must create itself. In *Endymion* I leaped headlong into the sea, and thereby have been better acquainted with the soundings, with the quick sands, and the rock, than if I had stayed upon the green shore, and piped a silly pipe, and took tea and a comfortable advice. I was never afraid of failure; for I would soon fail than not be among the greatest. But I am nigh getting into a rant.[107]

One of the other important aspects that concerns Keats is his views about marriage. In this regard Colvin finds him "cleaving exultantly to his high vocation and to the idea of a life dedicated to poetry alone",[108] as Keats says to his brother George, now settled in America:

> Notwithstanding your Happiness and your recommendation I hope I shall never marry. Though the most beautiful Creature were waiting for me at the end of a Journey or a Walk...I should not feel—or rather my Happiness would not be so fine as my Solitude is sublime. Then instead of what I have described there is a sublimity to welcome me home. The roaring of the wind is my wife and the Stars through the windowpane are my Children. The mighty abstract Idea I have of Beauty in all things stifles the more divided and minute domestic happiness—an amiable and sweet Children I contemplate as a part of that Beauty, but I have thousand of those beautiful particles to fill up my heart. I feel more and more every, as my imagination strengthens, that I do not live in this world alone but in a thousand worlds. No sooner I am I alone than shapes of epic greatness are stationed around me, and serve my Spirit the office which is equivalent to a King's bodyguard—According my state of mind I am with Achilles shouting in the Trenches, or with Theocritus in the Vales of Sicily. Or I throw my whole being into Troilus.... I melt into the air with a voluptuousness so delicate that that I am content to be alone. These things, combined with the opinion I have of the generality of women—who appear to me as children to whom I would rather give a sugar Plum than my time, form a barrier against Matrimony which I rejoice in.[109]

The letter strongly supports the opinion that Keats sacrificed his matrimonial life for the sake of poetry. It is never an easy decision to take. Only a person like Keats who is so intensely involved to his work of art can take such a decision. The decision is also indicative of the fact that Keats was a metaphysician by temperament and nature.

No letter of Keats is richer than this of February to May 1819 in variety of mood and theme and interest. It contains two of the freshest and most luminous of discursive passages of meditation on life and on the nature of the soul and the meaning of things: passages showing a native power of thought untrained indeed, but also unhampered, by academic knowledge and study, and hardly to be surpassed for their union of imaginative speculation. In one, starting from reflections on the unforeseen way in which circumstances, like clouds, gather and burst, reflections suggested by the expected death of the father of his friend Haslam, he calls up a series of pictures of instinctiveness of with which men, like animals,—the hawk, the robin, the stoat, the deer,—go about their purposes; considers the rarity of the exceptional human beings whose disinterestedness helps on the progress of the world; and then turns his thoughts on himself with the comment as follows:

> Even here, though, I myself am pursuing the same instinctive course as the veriest human animal you can think of, I am, however young, writing at random, straining at particles of light in the midst of great darkness, without knowing the bearing of any one assertion, of any one opinion. Yet may I not in this be free from sin? May there not be superior human beings, amused with graceful, though instinctive, attitude my mind may fall into as I am entertained with the alertness of the Stoat or the anxiety of a Deer?[110]

Analyzing the other part of the letter, dealing with Rousseau-Godwin theories of human perfectibility, Colvin says that it is a

> consideration of the physical frame and order of the world we live in, the flaws and violences which mar and jar it, and which its human offspring are likely to derive from and share with it until the end; and, provisionally accepting the doctrine of immortality, he broaches of his own a scheme of the spiritual discipline for the sake of which, as he suggests, the life of a man on this so imperfect earth may have been designed.[111]

The above analysis of Keats's letter proves further his interest in metaphysical matters, as he talks about the 'particles of light in the midst of great darkness', or the 'theories of human perfectibility' against the 'doctrine of immortality'.

So far as Keats's death caused by the Review is concerned and also about his temperament, S.T. Coleridge is on record as he shares his views about him with one Mr. Green. In fact, both were talking to each other about Keats's handshake with the former. Asked as to how the handshake was, by Mr. Green, Coleridge answers in the following words:

> I cannot describe it. There was a heat and dampness in the hand. To say that his death was caused by the Review is absurd, but at the same time it is impossible adequately to conceive the effect which it must have had on his mind...but all men are not born Philosophers, and all men have not those advantages of birth and education. Poor Keats had not, and it is impossible to conceive the effect which such a Review must have had upon him, knowing as he did that he had his way to make in this world by his own exertions, and conscious of the genius within him.[112]

By now, Keats's difficulties, economic as well as heath-related, had been increasing day by day. In such a condition, he decides to seek job as a surgeon. Recounting the matter to one of his correspondents Miss Jeffreys, describing about his problems and his commitments, Keats says:

> Your advice about the Indian man (of joining as a surgeon) is very wise advice, because it just suits me, though you are a little wrong concerning its destroying the energies of the Mind: on the contrary it would be the finest thing in the world to strengthen them—to be thrown among people who care not for you, with you have no sympathies farcing the Mind upon its own resources, and leaves it free to make its speculations of the differences of human character and to class them with the calmness of a Botanist. One of the reasons that the English have produced the finest writers in the world is, that the English world has ill-treated them during their lives and foster them after their deaths. They have not been treated like the Raphaels of Italy.... The middle

> age of Shakespeare was all clouded over; his days were not more happy than Hamlet's who is perhaps more like Shakespeare himself in his common everyday Life than any of his Characters—for all this I will not go on board as Indian man, nor for example's sake run my head into dark alleys: I daresay my discipline is to come, and plenty of it too. I have been very idle lately, very averse to writing; both for the overpowering idea of our dead poets and from the abatement of my love for fame. I hope I am a little more of a Philosopher than I was, consequently a little less of a verifying Pet-lamb. You will judge of my 1819 temper when I tell you that the thing I have most enjoyed this year has been writing an ode on Indolence.[113]

It is no less surprising that Keats was willing to produce more poetry, even as surrounded by so many serious problems. Certainly, he was guided by some uncommon inner strength, needed for such a will-power as he was having. The only reason for such a self-inspiration was his belief in the mortality of body as against of the immortality of soul. The body has to perish, howsoever strong or weak. This idea must have inspired Keats to continue his poetic activity, even as he was aware of his ever-diminishing health on account of his medical knowledge.

Here is another example of Keats's resolution to choose the way of fighting rather than despair, as he imparts another confidence in life to the same correspondent as mentioned above. He writes:

> I have been always till now almost as careless of the world as a fly—my troubles were of the Imagination—My brother George always stood between me and dealings with the world. Now I find I must buffet it—I must make my stand upon some vintage ground and begin to fight—I must choose between despair and Energy—I choose the latter though the world has taken on a quakerish look with me....[114]

On 25th of August, 1819, Keats writes to Reynolds, 'as usual more gravely and openly expressing his present feelings with regards to life and literature':

> The more I know what my diligence may in time probably effect, the more my heart distend with Pride and Obstinacy—I feel it in power to become a popular writer—I feel it in my power to refuse the poisonous suffrage of a public. My own being which I know to be becomes of more consequence to me than the crowds of Shadows in the Shape of men and women that inhabit a kingdom. The soul is a world itself, and has enough to do in its own home. Those whom I know already, and who have grown as it were a part of me, I could not do without: but for the rest of the mankind, they are as much a dream to me as Milton's Hierarchies. I think if I had a free and healthy and lasting organization of heart, and lungs as strong as an ox's, so as to be able unhurt the shock of extreme thought and sensation without weariness, I could pass my life very nearly alone though it should last eighty years. But I feel my body too weak to support me to the height, I am obliged continually to check myself, and be nothing.[115]

Again, reference to 'soul' and 'body' by Keats in the letter indicate to his interest in matters relating to metaphysics.

Keats's letters to his friends are a great help in the understanding of his own thinking and bent of mind. One of such friends is Leigh Hunt, about whom he says in his own philosophical style, (on 27th Oct. 1816):

> The greater part of my time has been spent in Leigh Hunt's society, who is certainly one of the most delightful companions. Full of poetry and art, and amiable humour, we argue with full hearts on every thing, but religion and Buonaparte, and we have resolved never to talk of these, particularly as I have been recently examining Voltaire's opinions concerning Christianity, and turmoiling my head to ascertain fully my right to put him into my picture! Though Leigh Hunt is not deep in knowledge, mortal, metaphysical, or

> classical, yet he is intense in feeling, and has an intellect for ever on the alert....[116]

On October 31, Keats writes to Cowden Clarke of his pleasure at 'the thought of seeing soon this glorious Haydon and all his creation'. After an evening of high talk at the beginning of their acquaintance, Keats praises Haydon as a man of qualities as well as a great painter in a letter written in a sonnet form in which he compared him with the literary giants like Wordsworth by saying that "Great spirits now on earth are sojourning...."[117]

Even at this early stage of his life Keats had shown his deep interest in serious matters of life. In one of his letters, in the form of an ode, sent to Haydon by Keats shows his "unfailing characteristic sincerity with his art and with himself to break into no stock raptures, but strives faithfully to get into words the confused sensations of spiritual infirmity and awe that have overpowered him."[118] The sonnet is as follows:

> My spirit is too week—mortality
> Weighs heavily on me like unwilling sleep,
> And each imagin'd pinnacle and steep
> Of Godlike hardship, tells me I must die
> Like a sick Eagle looking at the sky....[119]

He sends this with a covering sonnet to Haydon asking pardon for the immaturity of thinking in the following lines:

> Haydon! Forgive me that I cannot speak
> Definitely on these mighty things;
> Forgive me that I have not Eagle's wings....[120]

Haydon's acknowledgement is very enthusiastic and throws a great deal of light on Keats's inborn poetic gift, with metaphysical bent of mind, as he writes:

> Many thanks, my dear fellow, for your two noble sonnets. I know not a finer image than the comparison of a poet unable to express his high feelings to a sick eagle looking at the sky, where he must have remembered his former towerings amid the blaze of dazzling sunbeams, in the pure expense of glittering

clouds; now and then passing angels, on heavenly errands, lying at the will of the wind with moveless wings, or pitching down with a fiery rush, eager and intent on objects of their seeking....[121]

It is more than clear from the above correspondence between the two new fast friends, portraying Keats as a confused person with regards to 'these mighty high things' but at least he had his eyes very much set on 'these mighty things'. He had a genuine and sincere interest in such matters which he had shared with Haydon in a great deal.

Associating the 'letters' with Keats's metaphysical bent of mind, N.S. Sahu says, "Explicit or implicit in the letters are some of Keats's articles of faith and some of his central tensions or 'unreconciled opposites'. Juxtaposed with *Endymion*, it would not be fair to say that his letters reveal the ideas, and are more appealing than the diffuse and wayward poem. *Endymion* reflects not so much the burden of the conflicting and equally realized impulses but the confusion that is the product of semi-conscious instincts rushing through a self-imposed and only half-realized ideal. And, the 'Platonic' idealism of Keats's parable, the idea that the path to the one passes through loving apprehensions of many, was a sincere conviction, and his metaphysics of unity or reality was somewhat less real than his sensuous to actual and tangible."[122]

Thus, in a way, Keats wanted to reconcile the 'unreconciled opposites' through writing his letters. These 'opposites' clearly indicate to matters beyond physical world. The 'opposites' could not be reconciled by him, or for that matter, by human endeavour as they were controlled by some powers which were beyond human reach. And this is what the poet wanted to realize by his power of heightened imagination, a human faculty through which it was possible to resolve the 'unreconciled opposites'. As a result, it is unfair on part of Mr. Sahu to say that Keats's letters, or poetry, reflect less of the 'Platonic idealism' and more of sensuous response to the 'actual or the tangible'.

In fact, the very presence of the 'Platonic idealism' in his letters, as admitted by Mr. Sahu in his statement, is a proof of the fact of how much importance did the poet attach to it. Keats's deep interest in the works of Milton, Shakespeare, or Wordsworth, and his criticism of each of them also proves that his was not merely concerned with the sensuous pleasures of nature.

Therefore, the 'letters' speak volumes about Keats's mind and character, as well as his thoughts and beliefs, regarding life. If on the personal level, they reveal him as a sensitive, sympathetic and passionate human being; it is the metaphysical aspect of his character which finds a prominent place in them. Time and again, a genuine sense of concern for the 'higher matters' of life gets reflected in the letters, even as he was sharing his views about family matters with his brothers and sister. His obsession for poetry was, however, a recurrent theme of his letters, evident from them. The fact that he wrote most of the letters under compelling circumstances, or when he found himself unable to produce poetry, is a proof of his dedication to his profession.

In short, the 'letters' give us the fullest and most interesting portrait of a poet closely involved in the life around him. The man that is revealed through them is "profoundly original, challenging and deeply human".[123] The words 'profoundly original' and 'challenging' used for Keats are sufficient to suggest his interest in metaphysical considerations regarding life.

Thus, it will be no exaggeration to say that the 'letters' provide a true insight into Keats's metaphysical aspect of his personality and life.

5

Metaphysical Element with Reference to 'Ode on a Grecian Urn', 'Ode to a Nightingale', *Endymion* and *Hyperion*

First of all, 'Ode on a Grecian Urn' which exemplifies Keats's love for Greek Mythology in the most powerful way. His vision of the ancient world was intensely personal, and is shown at its most characteristic way in the grave and lovely poem 'Ode on a Grecian Urn'. "Here, contemplation of the events and figures portrayed on an ancient vase serves as a profound statement on the relationship of life and art, contrasting the urn's static perfection with the fervid imperfections of life, teasing us out of thought, as doth eternity."[1]

The last two lines in the poem ('Beauty is truth, truth beauty...'), however, do not make simple reading. These lines need to be read with the attentive seriousness which the poet brought to them. This is not a vague salute to beautiful things, but the impassioned philosophical belief that beauty had a profound moral value, and could guide, strengthen and console. Commenting on the power of Art, Keats himself had written in one of his letters (1817) that, "The excellence of every Art is in its intensity, capable of making all disagreeables evaporate, from their being in close relationship Beauty and Truth."[2] Writing to Benjamin Bailey regarding the poem, he said, "I am certain of nothing but the holiness of Heart's affection and the truth of the Imagination—what the imagination seizes as Beauty must be truth."[3]

Commenting on the puzzle of the last two lines, G.S. Fraser points out:

> If we take the last line and a half as spoken by Keats, there are two alternatives. Either Keats, as he has been doing throughout Ode, addressing the figures on the urn or he is, abruptly, confusingly and with a breach of decorum, addressing his readers for the first time in the ode. If he is addressing the figures on the urn there is no real puzzle; the truth and beauty, the existence and value, of figures in a work of art are identical. The whole poem has been saying that these figures are caught in a moment of ecstasy, free from human pain and struggle. The implication is that though art's message of some sort of ultimate identity of the true and the beautiful, the real and the ideal, makes art a 'friend to man', still we, 'this generation', as opposed to *ye*, the figure on the urn, need to know a great deal more than this, though we need to know this too. That was essentially how Matthew Arnold took it.[4]

The main question is whether the lines are spoken by the urn or by the poet. If by the poet, then why? As Keats is known for keeping his personality completely away from poetry. But, the lines appear to be addressed by the poet himself, as if speaking directly to the world in a manner of address. If so, then why did poet go against his own promise of keeping himself away from the work of art?

Continuing the argument further, G.S. Fraser says, "But if either the urn is addressing mankind to the end of the stanza or Keats is suddenly reinforcing the urn's message on his own behalf, then with Quiller-Couch, T.S. Eliot, and many others we cannot help feeling that 'Beauty is truth, truth beauty' is inadequate as a summary of *all* that we need in the way of saving wisdom."[5]

All-important question is as to what is the real meaning of the 'Beauty is truth, truth beauty', whether spoken be the poet or the urn. Attempting an answer to this complex question in an effective manner, Fraser says, "Keats's famous letter to Bailey, of which the most relevant portion is included in the compilation, makes it clear what some of the possible ranges of meaning could be. Keats was a man of swift intuitive perceptions and the thought of arriving at truth by a long laborious process of abstract reasoning repelled him. He was a man with a firm, though not orthodoxy Christian, belief in an afterlife. He thought of heaven as a repetition, with ever greater understanding, of the moments of beauty we have known on earth, just as he thought our highest experience on earth is the intense re-living of such moments. Such moments are not meaningless, are not mere reverie or fantasy, but give us a foretaste of what life in heaven will be like, or sudden intense glimpses of the ultimate harmony of things. There is some evidence that he thought of 'truth' not as the abstract correspondence of proposition and fact but as living pattern of identity in actual things, something like Hopkins's 'inscape', which imagination or intuition in a way that abstract reasoning or 'cold philosophy' (what we would now call science) never can."[6]

There must be something wrong with the last stanza, otherwise it would not have bothered so many so much. Whether it was flaw in syntax or not, Keats did not exactly describe about his intention of the 'lines', in his letter to Bailey. Hence the doubt on part of Fraser that:

> One could complain at the most, that there is a danger of taking 'Beauty is Truth, truth beauty' as an abstract philosophical statement (a truism to Platonists, but very worrying to Aristotelians) rather than a personal affirmation, based on Keats's experience as a poet and his very personal religious vision.[7]

Whether a philosophical or personal statement, as stated by Fraser, the crux of the matter is that the 'lines' ('Beauty is Truth'...) do have an undercurrent of a metaphysical message.

Keats's own comments on the background of the poem would serve as an original source, as far as the circumstances under which the poem must have been written. Writing to Benjamin Bailey, on dated 22 Nov. 1817, the poet says:

> ...But I am running my head into a Subject which I am certain I could not do justice to under five years study and 3 vols. octavo—and moreover long to be talking about the Imagination—...O I wish I was as certain of the end of all your troubles as that of your momentary start about the authenticity of the Imagination. I am certain of nothing but the holiness of Heart's affections and the truth of Imagination—What the imagination seizes as Beauty must be truth—whether it existed before or not—for I have the same Idea of all our Passions as of Love they are all in their sublime, creative of essential Beauty—In a Word, you may know my favourite Speculation by my first book and the little song I sent in my last—which is a representation from the fancy of the probable mode of operating in these matters—The Imagination may be compared to Adam's dream—he awoke found it truth. I am the more zealous in this affair, because I have never yet been able to perceive how anything can be known for truth by consecutive (sic) reasoning—and yet it must be—Can it be that even the greatest philosopher ever {when} arrived at its goal without putting aside numerous objections—However it may be, O for a Life Sensations rather than of thoughts! It is a Vision in the form of Youth, a Shadow of reality to come—Adam's dream will do here and seems to be a conviction that Imagination and its reflection is the same as Human Life and its spiritual repetition.... What a time! I am continually running away from the subject—sure this cannot be exactly the case with a complex Mind—one that is imaginative and at the same time careful of its fruits—who would exist partly on sensation partly on thought—to whom it is necessary that years should bring the Philosophic Mind—such a one I consider your's and therefore it is necessary to your Eternal Happiness that you not only drink {have} this old Wine of Heaven which I shall call the redigestion of

our most ethereal Musings on Earth; but also increase in knowledge and know all things....[8]

On dated 23 March, 1818, Keats wrote a verse letter, regarding the same subject as in the previous letter, but this time to J.S. Renolds. The letter is also significant in order to understand the background of the poem and the mindset of the poet. The contents are as follows:

The sacrifice goes on; the pontiff knife
Gleams in the sun, the milk-white heifer lows,
The pipes go shrilly, the libation lows....
For in the world we jostle—
But my flag is not unfurled
On the Admiral staff—and to philosophize
I dare not yet!—Oh never will the prize,
High reason, and the lore of good and ill
Be my award. Things cannot to the will
Be settled, but they tease us out of thought.
Or is it that imagination brought
Beyond its proper bound, yet still confined,—
Lost in a sort of Purgatory blind,
Cannot refer to any standard law
Of either earth or heaven?—It is a flaw
In happiness to see beyond our bourn—
It forces us in summer skies to mourn:
It spoils the 'singing of the Nightingale'.[9]

Both the letters have a lot to say about the theme of the poem. Evidently, the poet was undergoing lots of ups and downs with regards to the nature of human life and its real goal. So, the whole poem and particularly the last two lines reflect the philosophical thoughts that were haunting Keats's mind at the time of writing the poem. As far as the identity of the speaker of the lines is, it must be the poet himself, not the urn, as has been speculated by some critics, who would have spoken the lines, as it was the most vital issue that the poet was

addressing. In the views of the poet, it appears, when it comes to dealing with the issue that he was, the poet is forced to become the speaker. And this is exactly what Keats does with the last lines. He becomes the speaker to speak the 'Ultimate Truth'.

Elaborating on the theme of the Ode, Graham Hough says that it "takes up the thought of the seventh stanza of the *Ode to a Nightingale.* De Selincourt suggests as its motto a phrase of Leonardo's: Cosa bella mortal passa e non d'arte—Mortal beauties pass away, none, but not those of art.... The urn is taken as a type of enduring beauty; and again the immortality of art is only a quasi-immortality; for though ceramics last longer than those things they are not in any metaphysical sense more indestructible than mere human clay. There is no real analogy between the loves and pastoral felicities on the urn and 'breathing human passions'; the contrast between the permanence of the one and the transience of the other is another poetic casuistry. But this time it is directed to a different end. The poet's momentary emotional state enters less into the poem. He is concerned to establish at least one enduring value below the sphere of the moon, and he finds it in the existence of the art. It is the only way in which human feeling and natural loveliness can be given lasting significance. The happy boughs that cannot shed their leaves and the lover who can never kiss, but whose love can never fade are types of the only earthly paradise that exists; and the fact that it is not quite of the kind that men are looking for is not now in the foreground of consciousness."[10]

Graham Hough also has his viewpoint to give, regarding the 'last two lines' of the poem. In the first place, he does not agree that 'beauty is truth, truth beauty' is not all that the people should know on earth. He also does not agree with I.A. Richards's opinion who merely regards the lines as meaningless. He says that the "lines must be read in their context, and in the context of other odes." They are of course in the first place the expression of a moment of rapturous recognition of a beautiful object, and so far are equivalent to an exclamation of joy and reverence. But the sensuous resources of Keats's verse are so rich that he has no need to disguise his emotions of this kind as philosophical statements, unless he also means them in some sense to be so. And he says the same thing in the prose: 'I never can feel certain of any truth, but for a clear perception of Beauty.' The view is duly supported in the quote that follows:

> In this context, where transience and permanence are the two poles of the argument, 'truth' means 'that which has lasting value'. (The truth is great *and shall prevail*. What is true all the week is 'truer' than what is true only on Monday morning.) Keats is saying that beauty is 'truer' than love, pleasure and other forms of value, because they pass away while beauty can be embodied in a lasting quasi-permanent form. When poets say 'ye' they are often addressing themselves or other poets. The beauty is truth and truth beauty is all that the artist, as artist, knows, and all that he needs to know for the practice of his art.[11]

Cleanth Brooks is another critic, whose views are regarded as an authority on Keats's poetry. Throwing light on the 'urn riddle', Brooks says:

> There is much in the poetry of Keats which suggests that he would have approved of Archibald MacLeish's dictum. 'A poem should not mean/ But be.' There is even some warrant for thinking that the Grecian urn (real or imagined) which inspired the famous ode was, for Keats, just as a poem, 'palpable and mute', a poem in stone. Hence it is more remarkable that the Ode itself differs from Keats's other odes by culminating in a statement—a statement even of some sententiousness in which the urn itself is made to say that beauty is truth, and truth, and—more sententious still—that this bit of wisdom sums up the whole of mortal knowledge.[12]

Putting the criticism of T.S. Eliot, Middleton Murry and I.A. Richards, who more or less condemned the two lines of the poem as meaningless, Brooks says, "But the question of real importance is not whether Eliot, Murry, and Garrod are right in thinking that 'Beauty is truth, truth beauty' injures the poem. The question of real importance concerns beauty and truth in a much more general way; what is the relation of the beauty (the goodness, the perfection) of a poem to the truth or falsity of what seems to assert? It is a question which has particularly vexed our generation—to give I.A. Richards's phrasing, it is the problem of belief."[13]

The 'Ode', by its bold equation of beauty and truth, comments Brooks, "Raises this question in its sharpest form—the more so when it becomes apparent that the poem itself is obviously intended to be a parable on the nature of the poetry and of art in general. The 'Ode' has apparently been an enigmatic parable, to be sure: one can emphasize *beauty* is truth and throw Keats into the pure-art camp, the usual procedure. But it is only fair to point out that one could stress *truth* is beauty, and argue with the Marxist critics of the 'thirties for a propaganda art'. The very ambiguity of the statement, 'Beauty is truth, truth beauty' ought to warn us against insisting very much on the statement in isolation, and to drive us back to a consideration of the context in which the statement is set".[14]

It will be sufficient, however, continues Brooks, if it merely drives us back to a study of Keats's reading, his conversation, his letters. We shall not find our answer there even if scholarship does prefer on principle investigations of Browning's ironic question, "What porridge had John Keats? For even if we knew just what porridge he had, physical and mental, we should still not be able to settle the problem of the 'Ode'. The reason should be clear: our specific question is not what did Keats the man want to assert here about the relation of beauty and truth: it is rather: was Keats the poet able to exemplify that relation in particular poem? Middleton Murry is right: the relation of the final statement in the poem to the total context is all-important.[15]

The poem needs to be discussed in view of its paradoxical composition. The words 'mad' and 'ecstasy' occur in the poem, but it is the quiet, rigid urn, which gives the dynamic picture. And the paradox goes further, as the scene is one of violent love-making but the urn itself is like a 'still unravished bride', or like a child, a child 'of silence and slow time'. It is not merely like a child, but like a 'foster-child'. Likewise, 'Silence and slow time', it is suggested, are not true parents, but foster-parents. The foster-parents too seem to be too old to have borne the child themselves. Lastly, the urn is 'fresh and unblemished', so it is still young, for its antiquity, and time which has destroyed so much has but 'fostered' it.

On the use of such a bold paradox and its implications, Brooks says that "the first lines of the stanza state a rather bold paradox—even the dulling effect of many readings has hardly blunted it...." Attended to with care, it is a statement which is preposterous, and yet true—true on the same level on which the original metaphor of the speaking urn is true. The unheard music is sweeter than any audible music. The poet has rather cunningly enforced his conceit by using the phrase, 'ye soft pipes'. Actually, we might accept the poet's metaphor without being forced to accept the adjective 'soft'. The pipes might, although 'unheard', be shrill, just as the action which is frozen in the figures on the urn can be violent and ecstatic as in stanza I and slow and dignified as in stanza IV (the procession to the sacrifice). Yet, by characterizing pipes as 'soft', the poet has provided a sort of realistic for his metaphor: the pipes, it is suggested, are playing very softly; if we listen carefully, we can hear them; their music is just below the threshold of normal sound.[16]

This general paradox runs through the stanza, as the action goes on though the actors are motionless. As the song will never cease, so the lover cannot leave his song, and the maiden, always to be kissed, never actually kissed, will remain changelessly beautiful. "The maiden is," says Brooks, "indeed, like the urn itself, a 'still unravished bride of quietness'—not even ravished by a kiss; and it is implied, perhaps, that her changeless beauty, like that of the urn, springs from this fact."[17]

Elaborating on the theme of 'timelessness or immortality' through the static position of the urn, Mr. Brooks says that:

> The poet is obviously stressing the fresh, unwearied charm of the scene itself which can defy time and is

> deathless. But, at the same time, the poet is being perfectly fair to the terms of his metaphor. The beauty portrayed is deathless because it is lifeless. And it would be possible to shift the tone easily and ever so slightly by insisting more heavily on some of the phrasings so as to give them a darker implication. Thus, in the case of 'thou canst leave/ Thy song', one could interpret: the musician cannot leave the song even if he would: he fettered to it, a prisoner. In the same way, one could enlarge on the hint that the lover is not wholly satisfied and content: 'never canst thou kiss...*yet do not grieve'*. These items are mentioned here, not because one wishes to maintain that the poet is bitterly ironical, but because it is important for us to see that even here the paradox is being used fairly, particularly in view of the shift in tone which comes in the next stanza.[18]

The third stanza represents a kind of a recapitulation of earlier motifs. The boughs which cannot shed their leaves, the unwearied melodist, and the ever-ardent lover reappear. It is not sure that this stanza can be well-defended against the charge of a falling off from the firm precision of the earlier stanzas. There is, actually, a tendency to linger over the scene sentimentally. Therefore, "the repetition of the word 'happy' is perhaps symptomatic of what is occurring".[19]

The paradox is carried further in the case of the lover whose love is:

> For ever 'warm and still to be enjoy'd'. It appears to be ambiguous, as 'still to be enjoy'd' can be taken as an adjective phrase on the same level as 'warm'—that is, 'still virginal and warm'. But the tenor of the whole poem suggests that the warmth of the love depends on the fact that it has not been enjoyed as yet. That is to say, 'warm and still to be enjoy'd' mean also 'warm still to be enjoyed'. But, though the poet has developed his metaphors further in the third stanza, the ironic counterpoise is also developed further. But the reality is that the love which a line earlier was 'warm' and 'panting' becomes suddenly in the next line, 'All

> breathing human passion far above'. But if it is *above* all breathing passions, it is, after all, outside the realm of breathing passion, and therefore, not human passion at all.[20]

Keats has been criticized for letting the poem go out of his hands, as far as the last two lines are concerned. Mr. Brooks defends the poet against Garrod of this charge and says that "the purpose in emphasizing the ironic undercurrent in the foregoing lines is not at all to disparage Keats—to point up implications of his poem of which he was himself unaware. Far from it: the poet knows precisely what he is doing. The point is to be made simply in order to make sure that we are completely aware of what he is doing. Garrod, sensing this ironic undercurrent, seems to interpret it as an element over which Keats was not able to exercise full control". Continuing the argument Mr. Brook further says:

> Truth to his main theme [the fixity given by art to forms which in life are impermanent] has taken Keats farther than he meant to go. The pure and ideal art of this 'cold Pastoral', this 'silent form', *has* a cold silentness which in some degree saddens him.... In the last lines of the fourth stanza, especially the last three lines...every reader is conscious, I should suppose, of an undertone of sadness, of disappointment. The undertone is there, but Keats had not been taken 'farther than he meant to go'. Keats's attitude, even in earlier stanzas, is more complex than Garrod would allow: it is more complex and more ironic, and recognition of this is important if we are able to relate the last stanza to the rest of the 'Ode'. Keats is perfectly aware that the frozen moment of loveliness is more dynamic than is the fluid world of reality *only* because it is frozen. The love depicted on the urn remains warm because it is not human flesh at all but cold, ancient marble.[21]

The argument of the theme of timelessness continues, when Mr. Brooks says that "the marble men and women of the urn will not age as flesh and blood men and will: 'When old age shall this generation.' (The word 'generation', by the way, is very rich. It means on one level 'that which is generated'—that which springs from human loins—Adam's breed; and yet, so intimately is death wedded to men, the word 'generation' itself has become, as here, a measure of time.) The marble men and women lie outside time. The urn which they adorn will remain. The 'Sylvan historian' will recite its history to other generations."[22]

Concluding the discussion on the sublime nature of theme of the poem, Mr. Brooks says:

> Moreover, the 'truth' which the sylvan historian gives is the only kind of truth which are likely to get on this earth, and furthermore, it is only kind that we *have* to have. The names, the dates, and special circumstances, the wealth of data—these the sylvan historian quietly ignores. But we shall never get all the facts any way—there is no end to the accumulation of facts. Moreover, mere accumulation—a point our own generation is only beginning to realize—are meaningless. The sylvan historian does better than that: it takes a few details and so orders them that we have not only beauty but insight into essential truth. Its 'history', in shorts, is a history without footnotes. It has the validity of myth—not myth as a pretty but irrelevant make-belief, an idle fancy, but myth as valid perception into reality.[23]

In his analysis of the poem in the essay 'Symbolic Action in a Poem by Keats', Kenneth Burke says that "perhaps we might put it this way: If the oracle were to have been uttered in the first stanza of the poem rather than the last, its phrasing proper to that place would have been: 'Beauty is *not* truth, truth *not* beauty.' The five stanzas of successive transformation were necessary for the romantic philosophy of a romantic poet to transcend itself (raising its romanticism to a new order, or new dimension) an abolishing of romanticism through romanticism!"[24]

Pointing to the metaphysical aspects of the poem in terms of its motivation, Mr. Burke comments that:

> If we had only the first stanza of this Ode, and were speculating upon it from the standpoint of the

> motivation, we could detect there tentative indication of two motivational levels. For the lines express a doubt whether the figures on the urn are 'deities or mortals'—and the motives of the gods are of a different order from the motives of men. This bare hint of such a possibility emerges with something of a certainty in the second stanza's development of the 'pipes and timbrels theme'. For we explicitly consider a contrast between body and mind (in the contrast between 'heard melodies', addressed 'to the sensual ear', and 'ditties of no tune', addressed 'to the spirit').... Also, of course, the notion inaudible sound brings us into the region of the mystic oxymoron. And it clearly suggests a concern with the level of motives-behind-motives, as with the paradox of the prime mover that is itself at rest, being the unmoved ground of all motion and action. Here the poet whose sounds are the richest in our language is meditating upon *absolute* sound, the *essence* of sound, which would be soundless as the prime mover is motionless, or as the 'principle' of sweetness would not be sweet, having transcended sweetness, or as the sub-atomic particles of the sun are each, in their isolate purity, said to be devoid of temperature.[25]

Kenneth Burke tries to establish the presence of metaphysical elements in Keats's poetry, by contrasting his thoughts with those of Shelley. He says, "Here the futuristic Shelley is anticipating retrospection; he is looking forward to looking back. The form of thought is naturalistic and temporalistic in terms of *past* and *future*. But the form of thoughts in Keats is mystical, in terms of an *eternal present*. The Ode is striving to move beyond the region of becoming into the realm of *being*."[26]

Commenting on the Ode as a perfectly impersonal piece of art, where the personality of the artist is absolutely hidden from the work and known as 'Negative Capability' in poetry, Mr. Burke says, "Suppose that we had but this one poem by Keats, or knew nothing of its author or its period, so that we could treat it only by itself, as a series of internal transformations to be studied in their development from a certain point, and without reference to any motive outside the Ode. Under such conditions, I think, we should require no further observations to characterize the main argument in the second stanza…."[27]

For Keats writing poetry was a passion, or religion. Even his illness could not keep himself away from poetry. The illness, or the physical suffering which was Keats's companion all while living, inspired the poet, rather, to write with more passion. Throwing light on this aspect, Burke says, "But though the poet's body was *patient*, the poet's mind was an *agent*. Thus as a practitioner of poetry, he could *use* his fever, even perhaps encouraging, though not deliberately, esthetic habits that, in making for the perfection of his illness, would exact payment in the ravages of his body…. "Speaking of agents, patients, and action here, we might pause to glance back over the centuries thus: in the Aristotelian grammar of motives, action has its reciprocal in passion, hence *passion* is the property of a *patient*. But by the Christian paradox (which made the martyr's action identical with his passion) *patience* is the property of a moral *agent*. And this Christian view, as secularized in the philosophy of romanticism, with its stress upon creativeness, leads us to the possibility of a bodily suffering redeemed by a poetic art."[28]

Therefore, "The poem as a whole, makes permanent, or fixes in a state of arrest, a peculiar agitation. But within this fixity, by the nature of poetry as progressive medium, there must be a development. Hence the agitation that is maintained throughout (as a mood absolutized so that it fills the entire universe of discourse) will at the same time undergo internal transformations. In the third stanza, these are manifested as a clear division into two distinct and contrasted realms. There is a transcendental fever, which is felicitous, divinely above 'all breathing human passion'. And this 'leaves' the other level, the level of earthly fever, 'a burning forehead and parching tongue'. From the bodily fever, which is a passion, and malign, there has split off a spiritual activity, a wholly benign aspect of the total agitation."[29]

Attempting to conclude the Ode as an outcome of Keats's metaphysical attitude, Mr. Burke thinks that a work of art is possible because of God's will as it symbolizes 'good'. ('God willed the good *because* it is good.') He says that:

> In the scholastic formulas taken over from Aristotle, God was defined as 'pure act' (though this pure act was in turn the ultimate ground or *scene* of human acting and willing) and from the standpoint of pure dramatic symmetry, it would be desirable to have some kind of 'scene' even for God. This requirement is met, we are suggesting, in the doctrine that 'God willed the good *because* it is good'.... If even theology thus responded to the pressure for dramatic symmetry by endowing God, as transcendent act, with a transcendent scene of likely quality, we should certainly expect to find analogous tactics in this Ode ('Grecian Urn'). For as we noted that the romantic passion is the secular equivalent of the Christian passion, so we may recall Coleridge's notion that poetic action itself is a 'dim analogue of Creation'.... Keats in his way confronting the same dramatic requirement that the theologians confronted in theirs, when he has arrived at his transcendent act at the end of stanza III (that is, when the benign fever has split away from the malign of the bodily counterpart, as divorcing of spiritual action from sensual), he is ready in the next stanza for the imagining of a scene that would correspond in the quality to the quality of the action as so transformed....[30]

Whether the fourth stanza ("Who are these coming to the sacrifice? can e'er return."), is a vision of 'death' or of 'immortality' is the vital question to be asked, and must necessarily be conceived in terms of death (the necessity that Donne touches upon when he writes, '...but I think that I/ Am, by being dead, immortall.'[31] This is why, when discussing the second stanza, says Burke, "I felt justified in speaking of the variations of the love-death equation.... We have a deathly deathless scene, as the corresponding ground of our transcendent act. The Urn itself, as with the scene upon it, is not merely an immortal act in our present mortal scene; it was originally an immortal act in a mortal scene quite different. The imagery, of sacrifice, piety, silence, desolation, is that of communication with the immortal or the dead."[32]

So far as the lines "Heard melodies are sweat, but those unheard are sweater" are concerned, they indicate to the 'divine melody', supposed to have been put forth by God Himself, through the pipes of the musicians, painted on the Urn. Although, the poet uses the word 'sweater' for the 'unheard' melodies, he only meant 'sweetest' for them, as there can be no sweater melody than that produced by God Himself. The simple reason is that the 'heard' or human melodies are meant for the sensual ears, whereas the 'unheard' or divine melodies cannot be heard or enjoyed by the sensual ears, as they are incapable of doing so.

As a result, the divine melodies can only be enjoyed by divine ears, which the human beings cannot have, because of their human (imperfect) nature. So, by describing the 'unheard' melodies, the poet does not mean to refer to those songs which have so far not been heard by the man. Rather, the poet is trying to refer to those melodies which cannot be heard by men because of the sensual quality of their ears.

Describing the Ode as a manifestation of Keats's metaphysical outlook, Maurice Bowra states that it:

> Is built on a neat and recognizable plan in three parts: introduction, main subject, and conclusion. The first stanza gives the introduction, the second, third, and fourth stanzas the main subject, and the fifth the conclusion. The introduction presents the Urn in its mystery and shows what questions it poses to the poet. The main subject consists of the scenes on the Urn, not as a casual observer might notice them, but Keats sees them with the full force of imaginative insight into the 'metaphysical problems' which they raise and their hint of another life different from that which we ordinarily know.... The conclusion relates the experience gained from the Urn to its special order of reality and answers the questions which the poem has raised. Thus, it has

> what Aristotle has called a beginning, middle, and an end; it evokes a special state of mind and relates to this to ordinary life; it moves from eager curiosity to delightful amazement, exalted rapture, and devout solemnity. This ideal world of the imagination is given an unexpected strength by the comparison made between it and love as Keats actually knows it....[33]

For Keats the Urn is "beyond sound and change, in a noisy, changing world. We are brought at once into an order of things remote from our usual lives. The poet asks that we should see the Urn in all the mystery of its unchanging silence.... The Urn is a concrete symbol of some vast reality which can be reached only through knowledge of individual objects which share and reflect its character. The Urn is also 'foster-child of silence and slow time'. It is not their actual child, because they have not created it. But they have kept and preserved it, and that is why it is called 'foster-child'. Keats strongly felt the appeal of the uncalendered past and saw in the Urn a repository of wisdom of the ages."[34]

Associating the Urn with divinity, Bowra says that "the Urn is an 'ethereal thing' which raises and invites question. At the start the question does not look very difficult, but as Keats develops his theme, we see that they have a special point. He does not wish to know who the figures on the Urn are, but what they are, what they mean. In the next three stanzas he shows how much in these questions and in what relation to his theme of quietness and silence. Silence is emphasized at the start of the second stanza, when Keats challenges our curiosity by a paradox ('heard melodies sweet, but those unheard/ Are sweeter') expressed with a simplicity which makes it all the more striking. This is why, the unheard music, the melody of silence, is what Keats finds in the flute player on the Urn, and the passage from *Endymion* proves that this is no ingenuous trope. The music which we do not hear but only imagine is sweeter than any music actually heard because it is ideal of what music aught to be, the kind of music which we may conceive in fancy but which will never strike the 'sensual years'. In all the arts men reach towards such an ideal and know that, though they cannot ever attain it, it provided a standard and a criterion for what art they have."[35]

Again, the 'unheard music' that Keats talks about in his ode on 'Grecian Urn' "expresses with great force something which lies close to the centre of all truly creative experience. Great as was his physical sensibility and his appreciation of everything that came through his senses, he knew in the very moment of enjoying it that was not it was not every thing and not enough. Anything so vivid and yet so transient must be related to some larger reality which, being permanent and complete, gives a satisfying basis for it."[36]

Elaborating on the matter, relating to the world of metaphysics as dealt by Keats in his calling the Urn as a symbol of silence, Bowra says that:

> We may legitimately call this reality an ideal world, if by that we mean an order of things which gives substance and significance to the gifts of senses. And that Keats believed this is clear from the lines quoted from Book III of *Endymion*. His ideal world was not a scheme of abstractions but a source of living powers beyond the senses, therefore silent, but more real than the most entrancing gifts of the senses through the devotion which it commands and assurance with which he believes that it endures for ever. Nor is this belief irrational.... Great art cannot but suggest something beyond its immediate or even its remoter meanings, an indefinable 'other', which is the most important thing it has to give. In our appreciation and enjoyment of this, we almost forget the details of an actual work of art and pass beyond them into a state which may be called silence because it speaks not to the ear but to the spirit. If we feel this is reading poetry, we can imagine how much more keenly Keats felt it in writing. In his inspired moments of composition, he sought to give expression in audible and musical words to that other indefinite and more powerful music which makes poetry what it is.[37]

Keats's notion of silence is however, combined with his notion of time, as is evident from the following quote:

> The paradox of all art is that it gives permanence to fleeting moments and fixes them in an unchanging form. His ideal Urn embodies it. Preserved and sanctified by time, it keeps is original freshness and appeal. The work of art has its own life, which is more vivid than the actual life.... The paradox of the Urn, as of all true works of art, is that it transcends time by making a single moment last for ever and so become timeless.... The timelessness of his achievement is true reflection of something known to the artists (as in the case of Keats) when they work at the highest pitch of inspiration.... In the act of creation, when all faculties are harmoniously at work together, time does not so much stand still as vanish. The artist is not conscious of it because he is caught in an activity so absorbing that it is complete in itself, with no sense of before and after.[38]

It is for this reason that the context of 'pursuit and sacrifice' in the poem have a peculiar appeal, as Keats presents them, because they embody this sense of timeless rapture. Bridges was right up to the point when he said that the 'Ode on a Grecian Urn' deals with "the supremacy of ideal art over nature, because of its unchanging expression of perfection". But the Ode deals with more than that. "It shows the meaning to human beings of the mood in which such an art comes into existence, and takes beyond the actual work of art to the creative vision which has made it."[39]

This does not mean that the question of timelessness raised by the Urn is a philosophical problem beyond Keats's reach. Many critics also think so. But the fact is that he raised the question knowingly and with the belief that he can reach to its core. He means that work of art is like Urn seduces us from the ordinary life of thought in the extraordinary life of the imagination. And this is very much an act of philosophizing, although he had shown his disinterestedness regarding philosophy to his friend Reynolds in one of his letters quoted above. He seems to have done so to give preference to 'experience' rather than to 'philosophy' on his belief that "the mystery of things cannot mastered by an act of will but 'out of thought', from the ordinary ways of thinking into the approach of the imagination. By thought he means the discursive, analytical activity of the intellect. The words in the Ode represent a similar view. The Urn belongs to an order of things which is beyond such thought. It is as remote as the eternity which in its timeless existence it represents."[40]

The fact that the 'Urn' is the 'foster-child of silence and slow time', is because 'silence' and 'time' have not created it, but they have kept and preserved it. And is why it is called their 'foster-child'. In fact, Keats felt strongly the appeal of the unaccounted past and saw in the urn a repository of wisdom of many ages. But he saw more than that. He combines the urn with slow time. He did so clearly to associate the urn with what he calls 'ethereal things', a term which he has discussed with Bailey in a letter (the letter quoted in chapter 4).

In other words, the 'ethereal things' mean so much to Keats and because he pursues them so ardently. And that Keats believed in the 'ethereal things' is clear from the letter written to Bailey. Therefore, the intention of the poem is to view art as the source of the highest form of wisdom. It is in this sense that the Urn becomes a 'silent form'. It does not cry out for its existence to man, still it exists silently. From this point of view, the Urn makes a spiritual communication to man. It is for the man to understand the message.

Thus, "the Ode like the 'Ode to a Nightingale' is Keats's celebration of religious experience almost terrifying to him. Truth and beauty, or the spiritual and the sensuous are then different in mode and not in kind, and intensity of experience at some ultimate point etherealizes the sensuous (the condition of the mutable world) into spiritual (the condition of the immutable)."[41]

Therefore, the Ode is one of the most representative of Keats's poems in which his metaphysical thoughts get an outlet in the most spontaneous and powerful way. It bears a testimony to the fact that Keats is more than a mere romantic. If at all a romantic, he was a poet with metaphysical leaning for sure. Hence, the 'Beauty-truth' riddle, as it is so-called by many critics, is, therefore, not a riddle as such. It is, rather, a conscious statement made by the poet, through the Urn, on account of his beliefs in metaphysical matters.

Talking about 'Ode to a Nightingale', the poem was written at time when the poet had lost his brother, Tom, only few months ago. The brother had died from a 'painful and distressing illness, and the memory of this is in the third stanza'.[42] Commenting on the theme of the poem, Graham Hough says that "the poem is not, as is sometimes said, a contrast between his own despondency and the happiness of the bird. It is the contrast between his own immediately experienced happiness in the bird's song, his imaginative participation in an untroubled natural life, and less immediate but more enduring knowledge of sorrow. Happiness is momentary and transient: the only thing certain is 'the weariness, the fever and the fret'...."[43]

"The heart-ache and the drowsy numbness", analyzes Hough, of the opening lines do not describe mere dejection, but a sort of drugged state, which can only be maintained by further intoxication. Wine is traditional soother of men's cares, the traditional means of prolonging a drowsy sensuous enjoyment; and Keats sometimes said that he enjoyed claret. But though he had his Anacreontic intervals, they are no real answer for him, and in the fourth stanza he realizes that the only way of escaping to share the happiness of the bird is 'on the viewless wings of Poesy'.... Poetry means first of all imagination—in the bird's life: secondly, it means the actual poetry he is writing—the incantatory loveliness of the fourth and fifth stanzas does make this moment permanent, in a sense: but not in the sense that the living and suffering human being really desires. The only way in which it can be made eternal is to die at the moment of greatest sensuous happiness. 'I have been half in love with easeful death.'"[44]

Much ink has been split on the romantic poets in general and Keats's in particular. W. Empson says that "Keats's longing for death and his mother has become a by-word among the learned."[45] Analyzing the Freudian death-wish in the context of Keats, Graham Hough says that it:

> Is the desire of the cell to resist the encroachments of outside experience to remain enclosed in its own kind of contentment. So, the romantic poet's desire for death is not a longing for extinction, it is the desire to make a happiness that he knows to be transient last for ever. And Keats is only half in love with easeful death—the other half of his consciousness knows well enough that this answer is only the negation of any possible answer. But art offers a type of permanence; and by a startling transformation in the seventh stanza the nightingale becomes a symbol of the artist and its song a symbol of art.[46]

However, it appears to be an audacious paradox that a nightingale should become a symbol of immortality, which has a considerably shorter life than man. But "its song is only immortal in the sense that through history there have always been nightingales' songs and that they have always had the same power of enchantment.... It is only in this sense that immortality can predicted of poets; in fact, the poet's position is stronger, for his individual song endures."[47]

Therefore, there is no breach in the poetic logic. But the argument is casuistry none the less, because the special case of poetic immortality is used or is on the point of being used, as if it offered the kind of happiness that Keats as a man seeks. But it does not, and cannot do so.... So the last word of the seventh stanza, 'forlorn', recalls Keats the poet who creates, foreseeing a poetic immortality, to Keats the man who suffers, foreseeing only sickness and sorrow and an early death.... The song of the nightingale fades, and Keats finishes where, unlike Shelley, he generally finishes, with his feet on the ground. On the level of ordinary human experience there is no solution to the conflict. The poet who creates can offer little consolation to the man who suffers; but on the level of poetic creation the conflict disappears. Transitory human happiness is given permanence in a different sense by being embodied in art.[48]

The nightingale is a bird that cannot die. ("Thou wast not born for death, immortal Bird.") And the use of capital letter B for the bird in the poem also emphasizes the poet's intention of describing the singing nightingale as symbol of 'immortality'.

It will be worthwhile to have a look on two of Keats's letters written to Fanny Keats on dated 1st May, 1819, and to Georgiana Keats, on dated 15th January, 1820, respectively, as a background to the poem. The contents of the first letter are as follows:

> ...O there is nothing like fine weather, and health, and Books, and a fine country, and a contented Mind, and Diligent-habit of reading and thinking, and an amulet against ennui—and please heaven, a little claret-wine cool out of a cellar a mile deep—with a few or a good many ratafia cakes—rocky basin to bathe in, a strawberry bed to say your prayers to Flora in....[49]

In the second letter, written to Georgiana Keats, Keats says:

> George is busy this morning in making copies of my verse—He is now making one of an Ode to the nightingale, which is like reading an account of the black hole of Calcutta on an ice bergh.[50]

Both the letters convey a feeling of happiness on part of the poet while writing the poem. But reality was otherwise. The poet had seen his brother Tom's death because of consumption, leaving himself utterly sorrowful on the tragedy on the one hand, and foreseeing his own similar fate, on the other. The line "Where youth grows pale, spectre-thin, and dies", clearly indicates to his brother's unfortunate death.

Therefore, the poem is an outcome of the poet's unhappy state of mind contrasted with the nightingale's song which sounds heavenly. On hearing the song, the poet immediately thinks of an escape into the world of the bird. For the purpose, the poet firstly thinks of taking wine, ("O! For a beaker full of Warm-South") for the escape. Then, thinking wine as incomplete medium for the purpose, finally decides to go to the bird 'on the viewless wings of Poesy'.

Commenting on the 'escape', in his essay "The Composition of 'Nightingale'", M.R. Ridley says, "In the fourth stanza the determination to escape becomes yet more urgent, but the agency of the second stanza is rejected, and the escape is to be on the only wings of a dove on which he knew that he could fly away and be at rest, the wings of poetry, and by the fifth line the escape is achieved, and he is with the Nightingale in the depths of the forest, a forest so dark that even the presence of the thronged moon is conjectural...."[51]

The poet seems to have seen quite a few birds, as if he had been looking for one so enchanting as to become a subject for poetry. The search culminates in the Nightingale. Ridley says, "We get a hint of the same background-throwing imagination in an early letter, where he has been looking at less poetic birds at Carisbrooke: 'I daresay I have seen many descendant of some old cawer who peeped through the Bars at Charles the First', but here he carries the imagination to its limits; the song is the same and deathless through the years, even though it were the ancestor of this particular nightingale that sang to Emperors...."[52]

Even 'Ruth' finds a place in the poem, who comes right from the Bible. "We need hardly to look for a more recondite source for Ruth than the obvious one in the Bible."[53] As far as the 'casements' are concerned, Ridley says that "Keats had all his life a love of windows. One of his fellow students is recorded as saying, 'In a room he was always at the window peering into space so that the window seat was spoken of by his comrades as Keats's place'.... We find Keats's love of windows opening on the sea in the letters, 'the Window opening upon the Winander mere', and 'I should like the window to open onto the Lake of Geneva'; and his poetry is full of casements as in the famous stanza of 'The Eve of St Agnes' and the 'casement ope' of the 'Ode to Psyche', and open casements of the 'Ode to Indolence'."[54]

Keats appears to have been inspired by a Claude's painting named as 'The enchanting Castle'. Ridley describes it as "a castle by the sea, with plenty of casements; the sea is ruffled; in the middle distance is a boat, quietly rowing towards the castle; in the foreground is the placidly contemplative figure of a woman, and several equally placid deer. Any scene less perilous it would be hard to imagine...."[55]

As a matter of fact, the scene is a rarity on the earth. It looks so enchanting that it seems to belong to heaven. Giving an estimate of the Castle to his friend Reynolds, Keats says:

> You know the Enchanted Castle, it doth stand Upon a Rock, on the Border of a lake Nested in Trees, which all do seem to shake from some old Magic like Urganda's Sword. O Phoebus that I had thy sacred word. To shew this Castle in fair dreaming wise unto my friend, while sick and ill he lies. The doors all look as if they op'd themselves, the windows as if lach'd by Fays and Elves.[56]

Now, when the enchanting song of the Nightingale reaches the Enchanted Castle, the whole atmosphere becomes so serene as to be called celestial. In other words, through the scene resounded by the nightingale's magical song, the poet must be imagining a heavenly scene.

Unlike Shelley, who is envious of his Skylark's lot because it is 'blithe spirit' and therefore calls it a 'scorner of the ground', Keats feels pleasure in the Nightingale's happy lot? ("It is not through the envy of thy happy/ But being too happy in thy happiness.") Keats does not feel jealous of the happiness of his bird. He, rather, takes part in song of the bird and feels happier.

In terms of the nature of the birds, both Shelley and Keats regard them as 'heavenly creation'. If for Shelley the Skylark is 'a blithe spirit', then for Keats the Nightingale is 'immortal Bird'. On this account, both the poets are in agreement with each other. But, the real difference between the two lies in terms of the perception towards their respective birds. The Skylark is a hater of the earth and therefore once it flies from the ground up to the sky, it never returns to earth, as it hates it. In a way, the poet completely dissociates himself from the bird, on account of its being the 'scorner of the ground'. The bird disappears from the poem, giving way to the comparison and contrast between the bird and the man. He begins to contrast the happiness of the bird with the human suffering. ("We look before and after/ and pine for what is not.")

On the other hand, Keats enjoys the Nightingale's song in the best humanly possible manner. And once the effect of imagination comes to an end, the Nightingale seems to be flying away and away from the poet till it disappears. But, after the disappearance of the bird, unlike Shelley, he does not feel either dejected or envious or cheated by it. As far as the poet's addressing the bird as a 'deceiving elf' is concerned, it is very much a statement of realization rather than that of dejection.

There has been an intense discussion amongst the critics as to why Keats called the nightingale 'immortal'? John Holloway tries to find an answer in his essay 'The Odes of Keats', when he says that:

> No one seems quite to have explained the imaginative movement of the poem at the point where Keats called the nightingale immortal. Bridges regarded this passage as fanciful, and Miss Lowell as Platonic. Garrod, avoiding these errors, suggests that the nightingale is immortal because Keats thinks of it as a Dryad. But why is it appropriate to think the bird immortal for any reason? The answer is, perhaps, that at the climax of his poem Keats rightly allows a new ease of movement within the set of ideas he is controlling: he uses a freedom of contribution which characterizes poetry at high temperatures.... The nightingale momentarily assumes the quality of that ecstasy which it seems to experience, and which it induces in Keats. Within the apparently irresponsible movement of the stanza runs an exact line I am almost tempted to call logical development. Keats, entranced as he listens to the nightingale and responds to its apparent ecstasy, has an experience that seems to him to transcend experience; and in this stanza he claims that the nightingale's song is unrestricted by either time or space—which after all are pervasive features of experience. The voice of the nightingale, we might put it, is made immune first to history, and then to geography....[57]

Putting the poem on a different plane rather than in the category of romantic escapism, John Holloway comments that "...it (the poem) can establish a *rapport* with dead generation or with faery lands; and

> ...the same that oft-times hath
>
> Charm'd the magic casements, opening on the
>
> Foam of perilous seas, in faery land forlorn

is not Romantic escapism or idle gesturing. Word by word, this passage, in the free way of poetry, is indicating definite qualities of what was for Keats something he knew: the magic, the wideness, the heightened tension, the sadness, are things that we have by now traced elsewhere."[58]

However, Allen Tate does not agree with Keats in his description of the nightingale to be called immortal. In his essay "A reading of Keats", he says that "...It seems to me that the ambivalence of the nightingale symbol contains almost the whole substance of the poem: the bird, as bird, shares the mortality of the world; as symbol, it purports to transcend it. And I feel the pictorial technique has not been quite dramatic enough to give to the transcendence of the symbol life in some visibly presented experience.... Keats merely asserts: song equals immortality; and I feel there is some disparity between the symbol and what is expected to convey...."[59]

Touching upon Keats's death-wish and its implications, Tate says that the "dialectical tension underlying 'Ode to Nightingale', seems to me to be incapable of resolution, first in terms of Keats's mind as we know it from other sources, and, secondly, in terms of the pictorial technique, which dominates the poetic method. This method, which seems to reflect a compulsive necessity of Keats's experience, allows him to present the thesis of his dilemma, the ideality of the nightingale symbol, but not the antithesis, the world of common experience.... The resolution is suspended in the intensity of the images setting forth the love-death identity and reaching a magnificent climax in the stanza six ('Now more than ever seems it rich to die', etc). But the climax contains a little less than the full situation; it reaches us a little too simplified, as if

Keats were telling us that the best way to live is to die, or the best way to die is to live intensely so that we may die intensely. There may be concealed here one of the oldest syntheses of Christian thought that we die only to live...."[60]

Leonard Unger regards "delight as inseparable from melancholy", in his analysis of the Ode, "because it is not conceivable apart from the moral predicament. The answer to the question at the end of 'Ode to a Nightingale'—Do I wake or sleep?—is, both. In the structural imaginative arc of the poem, the speaker is returned to the 'drowsy numbness' wherein he is awake to his own mortal lot and no longer awake to the vision of beauty. Yet he knows that it is the same human melancholy which is in the beauty of the bird's 'plaintive anthem' and in the truth of his renewed depression. His way of stating this knowledge is to ask the question."[61]

In a way, Unger thinks that the question asked in 'Ode to a Nightingale' is answered in 'Ode on a Grecian Urn'. He says that "Such considerations (of asking question, 'Do I wake or sleep?') may clarify the truth-beauty passage. Whether they justify artistically Keats's use of these clichés of Platonic speculation is another matter."[62]

In an argument about the framework of the Ode, quoting Brook's and Warren's opinion in which they praise the form and the framework of the poem, Tate does not agree with them. According to him, there is no perfection in the poem. He says that the main function of criticism should be to:

> Refer to what poetry has accomplished in order to estimate what it can estimate, not what it ought to accomplish; we must heed Mr. Ransom's warning that perfect unity or integration in a work of art is a critical delusion, adding that 'Ode to the Nightingale' is by any standard one of the great poems of the world. Our philosophical difficulties with it are not the same as Keats's imaginative difficulties, which pertain to the order of experience and not of reason.... The poem is an emblem of one limit of our experience: the impossibility of synthesizing, in order of experience, the antinomy of the ideal and the real, and, although that antinomy

> strikes the human mind with a different force in different ages (Donne's dualism is not Keats's), it is sufficiently common to all men in all times to be understood.[63]

The above quotation establishes beyond doubt the deep connection between the two poems, as the later poem (Nightingale) carries the idea put forward in the earlier one ('Ode on a Grecian Urn') to a point of culmination, or a solution, with the realization of his strong death-wish ('So many times, I have been in half-love with easeful death') so that the Nightingale's magical song could be continued to be enjoyed eternally, and not momentarily, as in the present time.

However, the study of the Ode from the point of Vedantic philosophy would make an interesting criticism. Analyzing the poem from the Vedantic concept of Yoga, Dr. Amar Nath Prasad says that "In the beginning of the poem the poet is seen caught in the net senses. He wants to enjoy the permanent bliss of the nightingale. In other words, he wants to have the liberation of the self through him negation of the ability of the mind. He is in desperate search of light (Prakash), though his mind is thoroughly enthralled in the *rajas* and *tamas* activities of the mind...." Yoga says that the mind of a man is always wavering in its thoughts. It is so agile and unstable that it seldom listens to the voice of *atma* (Soul/Consciousness). The saints and sages try their best to listen to the voice of consciousness through penance, celibacy, and renunciation. When the process of *yoga* begins, there always a tussle between mind and soul. The voice of consciousness wants to fly free in the firmament of liberty and divinity, while mind, on the other hand, creates unwanted bumps in the sweat and sober path of the soul. This is what Keats feels (when he says):

> Away! Away! For I will fly to thee
>
> Not charioted by Bacchus and his pards
>
> But on the viewless wings of Poesy
>
> Though the dull brain perplexes and retards.[64]

Here, the term 'dull brain' is highly 'suggestive'. "Keats is never against intellect or philosophy which is sanctified by the process of *yoga*. He is dead against 'dull brain' which is guided by *Kriya* and *isthiti* (rajas and tamas). The brain of a man which is under the control of various waves guided by senses is dull and its most important feature is to interfere uninvited in the creativity of soul. Keats in his famous poem, 'Lamia' says the same thing:

Don't all charms fly

At the mere touch of cold philosophy."[65]

However, the poet is quite aware of the fact that through wine, "the 'blushful Hippocrene', he cannot enjoy the Nightingale's song for a longer period. In other words, with the help of these mundane visible things he cannot feel the permanent bliss and happiness which the great saints attain through process of *yoga*."[66]

In fact, the poet is so much tortured by trials and tribulations, cares and anxieties that he instantly wants to get himself completely relieved of them. "As a matter of fact, the activities of a great artist are very much parallel to those of a *yogi*. A true *yogi* is he who...who burns his impurities through the fire of *yoga* and then gives birth to immortal thoughts. Similarly, a great poet is basically a *yogi*.... In other words, in the terminology of T.S. Eliot, he has to escape from his personality. As a matter of fact, what T.S. Eliot says about impersonality or the 'continual self-sacrifice' or 'continual extinction of personality' is nothing but the English version of what Pantajali or our great saint poets mean by the 'negation of the self' to attain the cosmic music or *permananda*."[67]

Now, the idea of reaching the world of nightingale on the 'viewless wings of Poesy' becomes strong to the poet. As the wings of Poesy are viewless, they can easily transport the poet from the world of 'fret and fever' to that of 'happiness and divinity', where the Nightingale 'singest of summer with full-throated ease'. "This stage in *yoga*", says Dr. Amar Nath Prasad, "*sampurna-ananda* (the complete happiness). When a man, like Keats, reaches the zenith of this stage, the night becomes tender and glooms, verdurous. After attaining this cosmic music through poetry or art, Keats now feels a great sense of joy. The Queen Moon is on her throne. In yogic terminology, here the Queen Moon is the yogic mind of Keats which is now entirely sanctified from all its impurities through the fire of art...."[68]

Again, when the poet imagines the Queen Moon having appeared on the sky with all her 'Starry Fays', there should be a silvery light spreading on the earth. But, surprisingly there is no light. It is all dark ("But here there is no light". "This sentence", says Dr. Prasad "is richly suffused with vedantic philosophy of life and death, light and darkness. Usually 'light' stands for the good and darkness for the evil. But Keats feels here just the other way. He takes light as a variant of critical intellect, logic, 'dull brain', and 'cold philosophy', which 'clips on an angle's wing'. In other words, here darkness is a positive principle and light a negative one. Perhaps this is why Keats gives the epithet 'embalmed' before the term darkness.... Our age old Vedantic philosophy says that darkness is part and parcel of light. Light exists because of darkness. The womb of a mother full of darkness is a fine example. The mother earth under which seeds are buried in complete darkness incorporates the same rich philosophy of darkness."[69] Hence, the justification of Keats's 'embalmed darkness'.

Anyway, Keats is now in the world of the nightingale, the world of permanent bliss and cosmic vision, which is why:

> When a man reaches this stage through yogic process or through the wings of poesy, he gets an extraordinary strength to overcome all adversities. He transcends all human limitations and illusions and feels quite free and peaceful no matter how brutal and savage the rules of society are. This is what Keats feels when he goes to the world of the nightingale. Now his 'darkness' becomes 'embalmed' and death 'easeful'.... At the time of the composition of this poem, Keats was suffering from a malignant incurable disease.... But by the dint of poetic creativity, shunning everything related to sensual pleasures, the poet is able to embalm his darkness with the ointment of *yoga*. Consequently he begins to think that both life and death are two stages in human fulfillment. Now in this stage of eternal happiness while he was listening to the sweet eternal song of the

> nightingale he thinks that it is rich to die ('Now more than ever seems it rich to die').[70]

"Generally, it so happens that when we see a happy man we are inclined to envy him and be jealous of his success. But if the agile and egoist mind learns the art of *yoga* (the control of various thought waves) it attains the undisturbed calmness and begins to cultivate friendliness towards the happiness of others." Keats also forgets his grief and sorrow and shares the happiness of the bird:

> It is not through envy of thy happy lot,
> But being too happy in thy happiness.[71]

In brief, Keats gets delight in the divine song of the bird. "He shares the joy of the bird and after getting spiritual bliss he becomes unattached and indifferent to the wicked. Now the eternal happiness of art and beauty excel his previous love and attachment to his beloved, Fanny Browne. He also develops a sense of compassion for the unhappy that is, his fear of death is changed into 'easeful death'. Thus, it appears", concludes Dr. Prasad, "*Ode to a Nightingale* seems to be based on the great vedantic and yogic philosophy of our old age culture. It shows how a poet caught in the net of senses or earthly pleasures attains the supreme bliss or *parmanand* with the help of *yoga* or art. He goes to the glorious world which is unspeakable, and indestructible beyond everything. It is a world of 'charmed magic casements' which lightens the burden of various deviating thought waves and leads them to right path strewn with flowers of happiness, peace and prosperity."[72]

But, going back to the English critic, Kenneth Muir regards the song of bird as the song of the poet himself, as he says that:

> ...the song of the bird is the song of the poet. Keats is contrasting the immortality of the poetry with the mortality of the poet. He is saying with Horace, *Non omnis moriar*. This is the climax of the poem and the point where different themes are harmonized—the beauty of the nightingale's song, the loveliness of the Spring night, the miseries of the world, the desire to escape from those miseries by death, by wine, or by

> poetry. Whereas when Keats wrote the Epistle to Reynolds the problem of life spoiled the singing of the nightingale, the song now acquired a greater poignancy from the miseries of the world.[73]

However, Keats's 'death-wish', for example, can be viewed with his idea of the 'eternal'. It is not a cowardice wish. Rather, the poet wanted to die in the moment of the 'greatest sensuous happiness'. Therefore, the desire of Keats for death is not a 'longing' for an extinction but to make the moments 'eternal' by physical extinction, so that he could ultimately merge into the 'eternal'.

In a way, the whole poem oscillates between heaven and earth, not being able to reconcile them. It seems to be saying that 'Happiness' can be experienced only by the annihilation of 'self'. Thematically, both the poems, this and the 'Ode on a Grecian Urn', appear similar, in terms of materials. What is seen or felt in the immortal aspect of the former is seen or felt in the mortal aspect of the latter.

All in all, the bird stands a symbol of immortality for the poet. Associating the poem with the matters of 'ultimate truth', Mr. Sahu says that the bird, that had been distinguished from the mutable world, is now discovered to be in the presence of ideality, and in the fourth stanza, the nightingale has apparently soared to a higher level of symbolic meaning, since it is not only distinguished from the mutable, but is 'haply' partaking of ultimate truth, the 'completeness' towards which 'becoming' tends and which transforms one into an immortality. The night, the 'embalmed darkness' in which the mystery resides is tender with the nightingale, and to the bird the ideal Queen Moon, seated on her throne, has been pouring out of complete illumination. The moon, as Endymion discovered is 'that completed form of all completeness', the culmination (or perfection) of beauty-truth in its ultimate being....[74]

Thus, the poem is a kind of an expansion of thought introduced in 'Ode on a Grecian Urn'. It carries the argument, put forward in the Urn poem, to a finality with the help of movement. The poem is, therefore, an another example of

Keats's tendency to look into serious matters of human life as against the 'divine life'. Through the song of the nightingale, which is the symbol of 'eternity', the poet brings the miseries and transient nature of the world to light and wishes to die so that he could also become a part of the immortality as experienced by the bird. The poet's death-wish is, therefore, not a cowardice desire but a higher desire to be able to experience the divine truth, which is the 'ultimate reality', according to metaphysics.

According to Greek mythology, Endymion a beautiful shepherd-king of Mt. Latmos in Caria, is loved by Artimus (Diana, Cynthia) the moon-goddess. She contrives to throw the shepherd into a perpetual sleep and comes down every night to embrace him. Endymion is visited by the goddess a number of times in idyllic surroundings. During the intervals, maddened by his love, he is distracted by alternative moods of hope and despair. In his quest of the goddess throughout the earth, air and sea, among other experiences, he happens to meet famous mythological characters like Venus and Adonis, Glaucus and Scylla, Arethusa and Alpheus.

At last, the shepherd hears an Indian maid singing and declaring her love for him. He falls in love with her, though still yearning for his former love. As they are about to consummate their love, Mercury appears and causes two horses to spring from the earth, which carry them up into the air. Dreaming of heavenly scenes, Endymion perceives his love, the moon, and leaps towards her. But as he turns back to look at the Indian maid, the goddess fades from him. The maid wakes and the lovers are taken away into a world of their own.

But again as the moon appears, the maid dissolves away. Unable to resolve the conflict, the shepherd falls into the 'Cave of Quietude', a kind of sleep beyond pleasure or pain. Now he lands on earth to find the maid again and resolves to renounce his love, considering it as a mere dream. So, he embraces the earthly love, the maid. But, she declares that she is forbidden to be Endymion's love. As a result, the shepherd determines to live a hermit's life.

Endymion's story is a strong manifestation of Keats deep liking for Greek mythology. Apparently, he had this fascination because of his love for the 'antique', which is a part of the past. Somehow, by describing about the shepherd's love with the moon, the poet wants to relate to the divine love. Therefore,

> it is not only the beautiful ornamentation of the story with which Keats is concerned but the beauty of the essential truth underlying the story.... When we commune with the beauties of the world we rise merely above earthly trappings and achieve a oneness, a sense of identity with the thing we appreciate.... What then was he (Keats) trying to say? We must remember that he was not only a poet but one who explicitly disclaimed philosophy as his method of reaching the truth. He cannot explain in logical fashion but what he means conveys it poetically to our imagination. It is probably because we are hardly more enlightened on this subject at the end of the poem than at the beginning that Endymion does not succeed.[75]

"The difficulties of the poem are thus, particularly prominent in Book IV, as it seems to present poet's sense of depression and an inability to work out a coherent ending. Teased with the fleeting appearances of his dream-love (the moon-goddess), Endymion falls in love with mortal woman. He is torn between the two loves and can win neither as each fades when he thinks of the other. This is where he falls into the well of despair: There lies a den of remotest glooms/ Dark regions are around it...."[76]

But the next moment, "as if by magical powers, the shepherd finds himself in a 'Cave of Quietude', symbolically a state of spiritual calm beyond pleasure or pain, which has the power of resolving his anguish. It could well be described as an anguish of the poet himself. Contrasted with the shepherd's agony moments back, the same gloomy situation turns bright in the 'Cave of Quietude'.... Happy gloom/ Dark Paradise/ where pale becomes the bloom of health by due."[77]

From this state, 'which must reflect the personal experience of the poet',[78] Endymion awakes to find himself back to the earthly life. The legend, however, requires that he should win the moon-goddess and this is achieved by the two women mysteriously becoming one. "The conflict between the two loves seems to suggest the Platonic idea that we must love beautiful things as a means to loving principal of beauty itself; Endymion attains his ideal love through love of a mortal woman rather than through direct pursuit of the ideal."[79] Whatever the case, the shepherd comes up as a transformed person after the experience, with regards to his duties to his people: "Through me the shepherd realm shall prosper well;/ For to thy tongue I all health confide."[80]

While writing the poem, the poet was well aware of the size and the length of the project. Already, the poem was the 'test of the poet's Power of Imagination'. "In telling of the love between Endymion and the moon", says Keats, "I must make 4000 lines of one bare circumstance and fill them with Poetry." Even then, he thought, "it will take me but a dozen paces towards the Temple of Fame".[81] The above statement by the poet himself shows the degree of importance that he attaches to the poem, with regards to establishing him as a major English poet.

As a result, the subject that Keats chooses for the poem is a figure of the shepherd alienated from an ideal society by the burden of his visionary consciousness. By the time the festivities for Pan have come to their close, Endymion has been stultified by his anguish. His sister Peona leads him away from his people in a little boat to an island. 'Here, isolation and renovating sleep prepare Endymion's spirits for that act of confession during which he will admit to his love for the moon and begin to analyse his predicament. The outward form of the narrative becomes the vehicle for an inner quest. The progress away from the social and political world towards an intense subjectivity is clear.

In fact, the shepherd's visions had come to Keats in an opiated dream. Led on to enjoy a beautiful sunset (the last moments of a radiant Apollo shining over Latmos), there suddenly appeared before Endymion a magic bed of flowers ('dittany and poppies')[82], which were sacred to Apollo's sister the moon. Then, after the prince had fallen into a drugged or a visionary sleep, a beautiful moon appeared to him riding the sky. Eventually she retreats him into her 'dark and vapoury tent', where his visionary moon was metamorphosed into 'a bright something', a woman who is for Endymion the 'completed form of all completeness'. "This incarnation of feminine beauty", according to Stephen Coote, "then descended to enjoy his cares and give the prince intimation of life more ardent than that he has previously known."[83]

Giving the myth a realistic human dimension Stephen Coote analyzes that "Just as in the contemporary accounts of the origins of Greek Myth, those people who were fully alive to the natural world created, by the powers of fancy, a human form and a human voice in those scenes, which to a man of literal understanding may appear dead and lifeless, so Endymion's imagination transfigures nature and allows him to contemplate immortal truth and beauty.... Mortals yearn towards immortal, but as yet Endymion does not appreciate that these 'essences' also long for the earth and their incarnation in the human mind. For the moment his own mind can only aspire from heavenwards the return to earth broken and incomplete. Such a partial vision is dangerous, and Endymion's disillusioned spirit projects its own sickness on the world around him."[84]

Endymion clearly seems to stand for the poet's yearning for the 'ultimate truth', the term discussed in the first chapter. When, Peona tries to engage the prince by reminding him with his social commitments, his reply is significant, as far as metaphysical aspect is concerned. Endymion says in the poem, "He has longed to slake his 'thirst for the world's praise', but his visionary life is altogether more intense and imperious in its demands. The pursuit of true happiness, he insists, lies not in fulfilling outward ambition but in striving after a 'fellowship with essence', in a yearning after the beautiful and the true. The fulfillment of this state will be an annihilation of the ego to which a delight in nature and art can point the way."[85]

The prince suggests that "the awakening of the imagination to beauty through sensual love is a spiritual imperative so powerful that it may even be the motor power of the whole universe. The most profound human truth, therefore, lies not in the worldly pursuit of power but in the cultivation of the subjective and the spiritual, in an eager openness to a life of sensations in which the body and the soul may become one in joy while the imagination points to a happiness which, after our deaths will be repeated in eternity in a 'finer tone'."[86]

Told in a dream that Endymion must leave the 'normal human consciousness', he invokes the moon and then, in answer to mysterious summons, he descends underground to explore the 'silent mysteries of the earth'. "Here amid darkness, confusion and solitude, he must begin learning to sympathise with human love and pain as well as coming to understand how the poetic imagination perceives the relationship between the mortal and the divine"[87] says Stephen Coote.

The process begins with his encountering Venus and Adonis in the poem, where "The union of the mortal with the immortal is shown as sexually joyous, an enhancement of the imagination and as something intimately connected with the fecundity of the world. It is for the poets to perceive such truths and express them through myth. Now, as Endymion's reward for his growing insight, Venus promises him that, after all the wanderings, 'one day thou wilt be blest'."[88]

Now, Endymion's vision of his own goddess, the moon, follows. It is a vision "more intense and rewarding than those previously granted since, if it suggests the problems placed in the way of their union, it also asserts the identity of this image of womanly perfection with the moon herself. Above all, it expresses the passion she herself feels. The world of eternity is indeed in love with mortal man."[89]

That poet's predicament is similar to that of Endymion himself, is evident in the description of Stephen Coote about the poet, when says that "Keats would become taciturn, not because his was tired, nor even his mind was suddenly wrought to some bewitching vision, but from a profound disquiet which he could not or would not explain. The burden of pain clung as cruelly to him as to his own Endymion and was only with difficulty 'scared away by slow returning pleasure'."[90]

In fact, owing to Keats's metaphysical considerations, "these (ideas in the poem) concern that visionary power of the poet whereby his delight in the physical world is transformed through his imagination into an intimation of eternal truth and beauty, those 'essences' as Keats called them whose power over the inner self gives them an aura of the divine. In other words, the poem affirms that the most profound reaches of life lie in subjective experience and a vision of the sexual, psychological and spiritual wholeness symbolized by the union of the male and mortal Endymion to the eternal goddess of the moon. As Keats had already suggested in the *Poems*, it is through the creation of *such* myths that the poet can give coherence to the longings of mankind and present these to his audience through his art."[91]

Describing the central idea of the poem, Graham Hough says that it is one that is endemic in romantic literature—the pursuit in the world of ideal love who has been glimpsed dimly in vision. So far it is the same as that of Shelley's *Alastor*. Keats embodies it in a rehandling of the Greek fable of Diana's love for Endymion, a mortal shepherd.... That is to say, ideal beauty can only be achieved by love and sympathy for the beauty immanent in human life. The conclusion is quite different from that of Alastor, who not finding his veiled maid can only die disappointed. Keats does not accept the Shelleyan dichotomy between the world of experience and the world of imagination. Endymion achieves his quest but only by apparently compromising his love for a goddess by love for a mortal. Keats is recurring here to the idea we have met already I *Sleep and Poetry*, in the letter to Reynolds, and that we are to meet in the second Hyperion; the idea that the love of beauty, like other passions, cannot exist fruitfully in isolation, and that it can only fulfill itself through participation in the actual conditions of human life.[92]

Throwing light on Keats's attitude to life through the analysis of the poem, Graham Hough says, "Thus the leading idea of *Endymion* is not something mawkish, or undecided, but a quite vigorous existentialist principle before he is able to grasp it in any concrete embodiment. Convinced that he must leave the joys of 'the realm of Flora and old Pan', for 'the agony and strife of human hearts', he still does not know how to do it. The descriptive passages are rich, luxuriant and fertile in invention, but uncertain in purpose. Sometimes they (the passages) give the impression that he is perfectly content with this catalogue of 'luxuries', and content to let it obscure the ground-plan of the work; at other times he seems to be chasing all this loveliness of details some other kind of loveliness that he is not yet able to grasp. And the presentation of emotion is sentimental and monotonous—simply because it is unrealized, because Keats has not yet had had little experience of the divagations of the heart, little time even to look into his own. Perhaps if he had had more he would have found that narrative poetry was not to be the medium in which he was really to express himself most fully."[93]

"Throughout Keats's work (*Endymion*)", Colvin says, "the sources of his inspiration in his passages can almost always be recognized as dual, some special joy in the delights or sympathy with the doings of nature working together in him with some special stimulus derived from books. Of such a dual kind is the whole inspiration of *Endymion*." The poem, says Colvin, "is a joint outcome of his intense, his abnormal susceptibility to the spell of moonlight and of his pleasure in the ancient myth of the loves of the moon-goddess Cynthia and the shepherd-prince Endymion as made known to him through the earlier English poets."[94]

Describing the poem as an outcome of Keats's metaphysical thinking, Colvin very rightly says that "the moon was to Keats a very form what she has always been to popular astrology and tradition.... For Keats it was her transmuting and glorifying power that counted, not her pallor but her splendour, the magic alchemy exercised by her light upon the things of earth, the heightened mystery, poetry.... Now, as he settles down to work on *Endymion*, we shall find her, by reason of that special glorifying and mystifying magic of her light, become for him, at first perhaps instinctively and unaware, more and more conscious as he goes on, a definite symbol of Beauty itself—what he calls in a letter 'the Principle of Beauty in all things,' the principle which binds in a divine community all such otherwise unrelated matters as those we shall find him naming together as things of beauty in the exordium of his poem.... Hence the tale of the loves of the Greek shepherd-prince and the moon-goddess turns under his hand into a parable of adventures of the poetic soul striving after full communion with the spirit of essential Beauty."[95]

As a result, "the bewildering redundance and intricacy of detail in *Endymion* are obvious, the presence of an underlying strain of allegoric or symbolic meaning harder to detect. Keats's letters referring to his poem contain only the slightest and the rarest hints of the presence of such ideas in it, and in the execution they are so little obtruded or even made clear that they were wholly missed by two generations of his earlier readers.... Let it be borne in mind, then, that besides the fundamental idea of treating the passion of Endymion for Cynthia as a type of the passion of the poetic soul for essential Beauty, Keats wrote under the influence of two secondary moral ideas or convictions, inchoate probably in his mind when he began but gaining definiteness as he went on.... One (moral idea) was that the soul enamoured of and pursuing Beauty, cannot achieve its quest in selfishness and isolation, but to succeed must first be taken out of itself and purified by active sympathy with the lives and sufferings of others: the other, that a passion for the manifold separate and individual beauties of things and beings upon earth is in its nature identical with the passion for that transcendental and essential Beauty: hence the various love-adventures which befall the hero in dreams or in reality, and seem to distract him from his quest, are shown in the end to be in truth no infidelities but only attractions exercised by his celestial mistress in disguise."[96]

Therefore, one can say that: "In devising the adventures of his hero in accordance with these ideas, Keats works in part from his own mental exercise. He weaves into his tale, in terms always of concrete imagery, all the complex fluctuations of joy and despondency, gleams of confident spiritual illumination altering with faltering hours of darkness and self-doubt, which he had himself been undergoing since the ambition to be a great poet seized him.... He cannot refrain from also weaving in a thousand and one irrelevant matters which the activity and ferment of his young imagination suggest, thus continually confusing the main current of his narrative and breaking the coherence of his symbolism.... The scenery, indeed, is often not merely of a Gothic vastness and intricacy: there is something of Oriental bewilderment—an *Arabian Nights* jugglery with space and time—in the vague suddenness with which its changes are effected".[97]

The setting of the poem clearly reflects Keats's metaphysical thinking, as:

> The action of the first book passes on earth, and the second one beneath the earth. According to the cosmology fully set forth by the Ovid at the beginning of his first book, and therefore, thoroughly familiar to Keats, the proper region or sphere of fire was placed above and outside that of air and farthest of all from earth. The place is full of endless shadowy temple corridors, magical cascades spouting among prodigious precipices, and the gardens and bower of Adonais in their spring herbage and freshness. It is true again, that the third book takes us and keeps us under sea. But the reason is general one that Endymion typifies that poetic soul of man in love with the principle of Beauty, has to leave habitual things behind him and 'wander far/ In other regions, past the scanty bar/ To mortal steps', in order to learn secrets of life, death, and destiny necessary to his enlightenment and discipline. Where else should he learn such secrets if not in the mysterious hollows of the earth and on the untrodden floor of ocean?[98]

But why all this trouble, the reader might well ask, to follow the argument and track the wanderings of Endymion book by book, when everyone knows that the poem is admirable only for its incidental beauties, and nothing else? The answer is that the "Intricacy and obscurity of the narrative, taken merely as narratives, such as to tire the patience of many readers in their search for beautiful passages and to dull their enjoyment of them when found; but once inner symbolic meanings of the poem are recognized, even in gleams, their recognition gives it a quite new hold upon the attention.... It is not with simple matters of personification, of the putting of initial capitals to abstract quality, that we have to deal, nor yet with any obvious and deliberately thought-out allegory.... It is with a vital, subtly involved and passionately tentative spiritual parable, the parable of the experiences of poetic soul in man seeking communion with the spirit of essential Beauty in the world, invented and related, in the still uncertain dawn of his powers, by one of the finest natural-born and intuitively gifted poets whoever lived...."[99]

Therefore, this poem also has a bearing with Keats's interest in 'ethereal things'. That he "believed this is clear from the passage in Book III (of the poem), in which after attacking those people who are unable to see the true slendours of existence, Keats states his own case for them. So far from being unreal, he says in effect, they are remote and sublime realities, sought with effort and attained only by patient devotion."[100]

Associating the poem with the 'ethereal things', as well as with 'Ode on a Grecian Urn', as a mark of similarity in terms of theme, Maurice Bowra says it "shows that Keats is still thinking about the same problem. They are not the end but the means to some remoter and sublimer end, to those 'thronged seats' which are despised by many but mean everything to Keats. Also, the relevance of this passage in *Endymion* to the 'Ode on a Grecian Urn' is manifest. Just as in the Ode Keats passes beyond the music and the lovers, who are surely 'ethereal things' to something else, so in *Endymion* he sees that through his cult of such things he comes to something else and feels at one with the secret powers of nature...."[101]

Thus, apart from having 'metaphysical' undertones, the poem is internally connected with 'Ode on a Grecian Urn', as is evident from the above quotation, to further prove a pattern of definite thinking in all his later poems, which Keats always strived to convey to his readers.

As for *Hyperion*, its idea, based on a mythological theme was already in Keats's mind before he had finished *Endymion*, and soon he "embarked upon the idea, *The Fall of Hyperion*, with the theme of war between the Titans or the earlier generations of gods, and the later Olympians, who dispossessed them. The theme of supplanting of *Hyperion*, the old sun-god by Apollo, the New, is Keats's own invention. As, Endymion symbolizes the fate of the lover in the world, so the myth of Apollo and Hyperion perhaps symbolizes the fate of the poet as creator...."[102]

However, *Hyperion* exists in two versions, the second being the revision of the first, with the addition of a long induction in a new style which makes it a different poem. The chronology of the composition is obscure; it was contemplated long before it was written. Keats worked on it at intervals. Without discussing the evidence in detail, it can be said that the first version was written mostly before the great odes, the second mostly after them. And thus the two versions extend until increasing illness and despair finally made it impossible for him to work at all.

"After the publication of *Endymion*, in 1818, Keats went on a summer tour in Scotland, during which he studied Dante,"[103] and severely injured his health by exposure. He returned to look after his brother through his last illness. "It was apparently during this period, in September, that *Hyperion* was begun."[104] About the same time, Keats first met Fanny Brawne, with whom he was soon to be so hopelessly and disastrously in love. As a result, *The Eve of St. Agnes*, came out in the first flush of new emotion.

Therefore, work on *Hyperion* could not be continued on a regular basis. "In September, the month of the writing of *Ode to Autumn*, he writes that he has given *Hyperion* up, only to resume working on it in the winter of 1819, when his love for

Fanny Brawne, increasing in intensity as it was frustrated by illness, was gradually wearing him out. The period, covered by *Hyperion*, then, is the period of Keats's most intense experience, both of joy and sorrow, in actual life and of his most rapid development: and it is not surprising, therefore, that the second version shows greater changes from the first."[105]

In fact, as already told in the beginning of this discussion, "the idea of another poem on a mythological theme was in Keats's mind, before he had finished *Endymion*, and the subject-matter this time was the Fall of Hyperion. The theme of the war between the Titants, or earlier generation of gods, and the later Olympians who dispossessed them is often referred to in Keats's favourite literature, and he could have found the outlines of his story without referring to Lempriere"[106] for help. So, the specific theme, the supplanting of Hyperion, the old sun-god, by Apollo the new, is Keats's own material. "Apollo is also the god of poetry", says Graham Hough, "and as *Endymion* had symbolized the fate of the lover of beauty in, so the story of Apollo and Hyperion was perhaps going to symbolize the fate of the poet as a creator. Since the poem is unfinished, we cannot know. What is immediately clear is how much the design owes to Milton."[107]

"The poem opens in the regular epic manner, in the middle of the story. We find the Titans, like Milton's fallen angels, already outcast and shorn of their powers. Hyperion alone is not yet overthrown, and like Milton's Satan, he is the one hope of further resistance. The opening scene is followed by a council to discuss the lost dominions, in which Enceladus, like Moloch, pronounces his sentence for open war, and Oceanus, like Belial, stands for more moderate measures. Externally, at least, this is modeled on *Paradise Lost*, and marks a clear break with the meandering structure of *Endymion*."[108]

The first two books look like the opening of an epic, and it seems that Keats's original design, says Hough, "was a poem of epic scope, in which the war in heaven would have been narrated, as in *Paradise Lost*, in the form of an episode. But it seems likely that the plan changed, and the two books we are not a fragment of what should have ten, but of a more contracted design. Definite evidence is wanting, and the situation must remain obscure. We cannot avoid speculation, however: in spite of its condition, *Hyperion* remains Keats's most imposing piece of work, and the student of Keats must wish to know both why it was discontinued and how it would have gone on."[109]

One of the reasons given by the publishers for the discontinuance of *Hyperion* was the reception of *Endymion* by the critics. But, "this was untrue", Hough says, "and we have the evidence of chronology and a note from Keats himself to prove it. Keats said that he gave it up because of the excessive Miltonism of style—but he says it almost casually in passage where he is discussing other things; and there is not the slightest need to suppose that this was the only reason...."[110]

The first book presents a picture of the fallen Titans, with Saturn as the central figure, but Hyperion as the only one who remains potentially active. The second book, however, shows them in council, and the vital part of it is undoubtedly the speech of Oceanus. It is here that we begin to see the poem in a new perspective. According to the myth used in the poem, "Saturn was not the first power in the universe, nor the last. Chaos and darkness first produced light; light brought heaven and earth and life itself into being, and the Titans were the first-born of life. Heaven and earth are more beautiful than chaos and darkness:

> So on our heels a fresh perfection treads a power more strong in beauty, born of us, and fated to excel us. (II, 212)
>
> The Titans are not to repine or envy their successors: For 'tis the eternal law that first in beauty shall be first in might." (II, 228)[111]

Then Clymene follows and confirms Oceanus by testifying to the beauty of the young Apollo's music, which she had heard. "What does this mean for the poem as a whole?" inquires Hough. "It means that Hyperion is not after all to be a poem of epic conflict in the old sense—it is to be a poem of evolution, of the supersession of lower kind by higher; and the successors are to prevail because they are superior in beauty."[112]

In the Book III, the interest shifts from the Titans to the young Apollo. Mnemosyne (Memory) among the Titans forms relations with the younger gods. She had watched over the childhood of Apollo, and now she finds him wavering and uncertain of his course. In a speech with her, he finds he consciousness of his destiny and assumes his new-found godhead. At this point, the poem breaks off.

Commenting on the change in second *Hyperion* from the first one, Graham Hough says, "What has happened? It seems that what began as an epic poem about a mythological conflict has become a symbolical poem of a different kind. But in the process new difficulties have arisen. The conventional epic conflict would have afforded a wealth of scenes and incidents, outlined in Woodhouse's sketch of the proposed development of the poem. The new scheme, of an evolution of in beauty, presents far greater problems. It could hardly be embodied in events and actions, and would, therefore, not afford material for anything like the ten books originally proposed.... We have seen repeated evidence of a conflict in Keats's life between the longing for a state of changeless happiness ('that I may never know how change the moons') and on the other hand an urgent sense of the necessity for change and development, the necessity to emerge from the chamber of Maiden-Thought. But it is one thing to realize the need for a change, quite another thing to effect it. We are perpetually finding that a certain kind of experience is exhausted, or about to be exhausted, without knowing what is to take its place."[113]

The change in the tone and style of the poem, as indicated above, clearly reveals the change in style that Keats was searching for in his writing to give an expression to what was higher or deeper in meaning. "We are on the threshold of a new development", introspects Hough, "but the door is still shut. So it is with Keats. The thing that had been most real to him up to now was an impassioned sensuous contemplation, enjoyed in self-contained, timeless moments; and the longing to make them eternal. He can talk about leaving the realm Flora;

but he does not know the way out. He knows intellectually that the kind of beauty he has lived with up to now must be superseded by another kind ('Shapes of delight and mystery and fear').... But he can only see it in uncertain glimpses. So, faced with his poem about development and change, he can take us to the threshold of the new life, but he can go no further. And he is not happy with such a theme, for his deepest experience up to now has been of states that seem, while they last, to be timeless. The young Apollo assumes his god-like knowledge, his mind is filled with:

> Names, deeds, gray legends, dire events, rebellions,
> Majesties, sovran voices, agonies,
> Creations and destroyings. (III, 114)[114]

"But in Keats's own mind this knowledge is only potential; he is not yet in secure possession of it. And the poem remains unfinished because he does not know how it is to go on."[115]

Therefore, when Keats comes to revise the poem he knows no more than before how to continue it. So, *Hyperion* as it stands is not continued. The second version ends as the first did. But, he adds to it an induction, making his ultimate purpose clearer. Hough says that "he (Keats) cannot finish the poem, but he can show the direction in which it was to move. He does not do this by describing a distantly seen goal. Truths were not truths to Keats till they were not proved upon the pulses and he works now as ever by giving poetic embodiment to the actual state of his mind. The induction is one of the most remarkable pieces of writing in Keats's, and it is the beginning of a development of which he was not to see the end."[116]

Commenting on the influences of Milton and Dante on the writing of *Hyperion*, Hough says that "the Miltonic influence is as obvious in the verse and diction of the first *Hyperion* as it is in the design. Keats had been 'feasting upon' Milton in April 1818, shortly after the completion of *Endymion*, and the influence, mingled attraction and repulsion, goes on intermittently for the next eight months. On the Scotch tour, immediate before writing of *Hyperion,* he studied Dante in Cary's translation. Thus, he came under the spell of two austerer masters in poetry than any he had known before.... If there is anything Dantesque in *Hyperion*, it is later rather than the earlier version; but perhaps the remote effect of a reading of Dante can be seen throughout in the greater clarity and definiteness of the pictures. Keats was by now in strong revulsion from the bathos and vulgarity of Huntian manner, and it is natural, therefore, that he should turn to Milton, the obvious master of style of assured and conscious grandeur—above all, of an imitable style. There is no need to exemplify the Miltonic echoes in detail...."[117]

"Yet, the Miltonism are detachable, not organic: the basis of this is not Miltonic: it is still the verse of Keats, but immensely purged strengthened by contact with a severer master.... Indeed, *Hyperion* is Keats's most serious and considerable essay in the dramatic presentation of emotion—for the Titans are conceived in human terms, and their sorrows are human sorrows. There is far greater power, too, of discourse, of argument in verse, than ever before: there is no parallel in the earlier work to the speech of Oceanus; and Keats seems to be discovering, as Yeats did later, how useful this sheer rhetorical power can be; even to a poet whose aims are normally in another direction."[118]

However, that part of the second *Hyperion* which is merely a rehandling of the first does not present any profound changes, though they are quite good in number. Then changes are mostly for the purpose of removing effects of Miltonism. This accounts for the myth that Keats undertook the revision of the poem in the decline of his powers. Anyway, after the Odes, it is surely Keats's greatest verse.

"There is nothing like the first three hundred lines of the new *Hyperion* of Keats's earlier work", says Hough, "and I know of nothing like it in English blank verse at all. The new notes in black verse since Milton are not very numerous: there are innumerable Miltonics; there are the vital but rather graceless colloquial rhythms of Browning, and almost too professional mellifluousness of Tennyson. This (Keats's) is different from any. The rapidity and directness remind one of Dante.... Both in reflective and descriptive passages the verse seems to astride instead of to linger, as Keats's verse has mostly done hitherto. And the new-found decision of style reflects a new decision, in the handling of ideas."[119]

As far as the composition of the second *Hyperion* is concerned, it is cast in the form of dream, and the added opening describes this dream and its setting ("Fanatics have their dreams, wherewith they weave/ A paradise for a sect; the savage, too...").[120]

"This is an attempt to define the position of poetry", analyzes Hough, and says that "the poet has his dreams in common with other men, but he alone is able to secure them from oblivion. (Again, the thought of the *Ode to Grecian Urn*—only art can endure.) And the poet's dream differs from the fanatic's; it is for the world, the fanatic's only for a sect. We pass on to the dream itself, which begins in a wood—not a wild and gloomy one like Dante's, but a pastoral scene with a meal of fruits set out, of which the poet eats, then drinks from a cool vessel of transparent juice. He falls into a deep sleep and wakes to find that the scene is changed, that he is in a vast shrine, at the western end of which are steps leading up to an alter, with a gigantic image and a priestess ministering to the sacred flame. As he approaches, the veiled priestess addresses him:

If thou canst not ascend
These steps die on the marble where thou art." (I, 107)[121]

A stifling numbness overcomes the poet, seeing the vision, and he becomes immovable. Then a new life is poured into him. As a result, he draws closer to the alter and asks the priestess to explain the mysteries. She then reveals that the temple is Saturn's, the only remaining shrine of the old gods, and she is Montena, the only remaining priestess. "Montena is the Latin name of Mnemosyne, who occurs, of course, in the Hyperion story itself". "She is, as it were", says Graham Hough, "another avatar Mnemosyne, performing the same function for Keats Mnemosyne had done for Apollo. Then Montena unveils herself, whose description of looks and splendour is so effectively done so that it exceeds anything else in Keats, which is as follows:

Then I a wan face,
Not pined by human sorrows, but bright-blanch'd
By an immortal sickness which kills not;
It works a constant change, which happy death
Can put no end to; deathwards progressing
To no death was that visage; it had past
The lily and the snow, and beyond these
I must not think now, though I saw that face.
But for eyes I should have fled away." (I, 256)[122]

Gathering all the courage possible, the poet somehow dares to ask the priestess to be shown the hidden story that lies behind the survival of the mysterious temple. She consents to reveal it to him—and the story of Hyperion and the Titans, much as she had done before.

Therefore, *Hyperion* is in no uncertain manner Keats's final attempt to take poetry to the realm of metaphysical heights, as he could not continue it because of his untimely death. His poetic-self was never satisfied with the beauty of the Flora and Fauna only. It was always yearning for something more, something beyond the realm of Flora. *Hyperion*, is in a way, the culmination of Keats's search. That is why, Graham Hough, too, regards the poem as:

> Keats's last attempt to define the place of the poet in the world. It is not an exaltation of the poet, like Shelley's *Defence*. The poet is less than the man of active virtue, and Keats is still absorbed by the contrast between the realm of Flora and the other kingdom that he suspects to lie beyond it. He has still not crossed the boundary, but he knows more of what to expect on the journey. It is notable how much of Keats's poetry is about poetry, its functions, its glories and its limitations. It is he is perpetually trying to find a bridge between art and life, but is perpetually led back to art itself. Perhaps the solution for the artist is not to try to escape from the domain of art, but to explore it more closely.... In *Hyperion*, as always Keats makes no attempt to march

> forward to an intellectual conclusion; he shows us the steps and stairs of the mind by which a yet unseen conclusion may be reached. And he draws two distinctions—one between the practical and the visionary mind; and one between the creative visionary, the poet, and the mere dreamer who 'vexes' the world with visions that he can do nothing to transmute into reality. At this point, Keats's experience stops; and disease and an unhappy love were to cut short the possibility of further exploration.[123]

Commenting on the highly symbolic quality of the poem, Ram Bilas Sharma says that "it opens with the statement of the fact of the fanatic dreams as well as the savage. Next, he tells his own sorrow at their not having recorded their dreams like other poets and earned fame in their life. Having taken for granted that it is the genuine right of every poet to tell his dreams in poetry, he gives this right to every man who could dream and tell his dreams in his mother tongue. He is not even worthy to be called a man who lacks this capacity to dream, for without imagination he soul must be a clod. Since the right to dream and tell the dream in his mother tongue is not denied to the ordinary man, much less would it be denied to the poet who has the faculty to dream and express his dreams in poetry in the highest degree present in himself.... Why then the condemnation of the dreamer from the mouth of Montena? Montena condemns the dreamer because he dreams and makes his days full of misery without doing any good to humanity at large.... The dreamer is less than the humanitarian because he does not attempt to do any good to the world in the utilitarian sense. But the latter cannot also have sights of garden, the temple, the deity and all the visions that are vouchsafed to the weak dreamer at the sight of that goddess...."[124]

But the vital question is "Has the public benefactor, too busy with details of life, ever achieved this larger view of life, and grasped the truth underlying all those details that he had been so busy adjusting? He is certainly greater than dreamer because he does not wait to realize the whole truth but engages himself with a part of it for the benefit of humanity. But the dreamer is also greater than this philanthropist in achieving the whole truth which is ultimately of much more significance to humanity. He is not only a great man, he has the power to see the truth as a God sees it and this power would never have been his has he not been a weak dreamer in the beginning. Better weak dreaming for a while if it leads to the vision of beauty and truth in the end than doing good to the world which would leave him ultimately in ignorance.... This would seem to be the conclusion", thinks Mr. R.B. Sharma, "hinted at in Keats's dual visions of Montena and the Titans. The 'Fall' therefore is a strong vindication of the rights of the dreamer and affirms Keats's faith in beauty to the obliteration of all other considerations."[125]

Summing up the development of thought in the poem, Sidney Colvin remarks, "The reader remembers how Keats had broken off his work on the original *Hyperion* at the point where Mnemosyne, goddess of Memory and mother of the Muses, is enkindling the brain of Apollo by mysteriously imparting to him her ancient wisdom and all-embracing knowledge. Following a clue which he had found in a Latin book of mythology he had lately bought, he now identifies this Greek Mnemosyne with the Roman Moneta, goddess of warning or admonition; his vision takes him first into a grove or garden of trees and flowers and fountains, with a feast of summer fruits spread on the moss before an embowered arbour. The events which follow, and the converse held between the poet and the priestess, are in their ethical and allegoric meanings at many points obscure, and capable, like all symbols that are truly symbolic, of various interpretations. But the leading ideas they embody can be recognized clearly enough."[126]

The poem, therefore, seems to be "Keats's last attempt", argues Mr. Sahu, "to define the place of the poet in the world. It is no more a glorification of the poet, like Shelley's *Defence*. The poet is less than the man of dynamic virtue, and Keats remains caught in the dichotomy between the realm of Flora and the other kingdom that he presumably believes to exist beyond it. He has not yet crossed the boundary, but he is fully aware of what to expect on the journey ahead. It is quite obvious here to note how much his poetry is about poetry, its functions, its glories and its limitations. He is constantly striving to bridge the gap between art and life, but is constantly reverted back to art itself.... In *Hyperion* Keats makes no attempt to jump into an intellectual conclusion. He shows us the ways of the mind to arrive at the conclusion, which is yet unseen...."[127]

In a way, Keats, the poet, "discovers a distinctions between the practical and the visionary mind, and one between the creative visionary, the poet, and the mere dreamer, who 'vexes' the world with perceptions—that he can do nothing to transform into reality. At this point, Keats's exploration stops, and the diseases and an unhappy love are to cut short the possibility of his further quest...."[128]

Thus, *Hyperion* was the last major poem, which conveys the loftiest thoughts that Keats was capable of experiencing, in so far as it attempts to give a poet the highest honour in society by calling him the 'highest dreamer' in world. It is the poet alone, who is capable of dreaming about the 'metaphysical matters' because of his heightened sense of imagination. Therefore, on account of this power, a poet stands much higher in his perception of the 'mysteries of life', as compared to the common man, or the rest of the people at large. In a way, Keats gives a poet the status of a 'sage', who has prophetic powers. If a sage contemplates about the mysteries of life through his 'prophetic powers', then a poet is capable of doing the same through his the power of his 'heightened imagination'. Hence, the justification of the comparison of a poet with a sage.

Therefore, "it is to Keats that we may look for solution of the romantic conflict, and his solution is incomplete. It may perhaps be due to the fact that he died young, and his death was premature."[129] And, no doubt, it was. The quest itself on part of Keats is enough to suggest the greater heights that the poet was capable of achieving. In a way, Keats was ordained by God to come forth with such lofty ideas as he did. If so, then, one does not need longer span of life for having the kind of depth in thinking, as was evident in Keats. As a result, only a man of Keats's vision could have described a poet as the 'highest dreamer' in the world, and ceaselessly struggled to give him the 'highest honour' in the world, which was due to him, and which was, unfortunately, not accorded by the world to him, just because of an ignorance of recognizing his poetic powers, and not because of poet's unworthiness.

Hence, it would not be wrong to describe the *Hyperion* as the culmination of Keats's ultimate vision of life, which indicates to the 'ultimate reality'.

6

Conclusion

After an in-depth discussion of Keats's poetry from the metaphysical aspect of his mind, it will be in all fairness of things to say that his poetry definitely possess the 'metaphysical element' in his poetry. Right from the beginning of his poetic career, even when the sensuous beauty of nature was all in all to him, Keats was not satisfied with it. His poetic heart was yearning for something to say, but he did not know how to present what was going inside his heart. Which is why, beginning his career with the collection of the poems by the simple title *Poems* (March, 1817), Keats succeeds in taking his poetry to the great heights, with the publication of *Hyperion* (Oct., 1818), before setting out on an eternal journey.

It looks almost impossible to believe as to how a simple writer of 'Poems', who was interested only in the outer charm and beauty of nature, could have risen to the level of metaphysical heights in the poems like 'Ode on a Grecian Urn', where he speaks about 'beauty' as the 'ultimate truth', or in the poem *Endymion* in which the poet presents the idea that the 'divine love' is also possible if a human being (Shepherd) earnestly wished for that, by the power of his heightened imagination. By any stretch of imagination, these considerations on part of the poet cannot be sidelined as something fanciful or mere dreams.

The critics may diametrically differ in their criticism of the 'truth-beauty' matter, but one thing that can be established for sure is that it was not an out of contextual statement by Keats, as many critics think. Whether the poet said those lines or the poet makes the urn say them, is also not significant. The important point is that the poet concludes the poem with those lines. There could have been no better conclusion to the poem.

The idea that Keats had been undergoing a continuous mental growth in his poetic career is supported by one of the premier critics on Keats's poetry, Graham Hough, who says that "...It is possible that he (Keats) reached his full maturity in this dark period when he had not power to express it. Perhaps this new-found power would actually have led to drama. This is what Keats hoped himself...we cannot tell; there remains a real element of mystery about Keats's later work. Would he, if he had lived longer, have remained within the bounds of the pure aesthetic experience which had so far been most real to him: or would he have obeyed his continual promptings towards an interpretation of more general human experience: and is the later an essential part of his nature, is it simply a lingering relic of the endemic English Puritanism, with its suspicion of non-utilitarian beauty? ...It is certain the Keats of LA belle Dame and The Eve of St. Agnes who has produced the most numerous poetry progeny—the early Tennyson and the pre-Raphaelite being among them. The pre-Raphaelite indeed are his most obvious successors; and that, considering the narrowness of pre-Raphaelite scope, is as much to say that the works of Keats has never yet made its full impact on English poetry. Perhaps if he had reached maturity the pre-Raphaelite movement would have been a less abortive affair than it was, would have reached something of the dimensions of French symbolism. For myself, I find it easier to see him developing in this direction than towards the dramatic interpretation of life that he foresaw towards the end of his career."[1]

This different attitude separates Keats from his contemporaries. That is why; Graham Hough says that "in any case he (Keats) has reached a further point of insight into the nature of poet's problems than any other of the writers of his day. A whole new territory of poetic possibilities has been opened up by the romantic imagination. The rarity of complete and rounded achievement in Romantic verse, the fact that the

Romantic poets 'did not know enough', as Arnold complained is accounted for by the extent and the difficulty of the country they are exploring. Coleridge had asserted the primacy of the imagination; but had shown a few brilliant flashes how it could combine the creative freedom of a dream with truth to some of the deepest facts of human experience.... Wordsworth had exercised his power almost entirely on the bond between man and nature; and his strong grasp of the actual made him in many ways more akin to the eighteenth century than to the coming age. For the most part it is left to the second generation of Romantic poets to work out a relation between the actual and an imaginative ideal. Shelley leaves the dichotomy between the two almost unresolved. Byron frankly gives up the struggle and achieves his greatest successes on a lower level of insight altogether. It is to Keats if anyone that we must look for a solution of the Romantic conflict and his solution is incomplete."[2]

Describing Keats as a 'higher kind of dreamer', Ram Bilas Sharma tries to analyze his position as a poet when he says, "The theorist of art is assailed for rating art higher than humanity, for shrinking the struggle of the world and living in an unreal dreamworld of his own creation. Keats, too, while formulating a theory of exclusive devotion to beauty is faced with this problem of doing well to humanity. He anticipates the charge against such a poet of being a dreamer and of being useless to humanity in general. But the problem of doing good to humanity through art or poetry did not exist for Keats; while he is always thinking of doing good to the world at large and of the poet's proper function and the place in the social scheme, it can be definitely stated that the writing of poetry and doing good to the world, he understood as two separate things...."[3]

Regarding Keats's idea of 'truth and beauty', Mr. Sharma says that "he wants to believe that what is felt as beauty must also be truth but what he knows that what the mind arrives at by reasoning is in fact the real truth.... This truth is certainly not the scientific truth which understood by the reasoning faculty would still leave the disagreeable as it was. Indeed, the existence of the disagreeable itself is due to the reasoning faculty of the human mind. This is also a kind of truth, the truth of reason; but Keats does not mean this truth when he speaks of the truth co-existing with beauty. It is truth, imaginatively realized as beauty that destroys the existence of disagreeable in art...."[4]

In other words, "Beauty ultimately comes to mean realization of God. It is dependent on sensuous perception but purified by the heart and made to act for its moral benefit. A bad heart may still perceive beauty but would not be benefited by it as a good heart. To Keats as to Ruskin, beauty gives delight; to one it is sensitive and imaginative; to the other, besides these, it is also moral and in a sense religious. But their fundamental approach to the beauty is the same. It is non-utilitarian and imaginative."[5]

Thus, "Keats is the first apostle of Beauty who makes it an end in it for the artist. It is not an imitation of a literal fact of nature; its existence depends on imaginative realization morality, motives of doing well to the world and such desires of practical reforms are not the aims of an artist. Swinburne endorses the doctrine that to the artist, beauty is truth and he is to devote himself only to the worship of this beauty. Rossetti says in 'Hand and Soul that misery comes to the artist when he hears the voice of reason; hear what the heart says and paint what is beautiful this is the aesthetic teaching of that story....' Ruskin at one time makes truth the end of art, at another, the thing as it might most beautifully exist. He condemns utility but stresses on the moral effect of art. But the main line of thought is the same as that of Keats in its emphasis on the imaginative and non-utilitarian character of beauty. Morris followed Ruskin's teaching of happiness to the worker and the purchaser in the creation of work of art. His beacon-star however both in his poetical and social activities is beauty. The pre-Raphaelite in its devotion to beauty has therefore its proper predecessor in Keats."[6]

However, A.C. Bradley, one of the major critics on Keats, has his own analysis of Keats's principle of beauty. Defining Keats's Principle of Beauty, he says that "he (Keats) exalts sensation and decries thought or knowledge, what he is crying out for is beauty. The word 'sensation'...stands for poetic sensation, and, indeed, for much more. It is to speak broadly, a name for all poetic or imaginative experience.... For it is true that sometimes in the earlier letters we find Keats false to his better mind. Knowing that the more difficult is the fuller, he is yet, to our great advantage, so entranced by the delight or glory of the easier, that he rebels against everything would disturb its magic or trouble his 'exquisite sense of the luxurious'. And then he is tempted to see in thought only that vexatious questioning that 'spoils the singing of the nightingale', and to forget that it is necessary to the fuller and more difficult kind of beauty...."[7]

Regarding Keats's perception of 'truth and beauty' riddle, Bradley says that "he was far from being indifferent to truth, from considering it unimportant for poetry. In an early letter, when he criticizes a poem of Wordsworth's, he ventures to say that 'if Wordsworth had thought a little deeper at that moment he would not have written it', and that 'it is a kind of a sketchy intellectual landscape, not a search after truth'."[8]

"The whole thing must, I think," Bradley says, "have appeared to you, who are a consecutive man, as a thing almost of mere word, but I assure you that, when I wrote it, it was the regular stepping of Imagination towards a truth. And many passages show his conviction that for his progress towards this truth 'thought', 'knowledge', 'philosophy', are indispensable; that he must submit to the toil and solitude that they involve, just as he must undergo the pains of sympathy; that 'there is but one way for him', and that this one 'road lies through application, study, and thought'."[9]

"On the other hand", continues the critic, "he had, in the first place, as we saw, a strong feeling that a man, and especially a poet, must not be in a hurry to arrive at results, and must not shut up his mind in the box of his supposed results, but must be content with half-knowledge, and capable of 'living in uncertainties, mysteries, doubts, without any irritable reaching after fact and reason'. And, in the second place, a poet, he felt, will never be able to rest in thoughts and reasonings which do not also satisfy imagination and give a truth which is also beauty; and in so far as they fail to do this, in so far as they are mere thoughts and reasonings, they are no more than a means, though a necessary means, to an end, which end is beauty,—that beauty which is also truth. This alone is the poet's end, and therefore his law."[10]

Quoting Keats's opinion about beauty in which he says that "with a great poet the sense of beauty overcomes every other consideration, or obliterates all consideration," Bradley continues that "Thought, knowledge, philosophy, if they fall short of this, are nothing but a 'road' to his goal. They bring matter for him to mould to his purpose of beauty; but he must not allow them to impose their purpose on him, or to ask that it shall appear in his product. These statements formulate Keats's position more than he formulates it, but I believe that they represent it truly. He was led to it mainly by the poetic instinct in him, or because, while his mind had much general power, he was, more than Wordsworth or Coleridge or Shelley, a poet pure and simple."[11]

Establishing Keats's position as romantic poet above his contemporaries, on account of his superior thinking, Bradley says that "Keats was by nature both dreamer and a poet, and his ambition was to become poet pure and simple. There was, in a further sense, a double strain in his nature. He had in him the poetic temper of his time, the ever-present sense of an infinite, the tendency to think of this as an ideal perfection manifesting itself in reality, and yet surpassing reality, and so capable of being contrasted with it. He was allied here especially to Wordsworth and to Shelley, by the former of whom he was influenced.... But there was also in him another tendency; and this, it would seem, strengthened at the expense of the first, and would in time have dominated it. It was perhaps the deeper understanding and more individual. It may be called the Shakespearean strain, and it works against any inclination to erect wall between ideal and real.... Keats had the impulse to interest himself in everything he saw or heard of, to be curious about a thing, accept it, and identify himself with it, without first asking whether it is better or worse than another, or how it is from the ideal principle...."[12]

It is this impulse that makes Keats say that "if a sparrow comes before my window, I take part in its existence and pick up the gravel" or that "when she (the Indian Maid) into a room she makes an impression the same as the beauty of a leopardess."[13]

That is why, "a poet is the most unpoetical of anything in existence, because he has no identity. He is 'continually in, for, and filling some other body'. That is not," says Bradley, the description of Milton or Wordsworth or Shelley; neither does it apply very fully to Keats; but it describes something at least of the spirit of Shakespeare.... But Keats had that magic in fuller measure, perhaps, than any of our poets since Milton; and sharing the idealism Wordsworth and Shelley, he possessed also wider sympathies, and if not a more plastic or pictorial imagination than the latter, at least a greater freedom from the attraction of theoretic ideas.... "To what results might not this combination has led if his life had been as long as Wordsworth's or even as Byron's? It would be more than hazardous," says Bradley, "to say that he was the most highly endowed of all our poets in the nineteenth century, but he might well have written its greatest long poems."[14]

It may be right that Keats was a dreamer, but his dreams were not mere dreams. They carried substantial meaning with them, as far as the mysteries of life are concerned. These dreams, the poet thinks, might take their colours:

> From something of material sublime,
> Rather than shadow our own soul's day-time
> in the dark void of night.[15]

In other words, the dreams should mirror objective reality rather than the frustration, and conflicts of the dreamer. Keats confesses that he dare not yet philosophize (quotation used in the chapter 4) and doubts whether he will ever attain to the prize of "High reason, love of good and ill."[16]

But it is clear that the poet was very seriously thinking on these matters towards the end of his life, which make the basis the presence of metaphysical element in his poetry. Analyzing the part of quotation, in which Keats talks about the "love of good and ill", Kenneth Muir rightly says that by this Keats "meant not the knowledge of good and evil, but rather a recognition that particular evil is universal good, an ability to see 'the balance of good and evil'. But Keats could not then make his experience of life fit to a philosophical theory. Things—the problems of life—'tease us out of thought', as the Urn and Eternity were to do. But, when the poet turns from the imaginary world of his creation to the actual world his imagination is 'Lost in a sort of Purgatory blind'."[17]

Critics like Cleanth Brookes and T.S. Eliot might have condemned Keats's 'Truth-beauty' riddle in his 'Ode on the Grecian Urn' as meaningless or 'far-fetched', but truth of the matter is that even his earlier odes possess sufficient evidences of his philosophical thoughts in them, born of out of Keats's bitter gloomy atmosphere in the family. Kenneth Muir argues that "Keats is dissatisfied with escapist poetry, and not strong enough to cope with the problems good and evil.... The 'Chamber of Maiden Thought' becomes gradually darken'd and he feels the 'burden of the Mystery'. Such speculations inevitably interfere with the enjoyment of the present, so that in the Epistle Keats declares that 'It spoils the singing of the Nightingale'.... In the concluding section of the Epistle we learn that the particular problem which was agitating Keats at this time was the struggle for survival in the animal kingdom—'an eternal fierce destruction symbolized not merely by shark and hawk, but by the Robin. When he came to write the Odes a year later the death of Tom had become for Keats the prime example of nature's cruelty. But we can see in the careless and disconnected thoughts of the Epistle that many of the themes treated in the Odes were already in his mind."[18]

A look into the first of the great Odes 'To Psyche' would throw more light on Keats's initial thoughts and beliefs. Through the poem, he was "apparently looking for a surrogate for religion. He speaks nostalgically of 'the fond believing lyre', and looks back to a pantheistic world when air, water and fire were holy. He is mainly concerned with the relationship between the Psyche and Cupid. In becoming her priest he builds a fane where she can receive her lover—not as formerly in darkness, with a bright torch. In other words Keats is proposing love as substitute for religion; but as Psyche is the soul, the poem may also be linked with his conception of the world as a vale of soul-making and with the deification of Apollo in Hyperion."[19]

Keats in an earlier poem, 'Bards of Passion', had imagined that in heaven the nightingale sings

> Divine melodius truth;
>
> Philosophic numbers smooth.[20]

But in the 'Ode to a Nightingale', "though the poet temporarily endows the nightingale's song with meaning, the bird is still 'a senseless tranced thing'. We are left thinking", argues Kenneth Muir, "that neither the beauty of nature nor the beauty of art can console us for the miseries of life. In the 'Ode on a Grecian Urn' Keats ties once more. These figures on the urn possesses the beauty, the significance, and the externality of art; and this in the third stanza explicitly, and throughout the poem implicitly, is contrasted with the transitoriness, the meaninglessness, and the unpoetic nature of actual life.... Yet the moral is not 'mortal beauty passes, but not that of art'."[21]

The moral is, however, that "the sorrows and the meaninglessness of life can transcend if we learn the lesson of the Urn, that 'Beauty is truth, Truth Beauty'."[22]

Perhaps, by saying so the poet wanted all the disagreeables, in the form of the miseries and the fevers and frets of life 'where youth grows pale, spectre-thin and dies', to evaporate, so that they could be truly related to 'Beauty and Truth'. Kenneth Muir believes that it was only a "natural development of his (Keats's) own earlier aphorisms—that beauty is an image of truth, and that therefore, if we see life steadily and see it whole, the disagreeables will evaporate as they do in a great work of art.... Art claims that life could be as meaningful as art. When we are experiencing a work of art we are prepared to give our assent, though at other times we may be skeptical."[23]

In this regard, Keats stands comparable to W.B. Yeats in his treatment of poetry. "Keats was aware, as Yeats was aware when he sailed to Byzantium, of the limitations of art. Even when he is congratulating the lover (in the context of 'Ode on a Grecian Urn') on the permanence of his unsatisfied love, he hankers after 'breathing human passion'; and when he is describing the scene of sacrifice which will remain for ever beautiful, he thinks of the desolate town, emptied for ever of its inhabitants. Art is invaded by human suffering. The cold pastoral, although perfect, is lacking in the warmth of reality. It is this undertone which prevents us from branding the message of the Urn as irresponsible, or 'uneducated', or 'intrusively didactic'."[24]

For Keats happiness was not an outcome of the moments of joy only. The real happiness is experienced only in the moments of extreme joy mixed with the moments of intense sorrow or melancholy, which is also the theme of the poem 'Ode on Melancholy'. Thus, the Ode "has links with several of other odes. Keats had proposed to honour Psyche (in 'Ode to Psyche') by making 'a moan upon the midnight hour', and his fane would have 'thoughts, new grown with pleasant pain'. The song of the nightingale has made him too happy, his heart aching, and his senses pained by a drowsy numbness. Likewise, there is a strain of melancholy, in the fourth stanza of the 'Ode on a Grecian Urn'...."[25]

There are some verses written by Keats which are fine examples of the juxtaposition of joy and sorrow. One of them is as follows:

> Welcome joy, and welcome sorrow,
>
> Lethe's weed and Hermes' feather...
>
> Infant playing with a skull...
>
> Nightshade with the woodbine kissing...
>
> Oh! The sweetness of the pain![26]

Kenneth Muir is, right, when he says that "horrors of this kind, and the beetle and the death-moth, and owl, are not only unnecessary as a means of arousing melancholy, they are to be shunned since they 'drown the wakeful anguish of the soul' and prevents us from experiencing to the full the subtler melancholy of which Keats is writing. Melancholy is to be sought in beauty and joy—in a rose, a rainbow, or the anger of a mistress. Because beauty is transient, because love and joy fade, enjoyment must be accompanied with melancholy. Beauty is lovely because it dies and impermanence is the essence of joy; so that only those who are exquisitely sensuous and able to relish the finest joys can behold the 'Veil'd Melancholy'. Keats is really writing about the poetical character. The fine sensitivity necessary for writing poetry", ponders Muir, "makes the poet vulnerable both to joy and sorrow. The realization that love and beauty are subject to time intensifies his joy in them."[27]

John Holloway, one more esteemed critic on Keats, throws light on the unity of thought in the odes of Keats. Analyzing the 'Ode on Indolence', the critic says that "Keats' mood is not subtle or complex, and it does not develop in the course of the poem. What is significant is that several turns of the phrase or thought in this Ode reappear in the others; and there are elements of something that is more complex and that does develop. Of these, the drowsy indolence is of course one; so is the idea that Ambition is worthless because coming 'From a man's little heart's short fever-fit'.... The indolent mood which is the source of the poem, and somehow mingles sleeping and waking, is not lethargy but in some sense a visionary state, not devoid of pleasure and pain, but transmuting them.... Pleasure and pain have not ceased entirely, but ceased only to be disturbances, superficial additions to life.... And this indolence is a positive thing, bringing a calm pervasive happiness that its crucial feature perhaps—seems near to a suspension of sense for some other more elusive but more illuminating kind of experience:

> O, why did ye not melt, and leave my sense
> Unhaunted quite of all but—nothingness?"[28]

The word 'nothingness' tells the whole story. Nothingness is a state of mind which is above the experience of either pleasure or pain, and that too while living. Generally, a person achieves the 'state of nothingness' or 'sthitpragyan' as mentioned in the 'Bhagwatgita', after practicing a deep meditation. Here, the poet seems to be aspiring just for that state of mind.

The idea of Heaven or the Divinity was always present in Keats's mind. That is why, while discussing the Beauty-Truth passage in 'Ode on a Grecian Urn', Leonard Unger said that "it is conceivable Keats is saying here what he has said elsewhere and in another way—in the Ode".[29] The lines of the poem are worth-quoting in terms of understanding an underlying connectivity in all of Keats's Odes. The lines are as follows:

> Bards of Passion and of Mirth
> Ye have left your souls on earth!
> Have ye souls in heaven too,
> Double-lived in regions new?
> Thus ye teach us, every day
> Wisdom, though fled far away.[30]

The commentary of Unger regarding the poem is significant in terms of Keats's position as a poet. He says:

> Keats is not didactic here, nor does he claim didactism for the bards. Their earth-born souls, their works, teach wisdom in speaking of the lives of men, and in bringing to men, generation after generation, an intensified awareness and thrill of being alive. It is the same wisdom which the urn will continue to teach 'in the midst of other woe'. Keats believed that the man's life, though rounded with a sleep, is the stuff of which 'a thing of beauty' is made. Art takes its truth from life and then returns it to life as beauty.... The paradox that 'teases us out of thought' is that in a work of art there is a kind of life which is both dead and immortal. But a melancholic truth, only the dead are immortal. If there is a heaven, Keats wanted to be very much like earth, with a Mermaid Tavern where the poet could browse 'with contented smack'.[31]

Therefore, "Delight is inseparable from melancholy because it is not conceivable apart from the mortal predicament. The answer to the question at the end of the 'Ode to a Nightingale'—'Do I wake or sleep?'—is, both. In the structural imaginative arc of the poem, the speaker is returned to the 'drowsy numbness' wherein he is awake to his own mortal lot and no longer awake to the vision of beauty. Yet he knows that it is the same human melancholy which is in the beauty of the bird's 'plaintive anthem' and in the truth of his renewed depression. His way of stating this knowledge is to ask the question. Such considerations may clarify the truth-beauty passage."[32]

Studying the 'truth-beauty' passage in view of Platonism, Leonard Unger says that "...Whether they justify artistically Keats's use of these clichés of Platonic speculation is another matter. Keats was no Platonist, if he had avoided those terms or if he had indicated more obviously, within the poem, that he was using the word truth in a sense close to the materialism of his times, 'Ode on a Grecian Urn' would have had a different career in the history of literary criticism. It is unlike that any amount of exegesis can rescue those last lines of the poem from associations with Platonic pietism, for Keats was not enough of a witty and conscious ironist to exploit successfully the philosophical ambiguities of truth. His romanticism was neither reactionary nor modernist in that way and he may not even have been clearly aware of the ambiguity involved.... If it could be proved that he was innocent of the ambiguity, and wanted only the philosophical prestige of the Platonic associations, then from his point of view the poem would not suffer from the difficulties which the merest sophistication can ascribe to it. Whether such ignorance of the law would be too outrageous to merit critical exoneration is a nice problem for critical theory."[33]

Thus, "the impatient dismissal of perfectibility ('...the nature of the world will not admit of it.'), with which Keats introduces his sermon on soul-making reveals behind his perception that life is cruel and that to understand it is to be disenchanted. Man, he affirms, is 'destined to hardships and disquietude of some kind or the other'.... It is this conviction, jointed with his awareness of the existentialism pathos of the human soul (the tragic hero is any man, however fortunate), that makes the celebration of the Psyche more than a piece of mythological embroidery; and in Psyche's final apotheosis there may be a dimly expressed Keats's longing, which was now almost without hope, for some kind of personal immortality (reference to Fanny Brawne)."[34]

Keats's use of mythological references has a close association with his 'Soul-making' Principle, described by him in one of his letters (quoted in the chapter 4). Referring to this 'Soul-making' process and defending it as Keats's firm belief, and associating it with Hinduism and some other religions, in his discussion of Psyche, Mr. Allott says that "we need to be aware how closely ideas on the meaning and the function of myth were bound up with Keats's attempt to make sense of the human situation. He tells George and Georgiana that his system of soul-making 'may have been the Parent of all the more palpable and personal Schemes of Redemption, among the Zoroastrians the Christians and the Hindoos'.... That is to say, in these intimate speculations Psyche has for him much the same degree of reality and unreality as 'their Christ, their Oromances and their Vishnu'. Figures drawn from religious myths—and to Keats Christianity was simply the last of the great mythologies—may be understood sympathetically, he thinks, of personification of certain kind of human need or self-knowledge (people 'must have the palpable and named Mediator and Savior'). This is Keats's personal extension of a mode of mythological explanation the commonplace."[35]

Apart from other aspects emphasized in the above statement, one is that concerns Hinduism. It is more than clear that Keats must have studied Hinduism in some detail, as is evident from his reference of 'Hindoos' along with 'Zoroastrians and Christians' in his description of the principle of 'Soul-making', discussed above. If so, then the validity of analysis of the Odes 'On Grecian Urn' and on 'The Nightingale', done on lines of Hinduism in the previous chapter, is stamped. Already, the poet is tempted to refer to an 'Indian Maiden' as an earthly substitute for Endymion's beloved Cynthia or the Moon-goddess, in Endymion. Therefore, it would not be unfair to say that Keats's interest in Indian mythology also proves his interest in the matters of metaphysical aspects.

These mythological references were obviously used by Keats to be able to connect them with human situations. In other words, He seemed deeply interested in associating human life with the divine life, as all the myths he made use of were in one way or the other related to gods or deities. The following lines are a proof of Keats's holistic considerations:

> When holy were the haunted forest boughs,
>
> Holy the air, the water, and the fire.[36]

There is one Sonnet of Keats, entitled 'Why did I laugh tonight?' which throws light of particular importance on the Odes. "This sonnet...from the Letters, must have been written shortly before 19 March, 1819, and therefore near the beginning of this creative period. It is important for three reasons: it hints at some of the antimonies which the present enquiry has emphasized, it declares that that ecstasy is inseparable from physical experience...and it has verbal parallels with no less than three of the Odes. 'Nothing ever becomes real until it is experienced', Keats writes immediately before copying out this poem for George and Georgiana Keats."[37]

However, the ode is worth-quoting, as its contents obviously provide a background to Keats's metaphysical thinking. Here is a portion of the sonnet:

> Why did I laugh tonight? No voice can tell:
>
> No God no Demon of severe response,
>
> Designs to reply from Heaven or from Hell
>
> Then to my human heart I turn at once—
>
> Heart! Thou and I are here sad and alone;
>
> Yet could I on this very midnight cease
>
> And the world's gaudy ensigns are in shreds;

Verse, Fame and Beauty are intense indeed
But Death intenser—Death is Life's high meed.[38]

Analyzing the sonnet as a link with the Odes, Mr. Holloway says that the "lines 9-10 repeat, perhaps, rather obscurely, the 'advantage in the body overpowering the mind' which Keats referred to in describing his indolent mood of 19th March; and it has often been noted how line resemble 'to cease upon the midnight with no pain' of 'To a Nightingale'. But critics have not usually noticed that the gaudy ensigns in shreds have clearly something in common with the 'cloudy trophies' of 'On Melancholy'...and more important, that the 'Verse, fame and Beauty' of line 13 are virtually the same as the 'Poetry, Ambition and Love' of 'On Indolence. Both by its wording and by its substance, therefore, this sonnet does something further to suggest that the Odes explore various phases of a single experience."[39]

He further says, "Any similar suggestion about 'To Autumn' must be very tentative. Keats composed the other poems within a brief period in the spring and early summer of 1819, and this not until several months later. It may well have arisen from quite independent poetic impulse. But it is not altogether fanciful, perhaps, to see it as a quite and gentle close to the whole sequence of the poems, standing to them all somewhat as the last three lines of 'On a Grecian Urn' stand to that single poem. Nor would it be difficult to point out details that are reminiscent of the Odes—Autumn drowsing with the fumes of poppies (drowsing, too, among the 'twined flowers', like Keats himself in 'On Indolence' or the goddess in 'To Psyche'), or Keats's rejection of the songs of spring, or perhaps even the morning choirs of gnats...."[40]

Talking about the development of thought in Keats's Odes, the above-mentioned critic says that "...it seems much more like an expression of the very frame of mind from which at this time, to varying degree on various occasions, Keats found the raptures of poetic inspiration generate themselves—and do so, moreover, exactly because he was not seeking them."[41]

Quoting Sir Maurice Bowra, the same critic says further that "writing 'the three stanzas in which Keats tells of the timeless moments depicted on the Urn arise from his own knowledge of what creation is' seems to suggest this also. And these are, of course, well-known passages in Keats's Letters which indicate that he regarded what might be called the embryonic condition of the mood conveyed by these poems as also the embryo of poetic inspiration.... In a word, the Odes are not only the products of what Keats called 'Negative Capability', but taken together are a uniquely full account of what it is like and how it develops."[42]

Commenting on the metaphysical growth of Keats's personality, Sidney Colvin says that although "vague, and floating his conception of that something (Beauty) might be, but it was extraordinarily intense, partaking of the concentrated essence of a thousand thrilling joys of perception and imagination. He had read no Plato, though he was of course familiar enough with Spencer's mellifluous dilution of Platonic and neo-Platonic doctrine in his four Hymns. In *Endymion*, as in the speculative of the letters, his mind has to go adventuring for itself among those ancient, for him almost uncharted, mysteries of Love and Beauty. He does not yet conceive himself capable of anything more than steppings, to repeat his own sober phrase, of the imagination towards truth.... He does not light, he does expect to light, upon revelations of truth abstract or formal, and seems to waver between the Adam's dream idea of finding in some transcendental world all the several modes of earthly happiness 'repeated in a finer tone' but yet retaining their severalness, and an idea, nearer to the Platonic, of a single principle of absolute or abstract Beauty, the object of a purged and perfected spiritual contemplation, from which all the varieties of beauty experienced on the earth derive their quality and oneness."[43]

Continuing the argument further, the above-mentioned critic says, "But in his search, he (Keats) strikes now and again, for the attentive reader, notes of far-reaching symbolic significance that carry the mind to the verge of the great mysteries of things: he takes us with him on exploratory sweeps and fetches of figurative thought in regions almost beyond the reach of the words, where gain with him glimmering adumbrations of the super-sensual through distilled and spiritualized remembrance of the joys of sense-perception at their most intense."[44]

So, on the basis of the above observation, it can be strongly and firmly observed that Keats was capable enough of taking us to those 'regions which are beyond the reach of the words'.

As far as Keats's comparison of human life with a large mansion is concerned, it is supposed to have been inspired by Wordsworth's spirit in his Lines composed a few miles above *Tintern Abbey*. Yet, the difference of presentation is markedly clear. Again, Keats seems to excel his greater contemporary in his delineation of the subject:

> Here is a typical case of the method of evocation as against the method of exposition. Wordsworth's lines are written with a high, almost an inspired, power of describing and putting into direct words the successive moods of a spirit gradually ripening and deepening in the power of communion with nature, and through nature, with all life.... But Keats, fully as he has pondered them, cannot be satisfied that they fit his own case until he has called up history of his similar experience in the form natural to him, the form of concrete similitudes or visions of the imagination—the Thoughtless Chamber, the Chamber of Maiden-Thought with its gradual darkening and its many outlets standing open to be explored. It is significant that such visions should still be of architecture, of halls and chambers in an imagined mysterious building.[45]

Talking about a change in the poet's attitude with regards to nature from his earlier perception of it, Colvin says, "A change, it should be added, was coming over Keats's thoughts and feelings whereby natural scenery in general was beginning to interest him less and his fellow creatures more. In the acuteness of childish and boyish sensation, among the suburban fields or seaside holidays, he had instinctively, as if by actual partnership with and self-absorption into nature, gained enough delighted knowledge of her ways and doings for his facilities to work on through a lifetime of poetry; and now, in his second chamber of Maiden-Thought, the appeal of nature, even at its most thrilling, yields in his mind to that of humanity. 'Scenery is fine, but human nature is finer'."[46]

The ideas expressed in *Hyperion* "are primarily the same ideas, developed in a deeper and more somber spirit, as had been present in Keats's mind almost from the beginning: the idea that in the simple delights of nature and art as unreflectingly felt in youth there is no abiding-place for the poetic spirit, that from the delights it must rise to thoughts higher and more austere and prompting to more arduous tasks: the further idea that to fit it for such tasks two things above all are necessary, growth in human sympathy through the putting down of self, and growth in knowledge and wisdom through strenuous study and meditation. Such ideas had already been thrown out by Keats in Sleep and Poetry; they had been developed with much more fullness, though in a manner made obscure from redundance, of imagery, in Endymion, especially in the third book: they had been expressed with a difference under the new and clearer symbolism of the two Chambers of Thoughts in Keats's letters to Reynolds from Teignmouth."[47]

Commenting on the development of ideas in Keats's poetry, leading him to the world of metaphysics, his biographer Sidney Colvin says, "About the same hour, the hour, as I think, of the finest achievement of Keats's genius as well as of its highest promise,—there had appeared in his letters and some of his verses the quite new idea, which would have been inconceivable for him a year earlier, of questioning whether poetry was a worthy pursuit at all in a world full of pain and destruction. Musing beside the sea on a calm evening of April, he anticipates the Tennysonian vision 'of nature, red in tooth and claw with ravin.'... In letters written during the next few weeks he insists over and over again alike upon the acuteness of his new sense that the world is 'full of Misery and Heartbreak, Pain, Sickness and oppression', and upon poet's need of knowledge, and again knowledge, and ever more knowledge, to take away the heat and the fever and ease 'the Burden of the Mystery.'..."[48]

The biographer continues that "the pressure of the sense of human misery, the hunger of the soul for knowledge and vision to enlighten it, though they naturally do not colour his impersonal work of the next year and a half, nevertheless set their mark, the former strain in special, upon his most deeply felt meditative verse, as in the odes to the Nightingale and the Grecian Urn, and reappear occasionally in his private confessions to his friends. Now, after intense experience both of personal sorrow and of poetic toil, and under the strain of incipient disease and consuming passion, it is borne in upon his solitary hours that such poetry as he has written, the irresistible poetry of beauty and romance, has been mere idle dreaming, a refuse of the spirit from its prime duty of sharing and striving to alleviate the troubles of the world."[49]

"It seems to him that every ordinary man and woman is worth more to mankind than such a dreamer (as Keats was). If poetry is to have any real value to the world, it must be a different kind of poetry from this: the true poet is something the very opposite of the mere dreamer: he is one who has prepared himself through self-renunciation and arduous effort and extreme probation of the spirit to receive and impart the highest wisdom, the wisdom that comes from full knowledge of the past and foresight into the future. Of such wisdom (as mentioned above) *The Fall of Hyperion* in its amended form, as revealed and commented by Mnemosyne-Moneta, the great priestess and prophetess, remembrancer and admonisher in one, was meant to be a sample,—or such an attempt at a sample as Keats at the present stage of his mental growth could supply. But the attempt, too arduous and Dantesque for his strength, was soon abandoned."[50]

No doubt, the work on the poem was abandoned. But, it would be incorrect to say that Keats abandoned the poem because of his inability to complete it as it carried such an arduous and complex a subject as to have gone out of his control. At least, the whole project of the poem must have already been well-thought out by the poet. Had he not done so, he would not have been able to begin and develop the poem to the point it had reached. The serious reason for the abandonment, therefore, seems to be Keats's failing health rather than anything else. There are instances, through the letters or conversations, to suggest that the poet, as he grew older, wanted to go the way of 'study, hard work and dedication for the sake of humanity', or to 'achieve more and more knowledge' to be able to do something for humanity.

It is interesting to see Keats's state of mind in the last days of his life, in terms of religion. Religion-wise, "Keats had been neither a believer nor by any means (except in the earliest days of his enthusiasm for Leigh Hunt) a scoffer; respecting Christianity without calling himself a Christian, and by turn clinging to and drifting from the doctrine of human immortality. Now, on his death-bed, says Severn, among the most haunting and embittering of his distresses was the thought that not for him were those consolations of orthodoxy which were within the reach of every knave and fool. After a time, contrasting the steadfast behaviour of the believer Severn with his own, he acknowledged anew the power of the Christian teaching and example, and bidding Severn read to him from Jeremy Tailor's Holy Dying and Holy Living, strove to pass the remainder of his days in a temper of more peace and constancy."[51]

The last words uttered by Keats to his friend Severn even as he was dying are important to know his faith. On 23rd of February, quoting Keats, Severn says, "...about four, the approaches of death came on. 'Severn—I—lift me up—I am dying—I shall die easy; don't be frightened—be firm, and thank God it has come.'"[52]

The words were spoken in such a calm and quiet mood, as if Keats had a foreknowledge of his death, and also as if he was passing on to another journey, the eternal one, and not dying as such.

However, considering the different experiences and the preoccupations of the modern age, "the new poetry may not be able to fully to share Keats's inspiring conviction of the sovereign, the transcendental truth of whatsoever ideas the imagination seizes as beauty. It may even be constrained to abjure the direct and conscious search for beauty as its primary aim and impulse. All the more indispensably will it need that quality of intensity which is capable, of making all disagreeables evaporate; that is to say, of purging the ugliness out of things squalid or horrible or revolting and fusing them into something which by its very white heat of truth shall be akin to beauty. Provided that its organ be the imagination working with sufficient intensity on whatsoever themes, the new poetry cannot but achieve some phase, some incarnation, of beauty by the way."[53]

"Those who care for poetry at all must always care for those refreshing and draughts, from the innermost, the perennial, wells of antiquity, of nature, and of romance, those meditations that search into the mysteries of joy and sorrow at the unchanging heart of things. Moreover they will never cease to interest themselves in the question,—if only this great spirit (Keats) had survived, what would have been those unwritten poems of which he saw in the sky the cloudy symbols, of which he felt the pressure and prescience forcing the blood into his brain or bringing about his heart an awful warmth 'like a load of immortality', and the perishing of which unborn within him was one of the two great haunting distresses of his dying days."[54]

The matter of speculation is as to what heights Keats would have acquired in his pursuits of metaphysical enquiries, had he lived longer with a better fortune. Mr. Colvin tries to seek an answer to this curiosity when he says:

> In letting speculation wander in this field, we are brought up by many problems as to what kind of manhood could have followed a youth like that of Keats, had he have better fortune and had the conditions and accidents of his life been such as to fortify his bodily constitution instead of sapping it. Youth, especially half-trained youth, is always subject to such storms and strains as those which Keats experienced with a violence proportionate to the fervour of his being.... To the sane and sweet, the manly and courageous, elements in his character we have found his friends bear unanimous evidence, amply supported by the self-revelation of his

letters. But self-revealed also we see the morbid, the corroding elements which lay beneath these, just as beneath his vigorous frame and gallant bearing there lay the susceptibilities that with ill-luck enabled lung disease to fasten on and kill him.[55]

Therefore, when Keats "lets his mind dwell on the opposed extremes of human impulse and experience from the grossest animal to the loftiest and purest spiritual, which the word-of-all-work, love, is used to cover, he is more savagely perplexed and out of conceit with life from any other cause or thought whatever. The ruling power in himself, as he declares over and over again, was the abstract passion for beauty, the love of the principle of beauty in all things. But even in the poem especially designed to embody and celebrate that passion, in Endymion, we find his conception of realized and sexual human love to be mawkish and unworthy. When the actual experience overtakes himself, he falls utterly a slave, enraptured and tortured and desperately resentful all at once, to the jealous cravings which absorb and paralyse all his other faculties. Would ripened manhood or a happier experience have been able to bring health and peace to his spirit on this supreme vital matter and to turn him into a master-poet of love, love both human and transcendental, such as at the outset he had longed and striven to be?" "Again, along with his admirable capacity for loyal devotion and sympathy in friendship, we find in him capacities of quite another kind, capacities for disillusionment, and for seeing through and chafing at human and social shams and pretensions and absurdities; and we ask ourselves, would this strain in him, which we find expressed with a degree of pettish and premature cynicism, for instance in the Cap and Bells and in some of his later letters, have matured with time in to a power either of virile satire or genial, reconciling comedy?"[56]

"And once more," argues Colvin, "would that haunting, that irrepressible sense of the of the miseries of the world which we find breaking through from time to time amid the beauty of the odes, or the playfulness and affectionate confidences of the letters, or dictating that tragic return against himself and achievements in the revised Hyperion,—could it and would it with experience have mellowed into such compassionate wisdom as might have made him one of the rare great healers and sages among the poets of the world?"[57]

Then, as if to prove beyond doubt the metaphysical thinking inherent in Keats's temperament, Sidney Colvin asserts that "Such speculations are as vain as they are inevitable. But the closer any reader can bring himself to the mind and soul of Keats by habitual reading and meditating on the poems and letters together, the more convinced he will be of his almost unlimited potential greatness. Let indulge ourselves at any rate by remembering that it is the greatest among his successors who have held the sanguine view as to the powers that were in him. Here are more words of Tennyson's,—'Keats with his high spiritual vision, would have been, if he had lived, the greatest of us. There is something magic and of the innermost soul of poetry in almost everything which he wrote.' Leaving with these words the question of what he might have done, and looking only at what he did, it is enough for any man's glory. The days of the years of his life were few and evil, but above his grave the double aureole of poetry and friendship shines eternally."[58]

Therefore, commenting on the serious objectives of Keats's poetry, Maurice Bowra says, "April and May 1819 were perhaps the most remarkable period of Keats's creative life, remarkable not so much for the quantity of his work as for its quality. In these months he wrote 'La Belle Dame Sans Merci', the 'Ode to Psyche', the 'Ode to a Nightingale', and the 'Ode on a Grecian Urn'. In these poems he found his true voice and perfection which he had been seeking. It was an astonishing outburst, and it came all the more unaccountably since, in the preceding months of February and March, Keats had written very little.... The great odes were new venture unlike anything that Keats had hitherto done, and he conducted it in a new spirit. The odes that follow certainly 'read the more richly' for the care which has gone to their composition and for the selection and concentration of imaginative experience in them.

In them Keats carries out the prescription of poetry which he gave to Shelley and loads every rift of his subject with ore."[59]

In a letter to Bailey, written on March 13th, 1818, Keats had put the view that "every mental pursuit takes its reality and worth from the ardour of the pursuer—being in itself a nothing—Ethereal things may at least be thus real, divided under three heads—Things real—things semireal—and no things."[60] Commenting on the deeper layer of the letter, Bowra says, "...ethereal things are real because they mean so much to us and because we pursue them so ardently. We may well conclude, though Keats does not say so in this letter, that things which have been pursued and loved through many generations are more than usually 'ethereal.'... And that Keats believed this is clear from a passage in Book III of *Endymion*, in which, after attacking those people who are unable to see the true slendours of existence, Keats states his own case for them. So far from being unreal, he says in effect, they are remote and sublime realities, sought with effort and attained only by patient devotion:

> Are then regalities all gilded masks?
> No, there are throned seats unscapable
> But by a patient wing, a constant spell,
> Or by ethereal things that, unconfin'd
> Can make a ladder of eternal wind...."[61]

The phrase 'ethereal things' occurs in the Keats's letter to Bailey, quoted above, and shows that he is always thinking about the same problem. "They (ethereal things) are, as we now see, not the end but the means to some remoter and sublimer end, to those 'throned seats' which are despised by many but mean every thing to Keats."[62]

"The relevance of this passage," argues Bowra, "in *Endymion* to the 'Ode on a Grecian Urn' is manifest. Just as in the Ode Keats passes beyond the music and the lovers, who are surely 'ethereal things', to something else, so in *Endymion* he sees that through his cult of such things he comes to something else and feels at one with the secret powers of nature...."[63]

As a result, "There are", Keats believes, "beyond the reach of the fate, some things which deserve a religious respect and devotion and belong to the essential elements of the world. These things are 'silent as a consecrated urn'. They do not speak directly to us, like an urn, have a message which we feel to be holy. These are times marked in the natural order of the universe—'spherey sessions'—when these powers keep state, and it is then that we must get into touch with them, and see what they have to reveal. That, in rude paraphrase, is meaning of Keats' lines in book III of *Endymion*, and they take us to the heart of the 'Ode on a Grecian Urn'. The Urn is the 'foster-child of silence' not merely because it is itself dumb, but because it is related to this mysterious hierarchy of supernatural powers which are hidden until we learn how to enter into their presence."[64]

Throughout his poetic career Keats was obsessed with the idea of 'Beauty and Truth', which becomes eloquent in the last two lines of the ode on Urn. For him "Truth is another name for ultimate reality, and is discovered not by the reasoning mind but by the imagination. The imagination has a special insight into the true nature of things, and Keats accepts its discoveries because they agree with his senses, resolve disagreeable discords, and overwhelm him by their intensity. He is convinced that anything so discovered is true in a sense that the conclusions of philosophy are not.... Keats calls this reality 'beauty' because of its over-powering and all-absorbing effect on him. In fact, he substitutes the discovery of beauty through the imagination for the discovery of facts through the reason, and asserts that it is more satisfactory and more certain way of piercing to the heart of things, since inspired insight sees more than the abstract ratiocination ever can. Keats's concern is with the imagination in a special sense, and he is not far from Coleridge in his view of it."[65]

For Keats 'imagination' does much more than to imagine in the ordinary sense about the things and life as such. For him "it (imagination) is an insight so fine that it sees what is concealed from most men and understands things in their full range and significance and character. The rationale of Keats's poetry is that through the imagination it finds something so compelling in its intensity that it is at once beautiful and real. The theory which Keats puts forward piecemeal in his letters receives its final form in the last lines of the 'Ode on a Grecian Urn'."[66]

Maurice Bowra tries to summarize Keats's philosophy of life as he says that "this was not a complete philosophy of life, nor did Keats intend it to be. It is a theory of art, a doctrine intended to explain his own creative experience. He was increasingly conscious that art is not everything, and in his last two years he became more uneasy about the detachment from life which his work imposed on him. In 'The Fall of Hyperion' Moneta suggests that the poet is but a 'dreaming thing' and must hold a lower place than those who are moved by human suffering. When he wrote the 'Ode on a Grecian Urn', Keats had not gone so far as to think that the truth which he sought through imagination was a dream. It was still a very important truth for him as a poet—but only as a poet. The Ode is his last word on a special activity and a special experience. Within its limits it has its own view of life and that is what Keats expresses...."[67]

The critic, bringing the argument to its finality, says that "the belief that 'Beauty is truth, truth beauty' is true for the artist while he is concerned with his art. It is no less true that, while he is at work, this is all that he knows for certain and that he needs to know for the proper pursuit of his special task. Unless he believes this, he is in danger of ruining his art...."[68]

E. Nageswara Rao also upholds the view that Keats was apparently on the path of innovation in themes and techniques when he died.[69] The opinion that Keats was interested in the intellect is held by "De Selinecourt's Warton Lecture and A.C. Bradley's 'Keats and Philosophy', which attempt to show the intellectual core in Keats.... Keats's use of myths was examined by Douglas Bush and Walter H. Evert while Albert Gerard stressed the modernity of Keats who reconciles experience with philosophic thought...."[70]

However, Keats's quest "for permanence in these (Endymion's) and other similar scenes always involves a longing for a merger with a figure, image, or a symbol of beauty. The longing is at times expressed by a mortal youth in relation to a goddess or other immortal, at other times by the poet himself or his persona in relation to Fanny Brawne of a symbol like the Nightingale or the Urn. The figure or symbol is almost always defined as a feminine presence.... But the Principle of Beauty in Keats's thought is less an abstract ideal than one represented by a feminine figure or symbol who takes various forms and in whose presence the poet imagines his heroes or himself seeking an affirmation of self. It is the need expressed in the quest that remains constant, not the image representing potential fulfillment."[71]

Michael E. Holstein calls Keats a poet-healer. A poet-healer is the one who has the power of sympathizing with the pain of others. And Keats had this quality with him. To prove the point, he says that "In 1820, suffering the physical and psychological agonies of his own advanced case of tuberculosis, Keats nevertheless spoke of his desire to help others face terminal illness: 'If my health would bear it, I could write a Poem which I have in my head, which would be a consolation for people in such a situation as mine.' Although that poem was never begun, in a sense it had already been composed many times before, since throughout his poetry Keats had written to remedy pain, suffering and death. He most clearly formulates his healing mission in The Fall of Hyperion: A Dream when the narrator argues that the poet is a 'sage;/ A humanist, physician to all men.' Here Keats combines wisdom and classical humanism in a healing role in which he had long sought justification for himself as a poet."[72]

Carrying forward the argument of the role of a poet-healer, the critic says that "Keats's special outlook to pain can be seen in contrast to other attitudes. For example, in classical tragedy pain and death illuminate the precariousness of existence, but themselves are terrible and arbitrary. The passion of Christ and the suffering of the martyred saints dominate the medieval art. Analyzed against Christian values, "suffering represents a purifying rite of passage, labour pains that deliver a soul from a lower to a higher spiritual order.... But with the loss of common measures like an ascetic religion or natural law, pain became more unintelligible—a part of the absurd, something to be resisted not venerated. The real suffering of ordinary people replaced the abstract agonies of gods, heroes, and kings."[73]

It was to Keats's purposes, then, to describe pain clearly if he wished to alleviate the suffering of humanity and of all the Romantic poets Keats renders the most vivid, direct portrait of sufferings. Wordsworth, because he is so interested in the inner life, generally ignores physical pain as a major subject.... Shelley regards pain as the result of an incorrect ethical orientation.... For Coleridge, it represents guilt and atonement. For Blake pain resembles a Platonic disharmony of parts.... Keats in contrast, does not slight, allegorize, or abstract pain. It was in the very reality of suffering that Keats took heart. Scenes of intense physical suffering appear in his poetry. Especially after 1818, even nature reminds him of the cycle of sickness and death, and in the thinking of the death of Burns, he is moved to lament the cycle that infect the world. If pain were all too human and all too common, perhaps it could also be remedied by a single man (Keats) acting in a humanitarian capacity.[74]

Keats's initial response to suffering was to offer his poetry a palliative that reproduces properties of wine, opiates, love, or reverie. But "if pain for Keats springs from psyche, or environment, its effects could be mitigated by distracting the mind from the material world and providing more spiritual alternatives. So, poetry for Keats contributed to the world through its intense experience and its commanding claims on reader's attention which deflect consciousness from pain."[75]

Being a physician-turned poet that Keats was, he must have had at the back of his mind the idea of using poetry as a medicine to the suffering humanity. That is why, "as his confidence in healing powers of poetry, he began to explore how poetry could do more for suffering humanity than merely distracting the mind from pain, how it could in fact actively promote health. The healing properties of poetry, as he describes them in Sleep and Poetry, derive from the benefits of nature and sleep, but eventually surpass them. Nature offers a place where healing occurs."[76]

Keats's own experience of suffering certainly deepened his understanding of suffering. "Pain took on a intensity and an inevitability for him as he found in it a complex relationship between body and mind. Keats became less willing to locate escape from suffering in romance or romantic love, which on the contrary, were seen as sources of suffering. The typical response Keats developed to suffering after 1817 is less concerned restoratives, antidotes, or escape from pain than with the mystery of pain."[77]

Keats's conception of physical love (or worldly love) is also important to understand. "Frequently he links unrequited love with illness: the 'wan, and pale' hero of *Endymion* suffers from a love-longing for Diana, love that is called a 'cankering venom'; and in Isabella the heroine falls sick in sympathy with her lover who is fevered with love. Keats's own trying relationship with Fanny Brawne bred its share of anguished cries from the poet who called on 'Physician Nature' to cure his sickness...."[78]

Hence, "La Belle Dame sans Merci" may reflect Keats's profound distrust of romantic love and romance. The poem explores immense gulf between the common-place world that the Knight used to inhabit and bewitched realms that infect his imagination. His pain springs not only from a distempered imagination but from an entire tradition of romance and romantic love, one that has seduced Kings and princes. Through the poem, the poet, attempts to free himself from this romantic tradition that earlier he thought provided antidotes to pain and that now he feels can poison an imagination.

Thus, in view of the above analysis of Keats's 'letters', his life and works along with his romanticism from the standpoint of 'metaphysics', it can be well-established that Keats's poetry very much carried the metaphysical element in it, as far as the 'contents' are concerned. But, he cannot be named as a metaphysical poet in the sense John Donne was, as Donne's metaphysics was mainly based on the 'style', in the form of 'conceits' and 'juxtapositions', used in the composition of his poems.

But, as far as the 'contents' of the poetry is concerned, Keats was beyond doubt, a metaphysical poet and not a romantic, as he is known to be. From the first to the last of his poetic growth Keats made a conscious effort to reach the greater heights of realization of human life through his addiction to the 'sensuous beauty' in nature, in the beginning. But, he ends up as a grave poet of 'beauty', who saw the element of beauty in all things, as having been created 'beautiful' by the Creator Himself. And this was quite an uncharacteristic approach on part of Keats, as far as romantic poetry is concerned. Romantic poets are known to describe the beauty of nature and find shelter in it to avoid the worries of life. But, Keats always defined nature according to the maturity of his mind. His ideas about nature kept changing with the passage of time.

Hence, the 'principle of beauty in all things', propounded by Keats, means that it is for seer to perceive 'beauty' in each and every particle of creation rather than 'ugliness', as God has made it so. These were the metaphysical considerations with which the poet was always obsessed and which, as a result, he wanted to give a voice through his poetry. Seen from the very beginning of his poetic career, from the Poems till, say, *Hyperion*, a systematic and certain metaphysical growth can easily be noticed in Keats's poetry. As a result, his poetry did succeed in conveying the profound and serious concerns, as regards the origin and purpose of life in the world.

Therefore, to conclude, it will be perfectly right to say that Keats does carry the metaphysical element in his poetry. The study, as a result, presents Keats as a metaphysical poet, not in the sense of "technique and manner" by which John Donne is known to be, but from the point of view of his "ideas and thoughts" that find an expression throughout his poems. Thus, the detailed discussion, through an in-depth analysis and internal-connectivity of his letters, life and poetry, claims to find a new Keats—the poet with a metaphysical leaning. From this angle, it will be right to call him a metaphysical poet, born in a romantic era, whose poetry is through and through replete with deep thoughts in connection to his personal life, life in general, and in relation of human life with permanence or 'eternity'.

References

CHAPTER 1

1. *New Encyclopedia Britannica* (Vol. 12); *Encyclopedia Britannica*, Inc., Chicago, p. 12.
2. *Ibid.*, p. 10.
3. A.S. Hornby, *ALD*. Oxford University Press, 1974, p. 533.
4. *New Encyclopedia Britannica* (Vol. 10), p. 10.
5. *Ibid.*, Vol. 12, p. 10.
6. *Ibid.*
7. *Ibid.*
8. *Ibid.*
9. *Ibid.*
10. *Ibid.*
11. *Ibid.*, Vol. 12, p. 11.
12. *Ibid.*
13. *Ibid.*
14. *Ibid.*
15. *Ibid.*, pp. 11-12.
16. *Ibid.*, p. 12.
17. *Ibid.*
18. *Ibid.*
19. *Ibid.*
20. *Ibid.*
21. *Ibid.*, p. 13.
22. *Ibid.*
23. *Ibid.*, p. 17.
24. *Ibid.*
25. *Ibid.*

26. *Ibid.*
27. *Ibid.*, p. 18.
28. *Ibid.*
29. *Ibid.*
30. *Ibid.*
31. *Ibid.*
32. *Ibid.*, p. 19.
33. *Ibid.*
34. *Ibid.*
35. *Ibid.*, Vol. 14, p. 248.
36. *Ibid.*
37. *Ibid.*
38. *Ibid.*
39. *Ibid.*, p. 250.
40. *Ibid.*
41. *Ibid.*
42. *Ibid.*
43. *Ibid.*
44. *Ibid.*
45. *Ibid.*
46. *Ibid.*, p. 251.
47. *Ibid.*
48. *Ibid.*
49. *Ibid.*, p. 254.
50. *Ibid.*
51. *Ibid.*
52. *Ibid.*
53. *Ibid.*
54. *Ibid.*
55. *Ibid.*, p. 11.
56. *Ibid.*, Vol. 12, p. 12.
57. *Ibid.*, p. 17.
58. *Ibid.*
59. *Ibid.*, p. 18.
60. *Ibid.*

61. *Ibid.*
62. *Ibid.*, p. 12.

CHAPTER 2

1. Sydney Colvin, *Life of John Keats*. New Delhi: Vishvapati Publications, p. 7.
2. *Ibid.*, p. 9.
3. Stephen Coote, *John Keats: A Life*. Hind Publishers Ltd., p. 7.
4. *Ibid.*, p. 12.
5. Bernard Groom, ed., *Selections from Keats*. London: Macmillan & Co. Ltd., p. ix.
6. Stephen Coote, p. 17.
7. *Ibid.*
8. *Ibid.*, pp. 17-18.
9. *Ibid.*, p. 23.
10. *Ibid.*, p. 20.
11. Bernard Groom, Introduction, p. x.
12. Stephen Coote, p. 10.
13. Bernard Groom, Introduction, p. x.
14. *Ibid.*, p. xi.
15. *Ibid.*, p. xiv.
16. *The Works of John Keats*, Introduction by Keats, Wordsworth Editions Ltd., Hertfordshire, 1994, p. xv.
17. Bernard Groom, Introduction, p. xv.
18. *Ibid.*, p. xiii.
19. *Ibid.*, p. xiv.
20. Graham Hough, *The Romantic Poets*; Bombay: B.I. Publications Pvt. Ltd., p. 161.
21. *Ibid.*
22. Sydney Colvin, pp. 85-86.
23. *Ibid.*, p. 114.
24. *Ibid.*
25. *Ibid.*, p. 116.
26. *Ibid.*
27. *Ibid.*, p. 117.
28. *Ibid.*, p. 118.

29. *Ibid.*, pp. 120-21.
30. *Ibid.*, pp. 121-22.
31. *Ibid.*, p. 125.
32. *Ibid.*, pp. 126-27.
33. *Ibid.*, p. 128.
34. *Ibid.*, pp. 128-29.
35. *Ibid.*, p. 136.
36. *Ibid.*, p. 135.
37. *Ibid.*, p. 136.
38. Stephen Coote, cover page.

CHAPTER 3

1. Colvin, *op. cit.*, p. 22.
2. Graham Hough, *op. cit.*, p. 156.
3. *Ibid.*, pp. 156-57.
4. Arthur-Compton-Rickett, *A History of English Literature*. USB Publishers & Distributors Pvt. Ltd., New Delhi, p. 343.
5. *Ibid.*, p. 346.
6. T.H. Ward, *The English Poets*. Macmillan and Co. Ltd., London, 1933, p. 428.
7. *Ibid.*, pp. 434-35.
8. *Ibid.*, p. 435.
9. *Ibid.*
10. *Ibid.*, p. 431.
11. E.N. Rao, *John Keats: An Anthology of Recent Criticism*. Pencraft International, New Delhi, p. 128.
12. Graham Hough, *op. cit.*, p. 157.
13. *Ibid.*, p. 157.
14. *Ibid.*, p. 158.
15. *Ibid.*
16. *Ibid.*, p. 161.
17. *Ibid.*
18. *Ibid.*, p. 162.
19. *Ibid.*, p. 158.
20. *Ibid.*, p. 170.

21. *Ibid.*
22. *Ibid.*
23. *Ibid.*, p. 171.
24. *Ibid.*
25. *Ibid.*, p. 172.
26. *Ibid.*
27. *Ibid.*, p. 162.
28. *Ibid.*, p. 172.
29. Raghukul Tilak, *Short History of English Poetry*. Prakash Book Depot, p. 212.
30. *Ibid.*, p. 215.
31. Stephen Coote, *op. cit.*, p. 77.
32. E.N. Rao, p. 128.
33. Stephen Coote, *op. cit.*, p. 91.
34. *Ibid.*, pp. 96-97.
35. *Ibid.*, p. 97.
36. *Ibid.*
37. *Ibid.*
38. A.C. Bradley, *Oxford Lectures on Poetry*. Macmillan & Co. Ltd., London, 1962, p. 224.
39. *Ibid.*, pp. 224-25.
40. *Ibid.*, p. 226.
41. *Ibid.*, p. 228.
42. *Ibid.*, p. 229.
43. *Ibid.*, pp. 230-31.
44. *Ibid.*, p. 235.
45. *Ibid.*, p. 234.
46. *Ibid.*
47. *Ibid.*, p. 235.
48. *Ibid.*, footnote-2.
49. *Ibid.*, p. 235.
50. *Ibid.*
51. T.H. Ward, p. 436.
52. *Ibid.*, pp. 436-37.

53. Graham Hough, *op. cit.*, p. 178.
54. *Ibid.*
55. *Ibid.*, p. 179.
56. *Ibid.*, pp. 179-80.
57. *Keats: Odes*, ed., G.S. Fraser; Palgrave Publishers Ltd., New York, p. 152.
58. *Ibid.*
59. *Ibid.*, p. 190.
60. Graham Hough, *op. cit.*, pp. 167-68.
61. *Ibid.*, pp. 168-69.
62. *Ibid.*, p. 169.
63. *Ibid.*
64. Introduction, *Recritiquing John Keats*, ed., Aupama Nagar and Amarnath Prasad, Sarup & Sons, New Delhi, 2005, p. xv.
65. *Ibid.*, Introduction, pp. xv-xvi.
66. *Ibid.*, p. 48.
67. *Ibid.*
68. *Ibid.*
69. *Ibid.*, pp. 48-49.
70. *Ibid.*, p. 49.
71. *Ibid.*, p. 60.
72. *Ibid.*
73. *Ibid.*, cover page.
74. *Keats: Odes*, p. 192.
75. *Ibid.*, pp. 192-93.
76. *Ibid.*, p. 193.
77. *Ibid.*, p. 201.
78. *Ibid.*, p. 172.
79. *Ibid.*, p. 209.
80. Colvin, *op. cit.*, p. 219.
81. *Ibid.*, pp. 219-20.
82. *Ibid.*, p. 220.
83. *Ibid.*, p. 222.
84. *Ibid.*, pp. 222-23.

85. *Ibid.*, p. 235.
86. *Ibid.*
87. *Ibid.*, pp. 236-37.
88. *Ibid.*, p. 237.
89. *Ibid.*, p. 238.
90. *Ibid.*
91. *Ibid.*, p. 240.
92. Maurice Bowra, *The Romantic Imagination.* Harvard University Press, 1950, p. 127.
93. N.S. Sahu, *John Keats: A Sensuous Poet.* Prakash Book Depot, 2000, p. 2.
94. *Ibid.*, p. 83.
95. *Ibid.*, pp. 84-85.
96. *Ibid.*, p. 86.
97. *Ibid.*, p. 92.
98. *Ibid.*, quoted from *A History of English Literature* (Compton-Ricket), p. 23.
99. *Ibid.*, quoted from Harry Blamires, *A Short History of English-Literature*, p. 23.

CHAPTER 4

1. Chatwin Deryn. *Methuen Notes on Keats's Poetry and Prose.* London: Methuen Paperback Ltd., 1978, p. 69.
2. Bernard Groom, introduction, p. xv.
3. E.N. Rao, *op. cit.*, p. 207.
4. *Ibid.*
5. *Ibid.*, p. 208.
6. *Ibid.*, pp. 208-09.
7. *Ibid.*, pp. 214-15.
8. *Ibid.*, p. 215.
9. *Ibid.*
10. *Ibid.*, p. 219.
11. *Ibid.*, p. 221.
12. *Ibid.*, pp. 221-22.
13. *Ibid.*, p. 222.
14. Bernard Groom, p. xvi.

15. Methuen, *op. cit.*, p. 69.
16. Stephen Coote, *op. cit.*, p. 77.
17. *Ibid.*, pp. 80-81.
18. *Ibid.*, pp. 79-80.
19. *Ibid.*, p. 81.
20. *Ibid.*, p. 83.
21. *Ibid.*
22. *Ibid.*
23. *Ibid.*
24. *Ibid.*
25. *Ibid.*, p. 10.
26. *Ibid.*
27. *Ibid.*, p. 77.
28. *Ibid.*, p. 101.
29. *Ibid.*
30. Sydney Colvin, *op. cit.*, pp. 143-46.
31. *Ibid.*, pp. 138-39.
32. *Ibid.*, p. 139.
33. *Ibid.*, pp. 139-40.
34. *Ibid.*, p. 147.
35. *Ibid.*, pp. 147-48.
36. ibid. p. 148.
37. *Ibid.*, pp. 153-54.
38. *Ibid.*, p. 154.
39. *Ibid.*
40. *Ibid.*, p. 155.
41. *Ibid.*, pp. 156-56.
42. *Ibid.*, p. 16.
43. Bernard Groom, p. xv.
44. E.N. Rao, *op. cit.*, p. 1.
45. A.C. Bradley, *op. cit.*, p. 210.
46. *Ibid.*, p. 212.
47. *Ibid.*, pp. 210-11.
48. *Ibid.*, p. 213.

49. E.N. Rao, *op. cit.*, p. 10.
50. A.C. Bradley, *op. cit.*, pp. 217-18.
51. *Ibid.*, p. 218.
52. *Ibid.*, p. 220.
53. *Ibid.*
54. *Ibid.*
55. *Ibid.*, p. 22.
56. *Ibid.*, pp. 222-23.
57. *Ibid.*, p. 223.
58. E.N. Rao, *op. cit.*, p. 11.
59. *Ibid.*
60. *Ibid.*
61. A.C. Bradley, *op. cit.*, p. 210.
62. Stephen Coote, *op. cit.*, p. 103.
63. Colvin, *op. cit.*, p. 215.
64. Stephen Coote, *op. cit.*, p. 86.
65. *Ibid.*
66. *Ibid.*
67. A.C. Bradley, *op. cit.*, p. 217.
68. *Ibid.*, p. 216.
69. *Ibid.*
70. *Ibid.*, p. 217.
71. Stephen Coote, *op. cit.*, p. 95.
72. *Ibid.*, pp. 95-96.
73. T.H. Ward, *op. cit.*, pp. 432-33.
74. *Ibid.*, p. 430.
75. *Ibid.*, p. 431.
76. *Ibid.*
77. *Ibid.*
78. *Ibid.*, p. 432.
79. *Ibid.*, p. 433.
80. *Ibid.*
81. *Ibid.*, p. 432.
82. *Ibid.*, p. 433.

83. *Ibid.*, p. 434.
84. *Ibid.*
85. *Ibid.*
86. *Ibid.*
87. *Ibid.*
88. *Ibid.*
89. *Ibid.*
90. *Ibid.*, p. 429.
91. Colvin, *op. cit.*, p. 360.
92. *Ibid.*, pp. 360-61.
93. *Ibid.*, pp. 435-36.
94. *Keats: Odes*, p. 33.
95. *Ibid.*
96. Colvin, *op. cit.*, p. 245.
97. *Ibid.*, pp. 247-48.
98. *Ibid.*, p. 250.
99. *Ibid.*, p. 252.
100. *Ibid.*, pp. 252-53.
101. *Ibid.*, p. 253.
102. *Ibid.*, p. 263.
103. *Ibid.*
104. *Ibid.*, p. 265.
105. *Ibid.*
106. *Ibid.*, p. 266.
107. *Ibid.*
108. *Ibid.*, p. 271.
109. *Ibid.*, p. 319.
110. *Ibid.*
111. *Ibid.*, pp. 319-20.
112. *Ibid.*, p. 345.
113. *Ibid.*
114. *Ibid.*, p. 348.
115. *Ibid.*, p. 356.
116. *Ibid.*

117. *Ibid.*, p. 346.
118. *Ibid.*, p. 63.
119. *Ibid.*, p. 657.
120. *Ibid.*, p. 665.
121. *Ibid.*, p. 66.
122. N.S. Sahu, *A Sensuous Mystic: John Keats.* Prakash Book Depot, Bareilly, 2000, p. 40.
123. Stephen Coote, *op. cit.*, Cover page.

CHAPTER 5

1. Colvin, *op. cit.*, p. 429.
2. *Ibid.*, p. 360.
3. *Ibid.*, pp. 360-61.
4. *Keats: Odes*, p. 33.
5. *Ibid.*
6. *Ibid.*, pp. 247-48.
7. *Ibid.*, p. 250.
8. Colvin, *op. cit.*, p. 248.
9. *Ibid.*, p. 252.
10. *The Romantic Poets,* p. 176.
11. *Ibid.*, p. 179.
12. *Keats: Odes,* p. 263.
13. *Ibid.*, p. 263.
14. *Ibid.*, p. 265.
15. *Ibid.*
16. *Ibid.*, p. 266.
17. *Ibid.*
18. *Ibid.*, p. 271.
19. *Ibid.*, p. 314.
20. *Ibid.*, p. 319.
21. *Ibid.*, pp. 319-20.
22. *Ibid.*, p. 345.
23. *Ibid.*
24. *Ibid.*, p. 348.
25. *Ibid.*, p. 356.

26. *Ibid.*, pp. 356-57.
27. *Ibid.*, p. 346.
28. *Ibid.*, p. 63.
29. *Ibid.*, p. 65.
30. *Ibid.*, p. 66.
31. *Ibid.*
32. *Ibid.*, p. 67.
33. Maurice Bowra, *op. cit.*, p. 129.
34. *Ibid.*, p. 130.
35. *Ibid.*, p. 132.
36. *Ibid.*, p. 133.
37. *Ibid.*, p. 135.
38. *Ibid.*, p. 136.
39. *Keats: Odes*, p. 24.
40. *Ibid.*
41. *Ibid.*, p. 25.
42. *Ibid.*
43. *The Romantic Poets*, p. 174.
44. *Ibid.*, pp. 174-75.
45. *Ibid.*, p. 176.
46. *Ibid.*, pp. 176-77.
47. *Keats: Odes*, p. 132.
48. *Ibid.*, p. 133.
49. Colvin, *op. cit.*, p. 68.
50. *Ibid.*
51. *Keats: Odes*, pp. 133-34.
52. *Ibid.*, pp. 136-37.
53. *Ibid.*, p. 137.
54. *Ibid.*, pp. 137-38.
55. *Ibid.*, p. 138.
56. *Ibid.*
57. *Ibid.*, pp. 139-40.
58. *Ibid.*, p. 143.
59. *Ibid.*, pp. 83-84.

60. *Ibid.*, p. 84.
61. *Ibid.*, p. 85.
62. *Ibid.*
63. *Ibid.*, pp. 85-86.
64. *Keats and the Pre-Raphaelites*, p. 127.
65. *Ibid.*, p. 128.
66. *Ibid.*, p. 129.
67. *Ibid.*, p. 130.
68. *Ibid.*, p. 132.
69. *Re-critiquing John Keats*, p. 84.
70. *Ibid.*, p. 90.
71. *Ibid.*, p. 92.
72. *Ibid.*, p. 95.
73. *Keats: Odes*, p. 140.
74. *A Sensuous Mystic: John Keats*, p. 87.
75. *Ibid.*, pp. 172-73.
76. *Ibid.*, p. 173.
77. *Ibid.*, pp. 173-74.
78. *Ibid.*, p. 205.
79. *Ibid.*, p. 138.
80. *Ibid.*, p. 139.
81. Colvin, *op. cit.*, p. 130.
82. Graham Hough, *op. cit.*, p. 180.
83. Stephen Coote, *op. cit.*, p. 125.
84. *Ibid.*, pp. 180-81.
85. *The Romantic Poets*, p. 178.
86. *Ibid.*, p. 181.
87. Stephen Coote, *op. cit.*, p. 128.
88. *The Romantic Poets*, p. 179.
89. *Ibid.*, p. 182.
90. Stephen Coote, *op. cit.*, p. 178.
91. *Ibid.*, p. 183.
92. *The Romantic Poets*, p. 179.
93. *Ibid.*, p. 184.

94. Colvin, *op. cit.*, p. 132.
95. *Ibid.*, p. 184.
96. *Ibid.*, p. 185.
97. *Ibid.*, p. 186.
98. *Ibid.*, pp. 186-87.
99. *Ibid.*, p. 187.
100. *Ibid.*, p. 188.
101. Maurice Bowra, *op. cit.*, p. 128.
102. *The Romantic Poets,* p. 180.
103. Colvin, *op. cit.*, p. 140.
104. *Ibid.*, p. 141.
105. *Ibid.*, p. 135.
106. *Ibid.*, p. 138.
107. *The Romantic Poets*, p. 180.
108. *Ibid.*, p. 181.
109. *Ibid.*, p. 186.
110. *Ibid.*, pp. 191-92.
111. *Ibid.*, p. 189.
112. *Ibid.*, p. 190.
113. *Ibid.*, p. 183.
114. *Ibid.*, p. 185.
115. *Ibid.*
116. *Ibid.*, p. 187.
117. *Ibid.*, p. 185.
118. *Ibid.*, p. 186.
119. *Ibid.*, p. 188.
120. *Ibid.*, p. 186.
121. *Ibid.*, p. 189.
122. *Ibid.*, p. 191.
123. *Ibid.*, p. 190.
124. *Keats & the Pre-Raphaelites*, p. 130.
125. *Ibid.*, p. 131.
126. Colvin, *op. cit.*, p. 249.
127. *A Sensuous Mystic: John Keats*, p. 156.

128. Stephen Coote, *op. cit.*, p. 114.

129. *Ibid.*, p. 128.

CHAPTER 6

1. Graham Hough, *op. cit.*, pp. 104-05.
2. *Ibid.*, p. 106.
3. Ram Bilas Sharma, *Keats and the Pre-Raphalites*. Anamika Publishers & Distributors (P) Ltd., 2005, p. 63.
4. *Ibid.*, p. 64.
5. *Ibid.*, p. 66.
6. *Ibid.*, p. 68.
7. Bradley, A.C., *op. cit.*, p. 150.
8. *Ibid.*, p. 152.
9. *Ibid.*, p. 153.
10. *Ibid.*, p. 154.
11. *Ibid.*, p. 156.
12. *Ibid.*, p. 158.
13. Colvin, *op. cit.*, p. 143.
14. A.C. Bradley, *op. cit.*, p. 160.
15. *Ibid.*, p. 165.
16. *Ibid.*, p. 166.
17. E. Nageswar Rao, *John Keats: An Anthology of Criticism,* Pencraft International, p. 210.
18. *Ibid.*, p. 255.
19. *Ibid.*, p. 260.
20. Ibid., p. 265.
21. *Ibid.*, p. 279.
22. *Ibid.*, pp. 174-75.
23. *Ibid.*, p. 175.
24. *Ibid.*, p. 182.
25. *Ibid.*, p. 191.
26. *Ibid.*, p. 195.
27. *Ibid.*, p. 135.
28. *Ibid.*, p. 140.

29. G.S. Fraser, *Keats: Odes* (ed.), Macmillan Press Ltd., 1971, p. 80.
30. *Ibid.*, p. 90.
31. *Ibid.*
32. *Ibid.*, pp. 90-91.
33. *Ibid.*, pp. 93-94.
34. *Ibid.*, p. 91.
35. *Ibid.*, pp. 172-73.
36. *Ibid.*, p. 173.
37. *Ibid.*, p. 153.
38. *Ibid.*, p. 157.
39. *Ibid.*, p. 191.
40. *Ibid.*
41. *Ibid.*, pp. 157-58.
42. Maurice Bowra, *The Romantic Imagination.* Oxford University Press, 1950, p. 135.
43. Colvin, *op. cit.*, p. 143.
44. *Ibid.*, p. 145.
45. *Ibid.*, p. 148.
46. *Ibid.*, pp. 106-07.
47. *Ibid.*, pp. 107-08.
48. *Ibid.*, p. 108.
49. *Ibid.*, p. 109.
50. *Keats: Odes*, p. 227.
51. *Methuen Notes*, p. 15.
52. Colvin, *op. cit.*, p. 89.
53. *Ibid.*, p. 186.
54. *Ibid.*, p. 189.
55. *Ibid.*, p. 16.
56. *Ibid.*, p. 25.
57. *Ibid.*, p. 48.
58. *Ibid.*, p. 83.
59. Maurice Bowra, *op. cit.*, pp. 83-84.
60. Stephen Coote, *op. cit.*, p. 83.

61. *Ibid.*, p. 85.
62. *Ibid.*
63. Maurice Bowra, p. 90.
64. *Ibid.*, p. 86.
65. *Ibid.*, p. 89.
66. *Ibid.*
67. *Ibid.*, p. 92.
68. *Ibid.*, pp. 89-90.
69. Nageswar Rao, p. 85.
70. *Ibid.*, p. 84.
71. Graham Hough, *op. cit.*, p. 165.
72. *Ibid.*, pp. 165-66.
73. Colvin, *op. cit.*, pp. 165-66.
74. *Ibid.*, pp. 166-67.
75. *Ibid.*, pp. 172-73.
76. *Ibid.*
77. *Ibid.*, p. 178.
78. *Ibid.*, p. 180.

Selected Bibliography

Primary Source

Arthur-Compton-Ricket. *A History of English Literature*. New Delhi: USB Publishers & Distributors Ltd.

Bowra, Maurice. *The Romantic Imagination*. New York: Oxford University Press, Oxford, 1950.

Bradley, A.C. *Oxford Lectures on Poetry*. London: Macmillan & Co. Ltd., 1962.

Chatwin, Deryn. *Methuen Notes on Keats's Poetry and Prose*. London: Methuen Paperback Ltd., 1978.

Fraser, G.S. *Keats: Odes* (ed.). New York: Palgrave (Formerly Macmillan Press Ltd.), 1971.

Gardiner, Helen. *The Metaphysical Poets*. London: Penguin Books, 1972.

Garrod, H.W. (ed.). *Keats: Poetical Works*. Oxford & New York: Oxford University Press, 1956. (All the textual references are taken from this book).

Groom, Bernard. *Selections from Keats, Introduction and Notes*. London: Macmillan and Co. Ltd., 1952.

Hornby, A.S. *Oxford Advanced Learner's Dictionary of Current English*. Oxford University Press, 1974.

Hough, Graham. *The Romantic Poets*. Bombay: B.I. Publications Pvt. Ltd., 1953.

Keats. *The Works of John Keats: With an Introduction and Bibliography*. London: Wordsworth Editions Ltd., 1994.

Nagar, Aupama and Amar Nath Prasad (ed.). *Recritiquing John Keats*. New Delhi: Sarup & Sons, 2005.

New Encyclopedia Britannica (vol. 10). *Encyclopedia Britannica*, Inc: Chicago.

——. (vol. 12).

——. (vol. 14).

Rao, E. Nageswara (ed.). *John Keats: An Anthology of Recent Criticism*. New Delhi: Pencraft International, 1998.

Sahu, N.S. *A Sensuous Mystic: John Keats*. Prakash Book Depot, 2008.

Sharma, Bilas Ram. *Keats and the Pre-Raphaelites*. Anamika Publishers & Distributors (P.) Ltd., 2005.

Sharma, R.S. and L. Misra. *Anthology of English Poems: From Shakespeare to Keats*. New Delhi: Oxford University Press, 2001.

Sidney Colvin. *Life of John Keats*. New Delhi: Vishvabharti Publications, 2007.

Stephen Coote. *John Keats: A Life*. Ludhyana: Hind Publishers, 2005.

Tilak, Raghukul. *A Short History of English Poetry*. Prakash Book Depot, 2002.

Ward, T.H. *The English Poets*. London: Macmillan and Co. Limited, 1933.

Williamson, George. *A Reader's Guide to the Metaphysical Poets*. London: Thames and Hudson, 1968.